BUDDHIST MURALS OF NORTHEAST THAILAND

Buddhist Murals
of Northeast Thailand
Reflections of the Isan Heartland

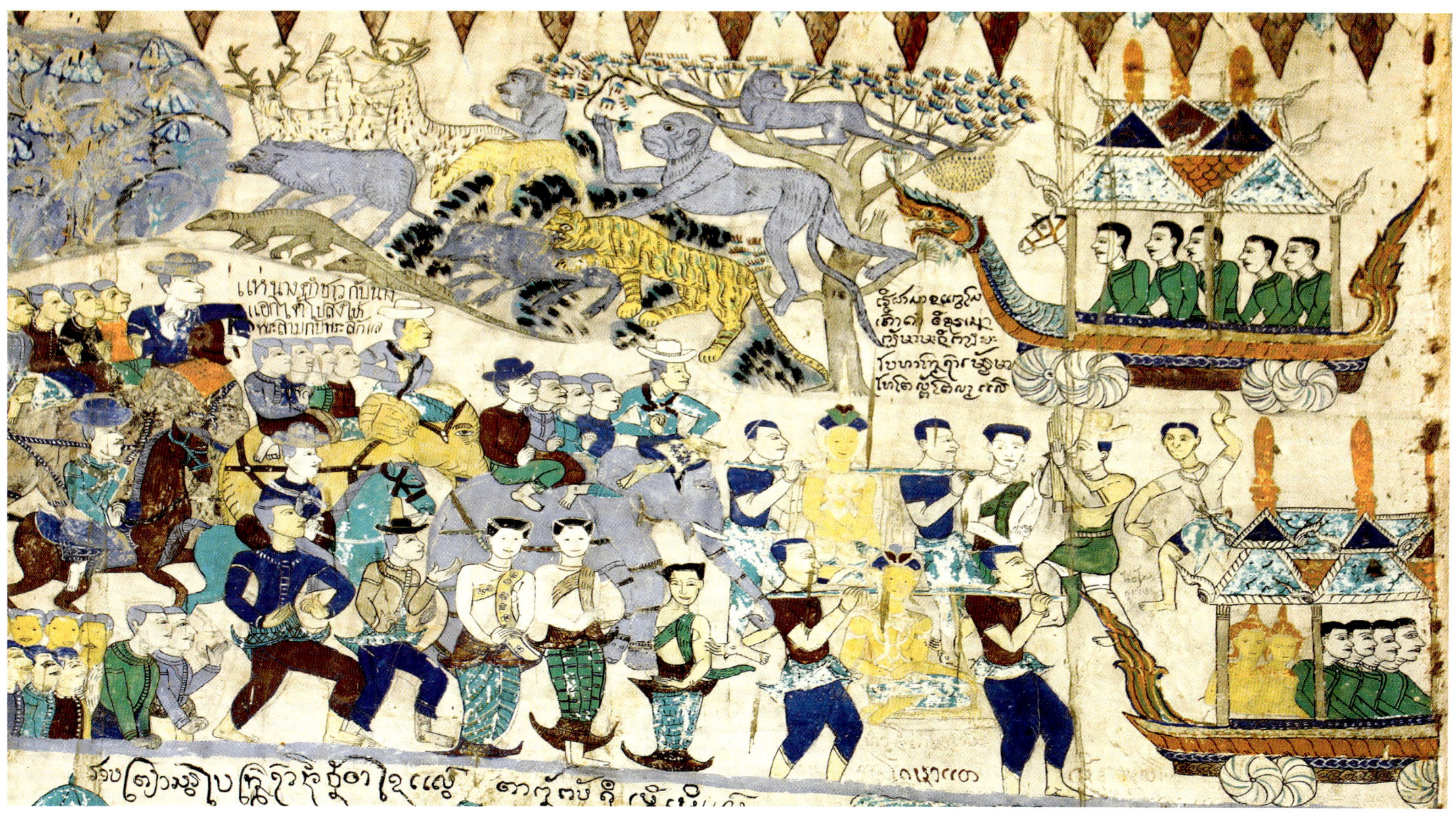

Bonnie Pacala Brereton and Somroay Yencheuy

MEKONG PRESS

Mekong Press was initiated in 2005 by Silkworm Books with the financial support of the Rockefeller Foundation. In 2007, the Mekong Press Foundation was registered as a nonprofit organization to encourage and support the work of local scholars, writers, and publishing professionals in Cambodia, Laos, Vietnam, and the other countries in the Greater Mekong Subregion. Books published by Mekong Press (www.mekongpress.com) are marketed and distributed internationally. Mekong Press also holds seminars and training workshops on different aspects of book publishing, and helps find ways to overcome some of the huge challenges faced by small book publishers in the region.

ISBN: 978-616-90053-1-5

© 2010 by Mekong Press
All rights reserved

Published in 2010 by
Mekong Press
6 Sukkasem Road, T. Suthep
Chiang Mai 50200 Thailand
info@mekongpress.com
http://www.mekongpress.com

Text by Bonnie Pacala Brereton and Somroay Yencheuy
thaiphon_yen@yahoo.com
Photographs by Bonnie Pacala Brereton (BB), Ivan Polson (IP), Robert Stratton (RS),
Somroay Yencheuy (SY), Leedom Lefferts (LL), and Jai Dokpromla (JD)

Typeset in Scala 10 pt. by Silk Type
Printed and bound in China

5 4 3 2 1

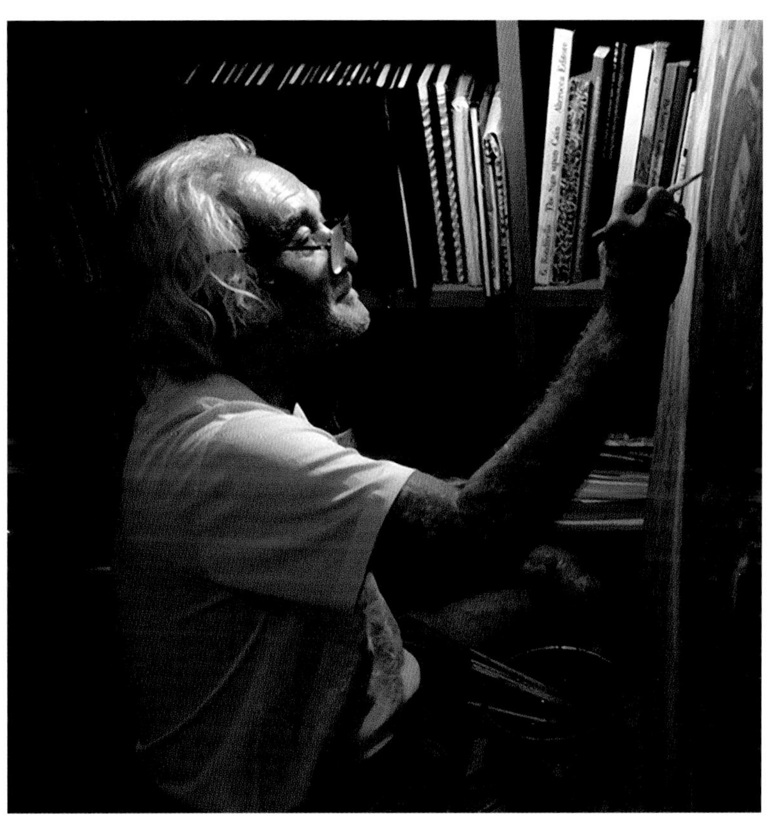

This book is dedicated to the late Achan Pairote Samosorn, whose pioneering research on Isan mural painting has been an inspiration to us. A native of Nakhon Si Thammarat province, Achan Pairote graduated from Silapakorn University in 1963 and taught at the Arts and Crafts School in Bangkok for seven years. In 1970 he began teaching at Khon Kaen University, where he taught until his retirement in 1999.

Achan Pairote was one of the first academics to realize the value of village murals. He began his quest back in the 1970s, long before the construction of Thailand's modern highway system, riding his motorcycle along narrow dirt roads to remote villages in search of obscure paintings. His pioneering work, *Chitrakam faphanang isan, E-Sarn Mural Paintings*, published in 1989, was the culmination of five years (1982–87) of intensive surveys, data collection, photographing, and analysis, sponsored by the Toyota Foundation.

As a gifted artist himself, Achan Pairote offered invaluable insight into the work of other painters. As a southern transplant in Isan, he grew to love his cultural surroundings and the people who created them. And as a kind and generous human being, he was willing to share his knowledge with those wanting to learn from him. For all these reasons and more, we will always respect and admire him and attempt to emulate the example he set.

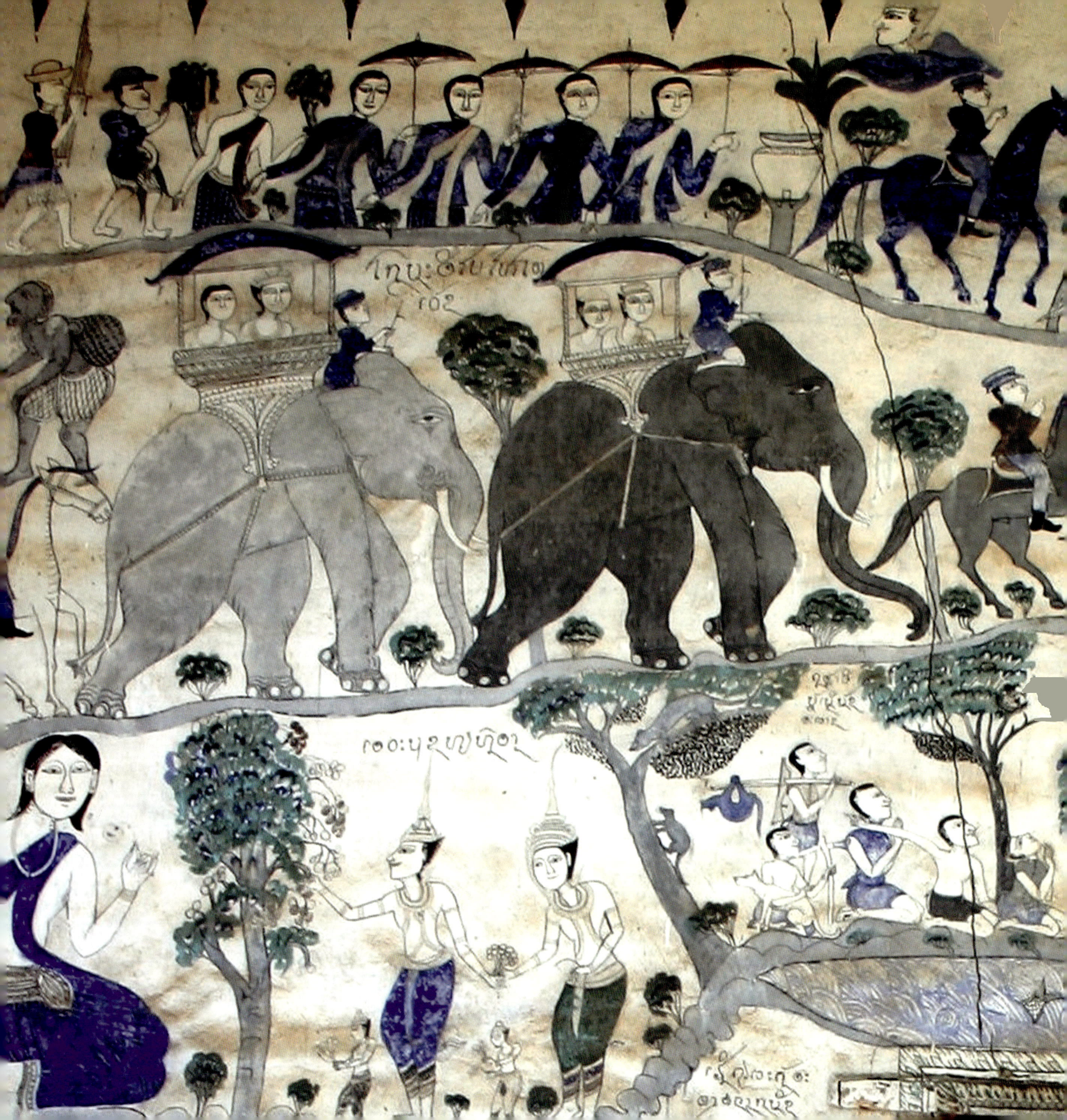

ເກນະຂົນໄທກ
ໂຍ
ເໄຍ:ບຂແຫຼຄຸໂຕາ
ຊຸຍຊຸ
ເຊຍກໂຕຖະຄຸ

CONTENTS

List of Figures ix

Acknowledgments xi

Introduction 1

The Setting 5

The Isan *Sim* (Ordination Hall) 9

The Isan Heartland as Seen in Murals 17

Texts, Tales, and Themes 25

Composition, Characters, and Postures 45

Artists and Sponsors, Tools, and Techniques 53

Material and Spiritual Culture 59

Eroticism, Bawdiness, and Buffoonery 69

Concluding Remarks: Painting as Pilgrimage 77

Appendix 1: Maps of Khon Kaen 79

Appendix 2: Maps of Maha Sarakham 81

References 83

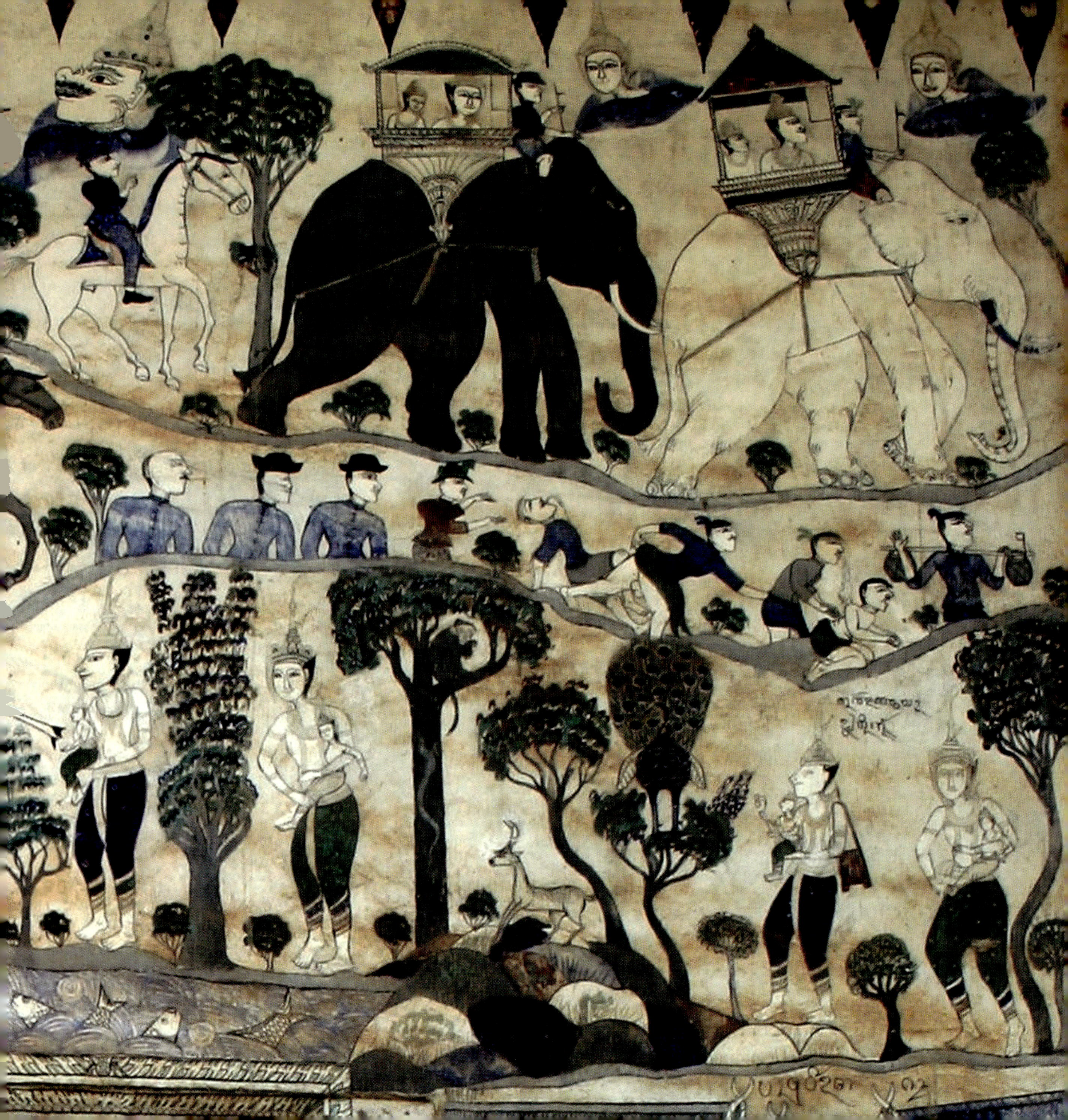

LIST OF FIGURES

Photographs by Bonnie Pacala Brereton (BB), Ivan Polson (IP), Robert Stratton (RS),
Somroay Yencheuy (SY), Leedom Lefferts (LL), and Jai Dokpromla (JD)

1. Map of Thailand showing the location of Isan.

2. Map of Isan. แผนที่ภาคอีสาน

3. Isan farmers harvesting rice. Maha Sarakham (SY). ชาวนาอีสานกำลังเกี่ยวข้าว จังหวัด
มหาสารคาม

4. Exuberant dancers and musicians. Wat Sa Bua Kaeo, Khon Kaen. เราสามารถพบเห็น
ภาพนักดนตรีและนักเต้นรำที่มีชีวิตชีวาได้ทั่วไปในภาคอีสาน ทั้งในจิตรกรรมฝาผนังและในชีวิต
ประจำวัน วัดสระบัวแก้ว จังหวัดขอนแก่น (BB)

5. Local forest creatures and the Brahmin Chuchok. Wat Ban Yang, Maha Sarakham.
ภาพสัตว์ป่าในท้องถิ่น และพราหมณ์ชูชก วัดบ้านยาง จังหวัดมหาสารคาม (SY)

6. Vessantara, Matsi, and their children in the forest. Wat Ban Yang, Maha Sarakham.
พระเวสสันดร พระนางมัทรี และพระโอรสพระธิดาในป่า วัดบ้านยาง จังหวัดมหาสารคาม (SY)

7. *Sim* interior. Wat Sanuan Wari, Khon Kaen. ภายในสิม วัดสนวนวารี จังหวัดขอนแก่น (BB)

8. Old *sim* with new Central-style roof. Wat Chai Si, Khon Kaen. สิมโบราณ พร้อมหลังคาใหม่
แบบภาคกลาง วัดไชยศรี จังหวัดขอนแก่น (BB)

9. Old and new *sim*. Wat Sanuan Wari, Khon Kaen. สิมแบบเก่าและแบบใหม่ วัดสนวนวารี
จังหวัดขอนแก่น (BB)

10. *Sim* renovation with local roof style, but Central-style tiles. Wat Sa Bua Kaeo, Khon Kaen.
สิมที่ได้รับการบูรณะ ประกอบหลังคาใหม่แบบท้องถิ่น แต่ใช้กระเบื้องแบบภาคกลาง วัดสระบัวแก้ว
จังหวัดขอนแก่น (SY)

11. *Naga* figures flanking stairway. Wat Sanuan Wari, Khon Kaen. บันไดนาค วัดสนวนวารี
จังหวัดขอนแก่น (SY)

12. *Singha* and human figures on railings. Wat Sa Bua Kaeo, Khon Kaen. รูปปั้นสิงห์และ
มนุษย์ที่บันไดทางเข้า วัดสระบัวแก้ว จังหวัดขอนแก่น (SY)

13. *Nariphon* tree. Wat Sanuan Wari, Khon Kaen. ต้นนารีผล วัดสนวนวารี จังหวัดขอนแก่น

14. *Nariphon* tree. Shadow puppet (JD). ตัวหนังประโมทัยรูปนารีผล (BB)

15. Owl couple. Wat Ban Yang, Maha Sarakham. นกฮูกผัวเมีย วัดบ้านยาง จังหวัดมหาสารคาม (SY)

16. *Phi* in forest. Wat Pa Rerai, Maha Sarakham. ผีในป่า วัดป่าเรไร จังหวัดมหาสารคาม (BB)

17. Smiling tigers. Wat Sa Bua Kaeo, Khon Kaen. เสือยิ้ม วัดสระบัวแก้ว จังหวัดขอนแก่น (SY)

18. Ferocious tiger attacking a man. Wat Ban Yang, Maha Sarakham. เสือดุโผนเข้ากัดคน
วัดบ้านยาง จังหวัดมหาสารคาม (SY)

19. Sin Sai story: battling with giants. Wat Sanuan Wari, Khon Kaen. เรื่องสินไช ตอน
สินไชรบยักษ์ วัดสนวนวารี จังหวัดขอนแก่น (BB)

20. The Great Departure. Wat Photharam, Maha Sarakham. มหาภิเนษกรมณ์ วัดโพธาราม
จังหวัดมหาสารคาม (IP)

21. Victory over Mara. Wat Ban Yang, Maha Sarakham. ภาพตอนตรัสรู้หรือมารวิชัย วัดบ้านยาง
จังหวัดมหาสารคาม (IP)

22. The Buddha's sickness and passing into nirvana. Wat Ban Yang, Maha Sarakham.
พระพุทธเจ้าทรงอาพาธ และเสด็จดับขันธ์ปรินิพพาน วัดบ้านยาง จังหวัดมหาสารคาม (IP)

23. Detail of the Buddha's sickness. Wat Ban Yang, Maha Sarakham. อาการอาพาธของ
พระพุทธเจ้า วัดบ้านยาง จังหวัดมหาสารคาม (SY)

24. Detail of the Buddha's cremation. Wat Ban Yang, Maha Sarakham. ถวายพระเพลิง
พระพุทธสรีระศพ วัดบ้านยาง จังหวัดมหาสารคาม (SY)

25. *Vessantara Jataka*: donation of elephant. Wat Sanuan Wari. เวสสันดรชาดก: พระเวสสันดร
ทรงบริจาคช้างปัจจัยนาคเป็นทาน วัดสนวนวารี จังหวัดขอนแก่น (BB)

26. *Vessantara Jataka*: donation of horses. Wat Sanuan Wari, Khon Kaen. เวสสันดรชาดก:
ทรงบริจาคม้า วัดสนวนวารี จังหวัดขอนแก่น (BB)

27. *Pha Lam Sadok*: the infant Nang Sida floating down the river on a raft. Wat Sa
Bua Kaeo, Khon Kaen. พะลามชาดก: ทารกนางสีดาถูกนำไปลอยแพ วัดสระบัวแก้ว จังหวัด
ขอนแก่น (BB)

28. Three-panel wall depicting Pha Wet's donation of Matsi and her return to him,
followed by their journey back to the royal city. Wat Ban Lan, Khon Kaen. ผนังสาม
ช่อง เล่าเรื่องพระเวสสันดรทรงบริจาคนางมัทรี และพระอินทร์ถวายนางคืน กับภาพสี่กษัตริย์นิวัติ
พระนคร วัดบ้านลาน จังหวัดขอนแก่น (IP).

29. Scene from *Pha Lam Sadok*. Wat Sa Bua Kaeo, Khon Kaen. ตอนหนึ่งจากเรื่อง พะลาม
ชาดก วัดสระบัวแก้ว จังหวัดขอนแก่น (BB)

30. Isan shadow puppet representing Sang Thong. หุ่นหนังประโมทัย ตัวสังข์ทอง (JD)

31. Sang Thong, Sin Sai, and Siho in forest, followed by their six ordinary brothers.
Wat Sanuan Wari, Khon Kaen. สังข์ทอง สินไช สีโห และพี่ชายทั้งหก วัดสนวนวารี จังหวัด
ขอนแก่น (BB)

32. *Phra Malai*. Wat Ban Yang, Maha Sarakham. พระมาลัย วัดบ้านยาง จังหวัดมหาสารคาม (IP)

33. Hell scene. Wat Chai Si, Khon Kaen. นรกภูมิ วัดไชยศรี จังหวัดขอนแก่น (BB)

34. Hell scene. Wat Sanuan Wari, Khon Kaen. นรกภูมิ วัดสนวนวารี จังหวัดขอนแก่น (BB)

35. Division of space in registers. Wat Ban Yang, Maha Sarakham. ผนังวัดบ้านยาง สังเกต
วิธีแบ่งพื้นที่ของฉากตามแนวนอน (IP)

36. Pha Wet holding an ascetic's rosary. Wat Ban Yang, Maha Sarakham. พะเวส ทรงถือ
ประคำ วัดบ้านยาง จังหวัดมหาสารคาม (SY)

37. Isan shadow puppets at a performance, Khon Kaen. การเชิดหนังประโมทัย จังหวัดขอนแก่น (BB)

38. *Pha pha wet* scroll used in Bun Pha Wet festivals. Wat Ban Lan, Khon Kaen. ม้วนผ้า ผะเหวด ใช้ในงานฉลองบุญผะเหวด วัดบ้านลาน จังหวัดขอนแก่น (RS)

39. Procession scene, *Vessantara Jataka*. Wat Photharam, Maha Sarakham. ขบวนแห่ วัดโพธาราม จังหวัดมหาสารคาม (IP)

40. Procession of celebrants at Bun Pha Wet festival, 1984. Khon Kaen. ขบวนฉลอง บุญผะเหวด จังหวัดขอนแก่น พ.ศ. 2527 (LL)

41. Women in *wat* at Bun Pha Wet festival. Khon Kaen, 2009. ผู้หญิงในวัด ช่วงงานบุญผะเหวด จังหวัดขอนแก่น พ.ศ. 2552 (LL)

42. Artist's self-portrait. Wat Sanuan Wari, Khon Kaen. รูปเหมือนศิลปิน วัดสนวนวารี จังหวัด ขอนแก่น (SY)

43. Dense composition filled with figures. Wat Sa Bua Kaeo, Khon Kaen. รูปวาดที่มี องค์ประกอบหนาแน่นด้วยภาพบุคคลจำนวนมาก วัดสระบัวแก้ว จังหวัดขอนแก่น (SY)

44. Loose composition. Wat Ban Lan, Khon Kaen. รูปวาดที่มีองค์ประกอบหลวม ๆ วัดบ้านลาน จังหวัดขอนแก่น (SY)

45 and 46. Murals cover entire surface. Wat Chai Si, Khon Kaen. จิตรกรรมฝาผนังของวัดไชยศรี จะวาดเต็มพื้นที่ว่างทั้งหมดบนผนัง (SY)

47. Border detail, Wat Sa Bua Kaeo, Khon Kaen. รายละเอียดของกรอบ วัดสระบัวแก้ว จังหวัด ขอนแก่น (BB)

48. Farming scene. Detail of Great Departure scene, Wat Photharam, Maha Sarakham. ภาพการทำนา วัดโพธาราม จังหวัดมหาสารคาม (BB)

49. Fishing scene. Detail of Great Departure scene, Wat Photharam, Maha Sarakham. ภาพการหาปลา วัดโพธาราม จังหวัดมหาสารคาม (BB)

50. Young women carrying water from well. Wat Ban Lan, Khon Kaen. ภาพหญิงสาวหาบน้ำ จากบ่อ วัดบ้านลาน จังหวัดขอนแก่น (RS).

51. Chinese merchants. Wat Photharam, Maha Sarakham. พ่อค้าจีน วัดโพธาราม จังหวัด มหาสารคาม (BB)

52. Elderly women. Wat Khon Kaen Nua, Roi Et. หญิงชรา วัดขอนแก่นเหนือ จังหวัดร้อยเอ็ด (SY)

53. High-spirited festival celebrants. Wat Pa Rerai Maha Sarakham. รอยสักบนขาผู้ชาย วัดป่าเรไร จังหวัดมหาสารคาม (SY)

54. Lustral water pouring ceremony. Wat Pa Rerai, Maha Sarakham. พิธีฮดสรง วัดป่าเรไร จังหวัดมหาสารคาม (SY)

55. Childbirth scene. Wat Ban Yang, Maha Sarakham. ภาพการคลอดบุตร วัดบ้านยาง จังหวัด มหาสารคาม (BB)

56. Funeral procession for Chuchok's cremation. Wat Ban Yang, Maha Sarakham. ขบวน ศพชูชก วัดบ้านยาง จังหวัดมหาสารคาม (BB)

57. Tug-of-war ritual. Wat Chai Si, Khon Kaen. การชักเย่อ วัดไชยศรี จังหวัดขอนแก่น (SY)

58. Detail of *mara vijaya* scene. Wat Khon Kaen Nua, Roi Et. รายละเอียดภาพมารวิชัย วัดขอนแก่นเหนือ จังหวัดร้อยเอ็ด (SY)

59. Great Departure. Wat Ban Yang, Maha Sarakham. มหาภิเนษกรมณ์ วัดบ้านยาง จังหวัด มหาสารคาม (IP)

60. Procession including carousing men. Wat Ban Yang, Maha Sarakham. ภาพขบวนคน ที่มีขี้เมาอยู่ด้วย วัดบ้านยาง มหาสารคาม (SY)

61. Amittada taunted by jealous neighbors. Wat Ban Yang, Maha Sarakham. อมิตตาถูก เพื่อนบ้านที่อิจฉาด่าว่า วัดบ้านยาง จังหวัดมหาสารคาม (BB)

62. Amittada taunted by jealous neighbors. Wat Sanuan Wari, Khon Kaen. อมิตตาถูก เพื่อนบ้านที่อิจฉาด่าว่า วัดสนวนวารี จังหวัดขอนแก่น (SY)

63. Chuchok's death by gluttony. Wat Sanuan Wari, Khon Kaen. ชูชกตายเพราะตะกละ วัดสนวนวารี จังหวัดขอนแก่น (SY)

64. Matsi encountering forest creatures. Wat Ban Lan, Khon Kaen. พระนางมัทรีทรงพบ สัตว์ร้าย วัดบ้านลาน จังหวัดขอนแก่น (SY)

65. An unusually handsome version of Chuchok. Wat Ban Yang, Maha Sarakham. ภาพนี้ วาดชูชกได้งามเป็นพิเศษ วัดบ้านยาง จังหวัดมหาสารคาม (SY)

ACKNOWLEDGMENTS

We would like to express our gratitude to the James W. H. Thompson Foundation for its generous support, without which the writing of this book would not have been possible. We also wish to express our appreciation to H. Leedom Lefferts, Jr. for his careful reading of the manuscript and his many useful suggestions. Thanks also go to Carol and Bob Stratton and Ivan Polson for their ideas and the generous use of their photos; and to Sommai Premchit and Chris Baker for their input. Most of all, we are grateful to the artists who created this lovely and lively legacy of the local Buddhist imagination.

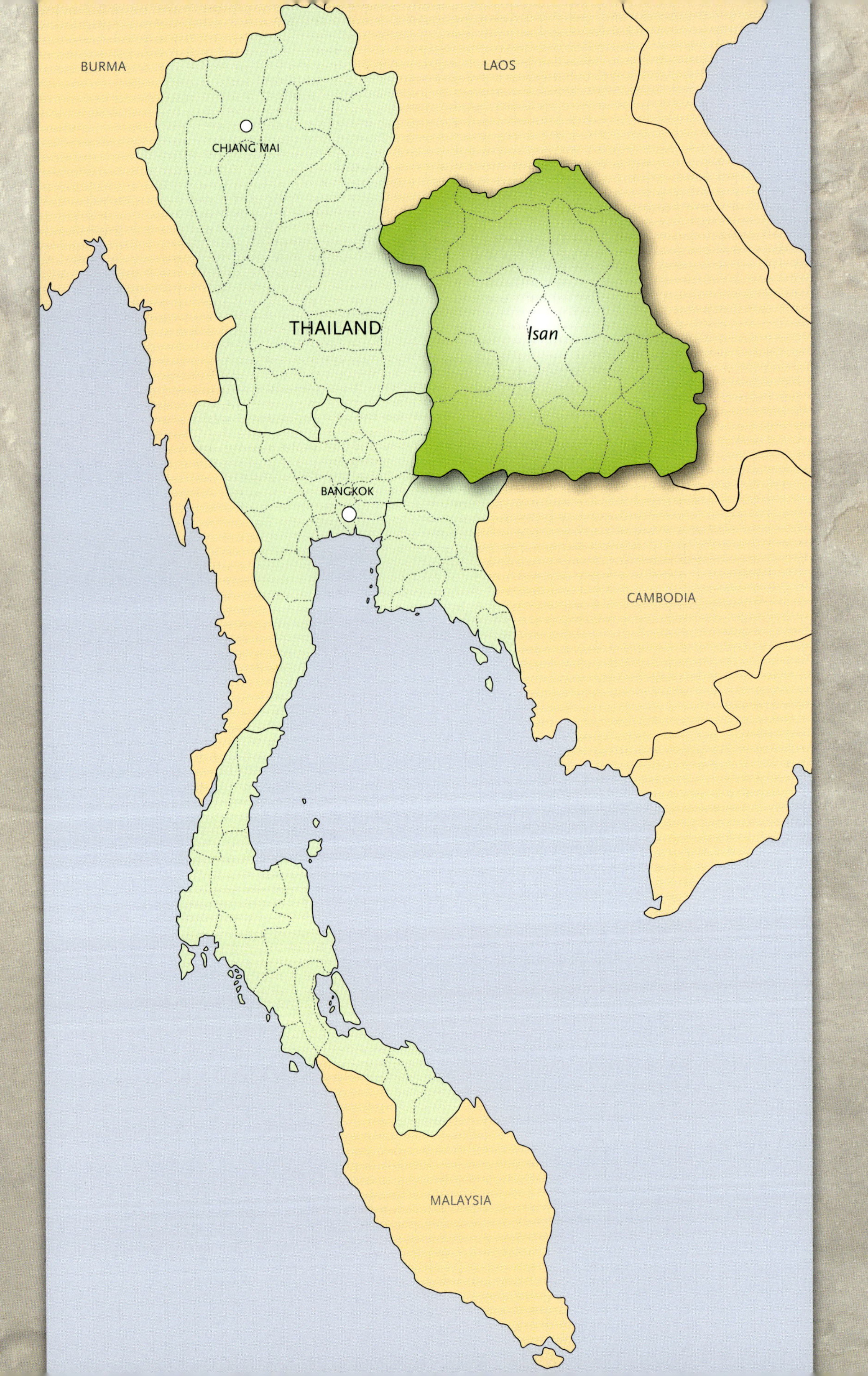

BURMA
LAOS
CHIANG MAI
THAILAND
Isan
BANGKOK
CAMBODIA
MALAYSIA

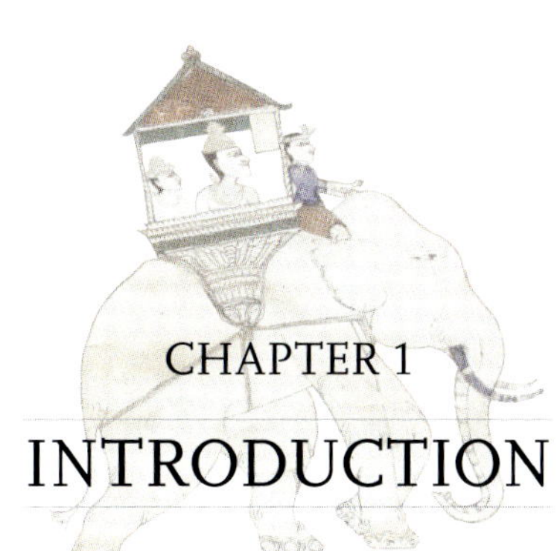

CHAPTER 1

INTRODUCTION

Isan, the northeastern region of modern Thailand (see figure 1, map of Thailand), is known for its high-spirited music, tasty food, intricate silk weaving, prehistoric pottery sites, and magnificent Khmer temple ruins. Tour companies also promote its dinosaur parks, snake farms, and at least one bat cave. Less known are the lively Buddhist murals that are part of its Lao cultural heritage. Despite their prolific number, distinctive compositions, and delightful narrative scenes, they are known to only a small number of Thai scholars and few of them have ever been seen by tourists—Thai or foreign.

These wall paintings provide a view of certain local Buddhist traditions, practices, and artistic expressions not found in other parts of the country. Many aspects of Isan culture are much more closely related to those across the Mekong River in Laos than to those found in Central Thailand. Some of these traditions—including local folktales, palm-leaf manuscripts, and the *Thai noi* writing system, which was used for religious texts—came under siege when the Thai government's highest priority became melding the country's diverse regions into a homogeneous nation-state. Countless measures were adopted that discouraged, suppressed, or belittled indigenous languages, cultural forms, and other forms of local identity, particularly in Isan.[1] The result was a devaluation of vernacular art and architectural forms among villagers and their unfortunate destruction and replacement by Bangkok-centric models.

Only a handful of titles on Isan murals have been published, all in Thai, with the exception of Pairote Samosorn's pioneering volume, *E-Sarn Mural Painting*, in Thai and English, published in 1989. Pairote, a Khon Kaen University art professor from Nakhon Si Thammarat, working contemporaneously with Wiroj Srisuro, an architecture professor and fellow southerner, located seventy-four temples with murals (several of which have since been demolished). From these examples, Pairote identified three groups or schools of Isan painting, each distinguished by distinct features, including composition, colors, and external influence.[2] These are (1) a distinctive local group, found in the central Isan provinces of Khon Kaen, Maha Sarakham, Kalasin, and Roi Et; (2) a Bangkok-influenced group, found in the Khorat area; and (3) a Lan Chang–Bangkok-influenced group, along the northern Mekong River[3] (see figure 2, map of Isan).

The present book focuses on murals at a cluster of seven monasteries in the local group, mainly in the provinces of Khon Kaen and Maha Sarakham. This subregion, which we call the Isan heartland, experienced less external (that is, Bangkok) influence than other parts of Isan. Consequently, its murals are among the most distinct in Thailand. The modest paintings found here are different from the renowned works of art found or originating in historic power centers like Sukhothai, Ayutthaya, Bangkok, and Lanna (or even those in major Isan cities), which were commissioned by the rich and famous—royalty, nobility, or wealthy entrepreneurs. The murals in this book are humble works created by ordinary villagers whose primary occupation was rice farming and whose descendants, for the most part, still grow rice (figure 3). Their paintings can be called "folk art," both for their robust expressiveness and because they represent the art of village folk. Indeed, local people refer to these paintings by the simple Lao/Isan term *"hup taem"* (colored or decorated pictures) rather than the elaborate Central Thai *"chitrakam faphanang"* (artistic/elegant murals). The folks in this case were Thais of Lao ethnicity. Many of their villages probably have been in existence for a long time; others were created only during the past two centuries by immigrants or prisoners of war from what is now the Lao People's Democratic Republic (commonly known as Laos) on the other side of the Mekong River. A comprehensive history of these people, their settlements, and their art has yet to be written.

The exact age of most of these murals is not known, but the oldest probably date back to the early twentieth century. While not as old as many of those in Thailand's Central Region (see figure 1, map of Thailand), they are nonetheless significant. Rather than representing weak

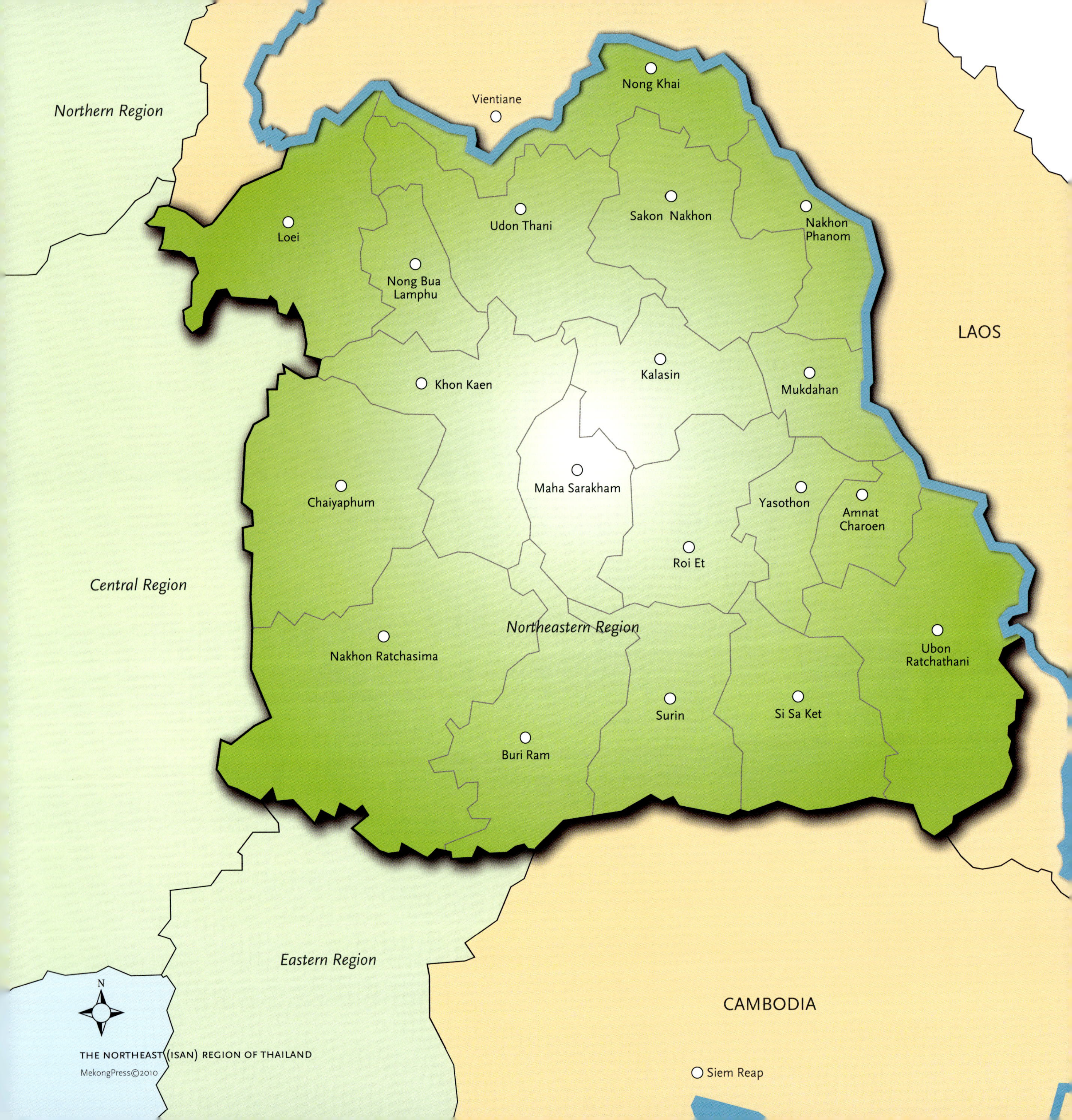

Northern Region
Central Region
Eastern Region
Northeastern Region
LAOS
CAMBODIA
Vientiane
Nong Khai
Loei
Udon Thani
Sakon Nakhon
Nakhon Phanom
Nong Bua Lamphu
Khon Kaen
Kalasin
Mukdahan
Chaiyaphum
Maha Sarakham
Yasothon
Amnat Charoen
Roi Et
Nakhon Ratchasima
Ubon Ratchathani
Surin
Si Sa Ket
Buri Ram
Siem Reap
N
THE NORTHEAST (ISAN) REGION OF THAILAND
MekongPress©2010

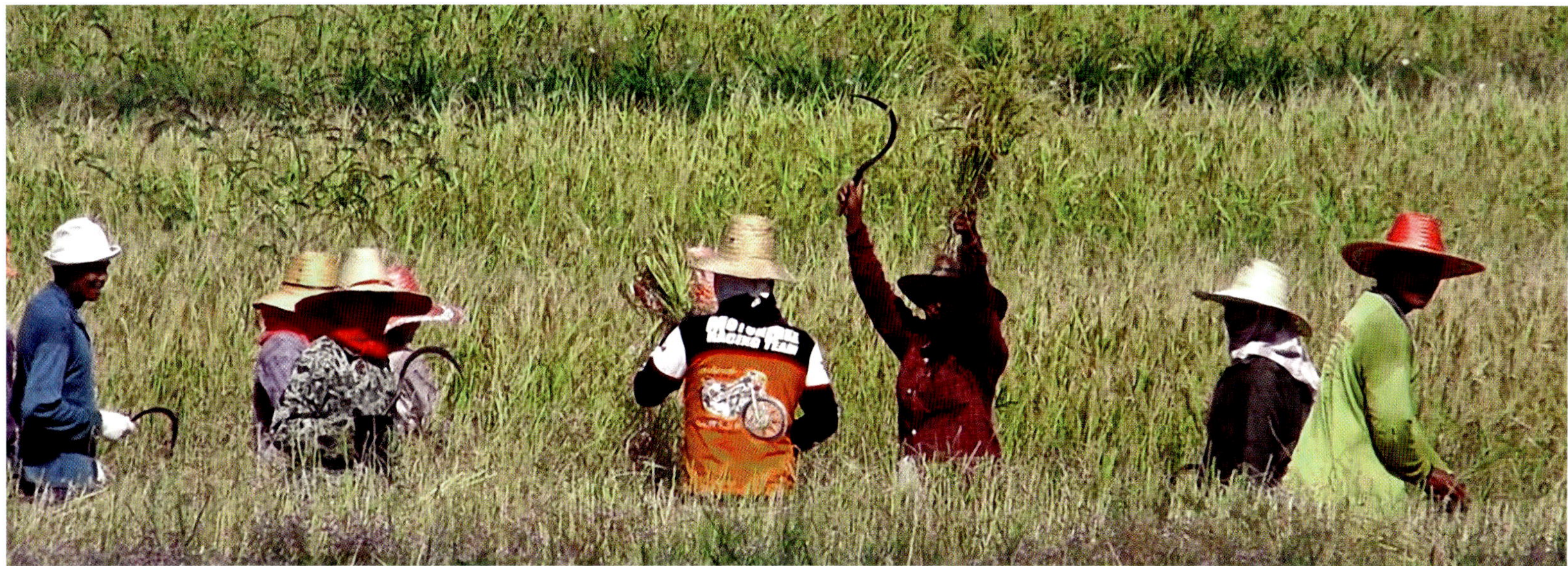

imitations of Central Thai murals, Isan heartland murals constitute a unique school of painting based on local aesthetics, customs, literature, and social values. Moreover, they document a way of life that is now nearly obsolete. Most aspects of the material culture that serves as a backdrop in the murals—including housing styles, farming and fishing techniques, clothing, and the natural landscape—have changed drastically through modernization.

The chapters that follow will locate some of the surviving Isan heartland murals in their geographic and cultural contexts, describe their stylistic features, summarize the stories they depict, and point to some of the distinct aspects of the local material and spiritual culture that they catalog. This book is, however, an introductory text rather than a comprehensive study. Its focus is primarily a subgroup of murals in the Isan heartland that share certain stylistic, thematic, and iconographic characteristics. They are located at Wat Sanuan Wari, Wat Sa Bua Kaeo, Wat Chai Si, and Wat Ban Lan in Khon Kaen province; and at Wat Pa Rerai, Wat Photharam, and Wat Ban Yang in Maha Sarakham province.[4] In addition, a few details

◄ **FIGURE 2.** Map of Isan. แผนที่ภาคอีสาน

▲ **FIGURE 3.** Isan farmers harvesting rice, 2008. Maha Sarakham. ชาวนาอีสานกำลังเกี่ยวข้าว พ.ศ. 2551 จังหวัดมหาสารคาม

from *wat*s in nearby Roi Et and Kalasin will also be mentioned. It should be noted that still other *wat*s in the latter two provinces have murals worthy of study but with different stylistic features. We have tried to keep this book as straightforward and accessible as the murals it describes. Our hope is that it will lead to a greater awareness of these murals as national treasures and stimulate further research, appreciation, and conservation.

NOTES

1. See Kamala (1997) and (2003).

2. Pairote (1989, 264–65). Of the small body of research on the subject, Pairote's work remains the most significant because he was the first to appreciate the value of local Lao village art.

3. Pairote (1989, 164) divides the *wat*s into three clusters based on their location, which correspond roughly, but not entirely, to the three groups. These are (1) the Mekong River cluster, in Loei, Nong Khai, Nakhon Phanom, and Mukdahan; (2) the central northeast cluster, in Khon Kaen, Udon Thani, Kalasin, Maha Sarakham, Roi Et, and Chaiyaphum; and (3) the southern northeast cluster, in Khorat, Buri Ram, Surin, and Si Sa Ket.

4. The names used in this book are the ones by which the *wat*s are popularly known. Some also have formal names that are used less frequently. Wat Sanuan Wari is also known as Wat Sanuan Wari Phatthanaram, Wat Ban Lan as Wat Matchim Witthayaram, Wat Pa Rerai as Wat Ban Nong Phok, and Wat Ban Yang as Wat Yang Suang Aram.

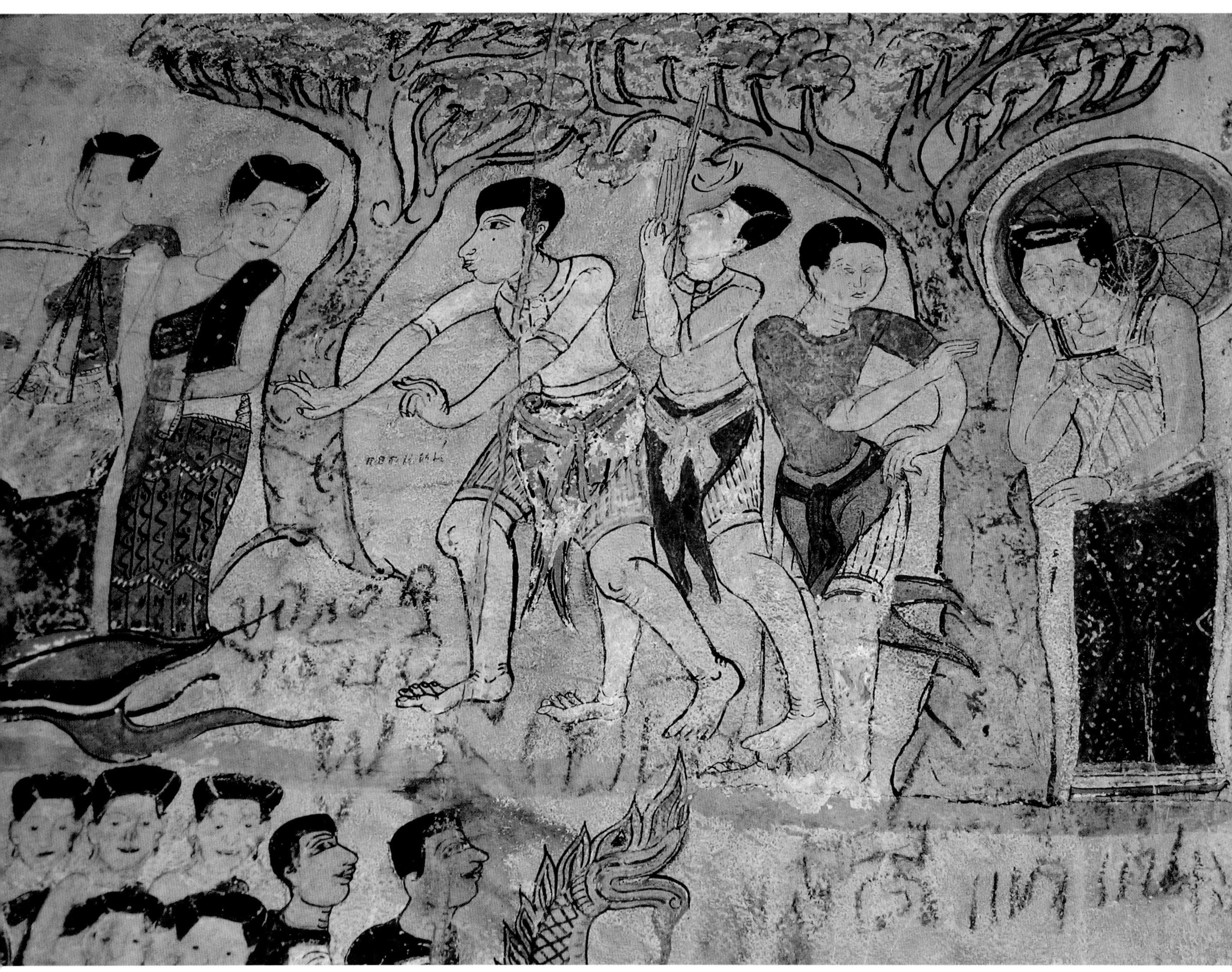

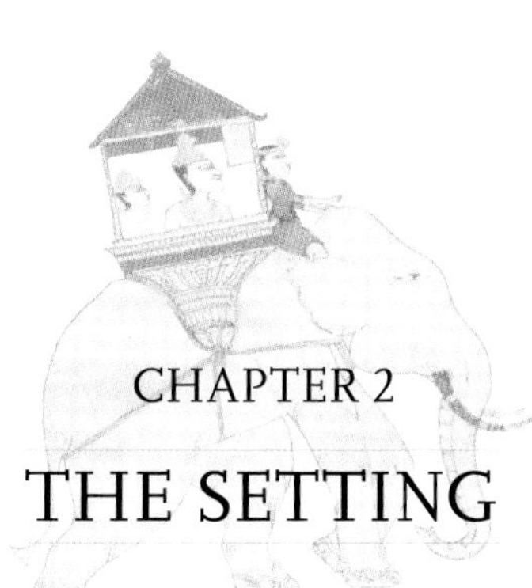

CHAPTER 2

THE SETTING

Northeast Thailand has been known as Isan since the reign of Rama V in the early twentieth century. The term, derived from Sanskrit, was created by the central government rather than the local people to refer to the region's location relative to the nation's capital. It is Thailand's largest region, comprising one-third of its area, or roughly 170,000 square kilometers. Geologically and climatically complex, it consists of the broad Khorat Plateau (which includes the east bank of the Mekong River, in what is now the Lao People's Democratic Republic), several extensive mountain ranges, and hundreds of kilometers along the Mekong River.

Isan's ethnic makeup is complex as well, with a Lao majority and pockets of Tai Dam and Phu Thai concentrated roughly in the center, various peoples who speak several Mon-Khmer languages in the south, and a small Vietnamese commerce-oriented minority at various urban spots along the Mekong River. In addition, many other numerically small ethnic groups are scattered throughout the region, while Sino-Thai merchants predominate in the urban centers.

Regarding its history, the general consensus seems to be that for many centuries much of what is now Isan probably consisted of widely dispersed small farming communities isolated from the major power centers that created the country's older, more famous Khmer-inspired art treasures. However, the existence of hundreds of prehistoric moated towns—more than in any other part of the country—suggests that many parts of the region were once both prosperous and populous (Thiva and Srisakra (1972). Archaeological and historical research from a local rather than a Bangkok perspective is needed to shed light on the region's past.

The earliest historical civilization in Isan appears to have been influenced by the Mon of Dvaravati, as seen in the extensive remains of *sema* stones discovered there. Mon influence was supplanted by that of the Khmer, whose Angkor-centered empire inspired the building of dozens of temples in southern Isan.

Following Khmer decline in the fourteenth century, the Lao state of Lan Chang, with its capital in Luang Prabang and led by King Fa Ngum, began to expand into the middle plains of the Mekong. Subsequently, numerous groups of Lao and other Tai-speaking peoples settled in what is now Isan. Their reasons for migrating were often tied to the machinations of power holders in their homeland or in the Thai capital. Some groups may have come to avoid conscription into service by Lao warlords, but many were forcibly moved to the region by Siamese conquerors. For several centuries the northern part of the region was influenced by the Lan Chang culture of what is now Laos, while the southern part retained Khmer influence, a situation that still exists today, as evidenced by local languages and ethnic groups.

Isan's dealings with Sukhothai and Ayutthaya seem to have been slight, although the latter occasionally marched across southern Isan to attack Cambodia.[1] It was only in the early nineteenth century that Siamese control began to be felt under the Ratanakosin dynasty centered in Bangkok. Previously the relationship between the Isan heartland and the Bangkok government generally had been loose and ambiguous. The rulers of northeastern towns paid homage to the Siamese king every year by sending gifts of tribute to the capital, but in the countryside there was little sense of belonging to the Siamese kingdom. While the Bangkok government did not directly govern the northeast, it appointed administrators, demanded tax, and occasionally called for laborers to be sent to Bangkok. Beginning in the third quarter of the eighteenth century, however, all able-bodied men aged eighteen to sixty were registered and tattooed, in order to prevent them from evading service to the Bangkok government.[2]

In the first quarter of the nineteenth century, the Siamese hold on the region came under threat from Chao Anouvong (also known as Anuruttharat), a member of the Lao royal family whom the Siamese had chosen to rule the Lao kingdom, which was then centered in Vientiane. Chao

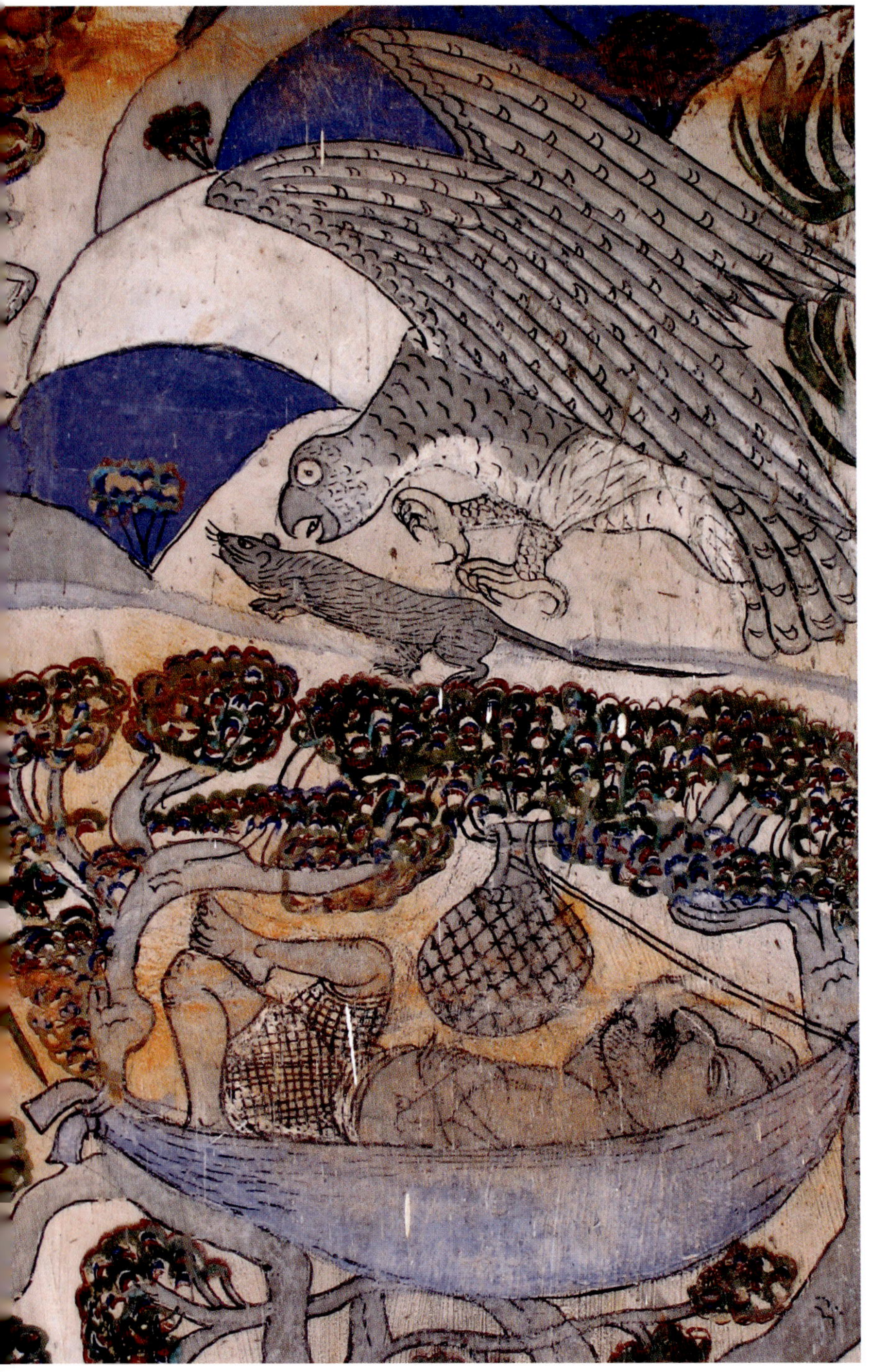

Anouvong apparently was an astute leader, who since the beginning of his reign in 1805 had undertaken major public works projects in his capital and cultivated the alliance of Vietnam. He also persuaded the Siamese to appoint his son to rule Champassak in southern Laos following internal political problems there. Anouvong thus controlled a considerable part of Laos. Seeking to gain complete independence from the Siamese, some twenty years after assuming the throne he and his troops captured Khorat and marched toward Bangkok. They were taken prisoner, however, and Anouvong was put on display in a cage in Bangkok before being executed in 1835. The Siamese totally destroyed Vientiane and captured most of the kingdom's population, resettling them not only in Isan but also in numerous provinces of the Central Region (Somkiart 2000, 56–58).

During the decades that followed, Bangkok's control over the northeast tightened as King Rama V faced the threat of the French Empire, which was expanding its influence in the region (Pairote 1989, 254). The old system of local control by local people was replaced by administrators sent from Bangkok. As outsiders from the capital, many of them tended to denigrate the local people and their cultural forms. Consequently, and not surprisingly, village abbots often failed to see the value of local Buddhist art and architectural styles and encouraged their replacement by Bangkok-influenced models.

NOTES

1. An important new collection of essays is Wilson (2009), with relevant chapters by Wilson, John Hartmann, and Marc Askew.

2. See Constance M. Wilson's detailed chapter, "Tribute, Insignia, and the Royal Gift: The Assimilation of Elites in the Khorat Plateau and the Middle Mekong Valley to Central Thai Culture during the Nineteenth Century," in Wilson (2009).

◄ **FIGURE 5.** Local forest creatures and the Brahmin Chuchok. Wat Ban Yang, Maha Sarakham. ภาพสัตว์ป่าในท้องถิ่น และพราหมณ์ชูชก วัดบ้านยาง จังหวัดมหาสารคาม

► **FIGURE 6.** Vessantara, Matsi, and their children in the forest. Wat Ban Yang, Maha Sarakham. พระเวสสันดร พระนางมัทรี และพระโอรสพระธิดาในป่า วัดบ้านยาง จังหวัดมหาสารคาม

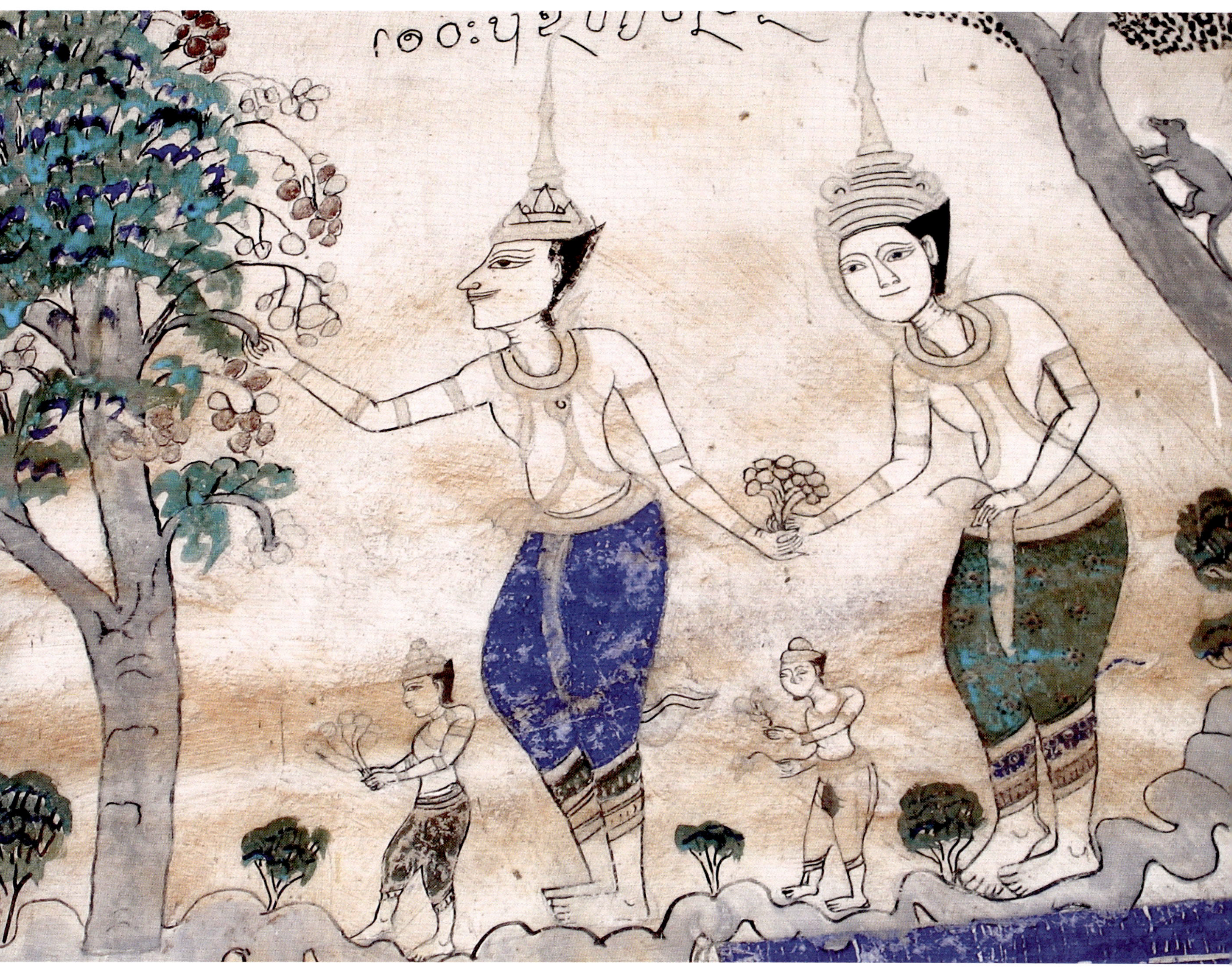

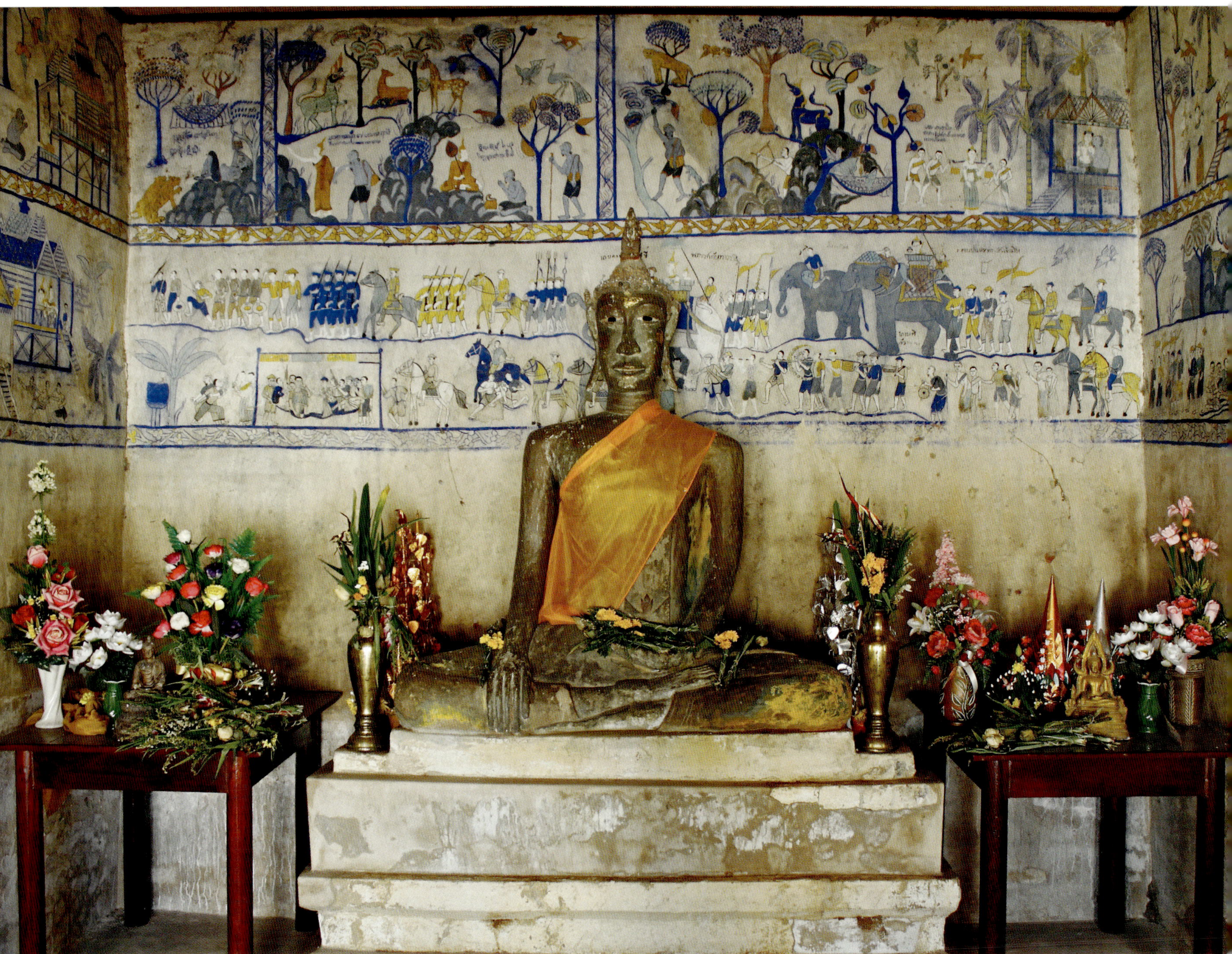

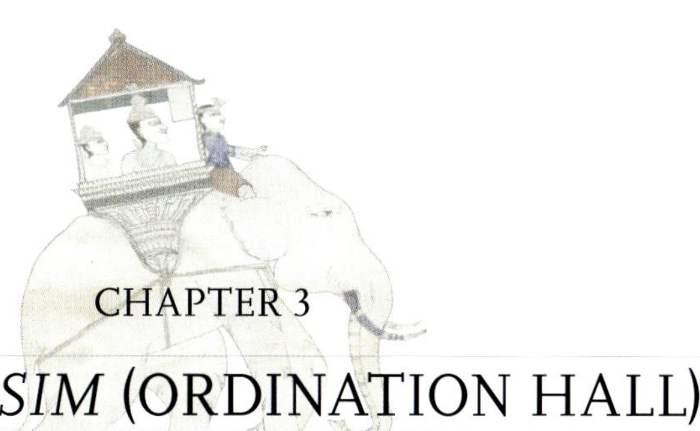

CHAPTER 3

THE ISAN *SIM* (ORDINATION HALL)

Most of the murals discussed in this book are painted on the exterior walls of ordination halls known in the Lao language as *sim* (a word derived from the Pali "*sima*," the boundary markers used to delineate the sacred space of the ordination hall). In other parts of Thailand the ordination hall is known as the *ubosot* or *bot*. Historically, when a village or group of villages was established, the residents would build a *wat* to serve as their religious, communal, and educational center. Not every monastery had—or even today has—an ordination hall, since ordinations are not an everyday occurrence. For those monasteries that do have one, it is in many respects the most important building on the compound.

Other buildings at a completely outfitted Buddhist monastery in Thailand include an assembly hall (*sala*) for the laity to gather, a Buddha image hall (*wihan*), and living quarters for the monks. One or more solid reliquary structures (*chedi*) containing the ashes of revered monks, or in some cases of the Buddha, might also be present. Numerous variations exist in the style and size of these buildings and any additional structures that might be present, depending on the community's financial means.

Despite the *sim*'s importance as a sacred space for ordinations, at many Isan village monasteries the old *sim* is the smallest building on the compound. Unlike the assembly hall, which is large enough to comfortably accommodate the entire congregation, the *sim* has little interior space (see figure 7, interior of Wat Sanuan Wari). The reason is

pragmatic: *sim* were constructed only large enough to hold those being ordained and the presiding monks. Its sacred interior was considered off-limits to women, since they could not be ordained. Consequently, murals depicting Buddhist stories were painted on the *sim*'s exterior in order to make religious teaching available to women.[1]

External murals are rare in other parts of Thailand. Some *sim* have interior murals as well, but only those at Wat Sanuan Wari will be discussed here, because they provide a model for understanding the composition of those on the exterior.

Nowadays, when one enters an Isan monastery compound the old *sim* may not be readily apparent, as most are overshadowed by their replacements—tall, narrow buildings constructed according to a standard plan distributed by the Thai Department of Religious Affairs (Ministry of Education) in Bangkok, and painted with gaudy synthetic colors. By contrast, the older *sim* are shorter, more diverse architecturally, and sometimes in need of repair. An example is the *sim* at Wat Sanuan Wari, seen in figure 9. It was recently renovated by the Fine Arts Department but, unfortunately, its new roof is made of galvanized metal rather than the original wooden tiles. Most old *sim* are no longer used for ordinations but rather for small, private merit-making sessions. Others have been torn down through a lack of appreciation of their value. This loss makes it difficult to develop a meaningful chronology of local painting.

Sim Design

Sim design includes numerous variables—height, length, width, proportions, profile, amount of molding around windows and doors, and still other features, as the examples in figures 8–10 illustrate.[2] Nevertheless, Isan heartland *sim* all have several features in common. They are all made of brick and mortar, and most were built by Vietnamese craftsmen who specialized in the medium.[3] Some have doors or decorative motifs carved of wood, or both. *Sim* usually have an elevated base

◄ **FIGURE 7.** *Sim* interior. Wat Sanuan Wari, Khon Kaen. ภายในสิม วัดสนวนวารี จังหวัดขอนแก่น

FOLLOWING PAGE

➤ **FIGURE 8.** Old *sim* with new Central-style roof. Wat Chai Si, Khon Kaen. สิมโบราณ พร้อมหลังคาใหม่แบบภาคกลาง วัดไชยศรี จังหวัดขอนแก่น

➤ **FIGURE 9.** Old and new *sim*. Wat Sanuan Wari, Khon Kaen. สิมแบบเก่าและแบบใหม่ วัดสนวนวารี จังหวัดขอนแก่น

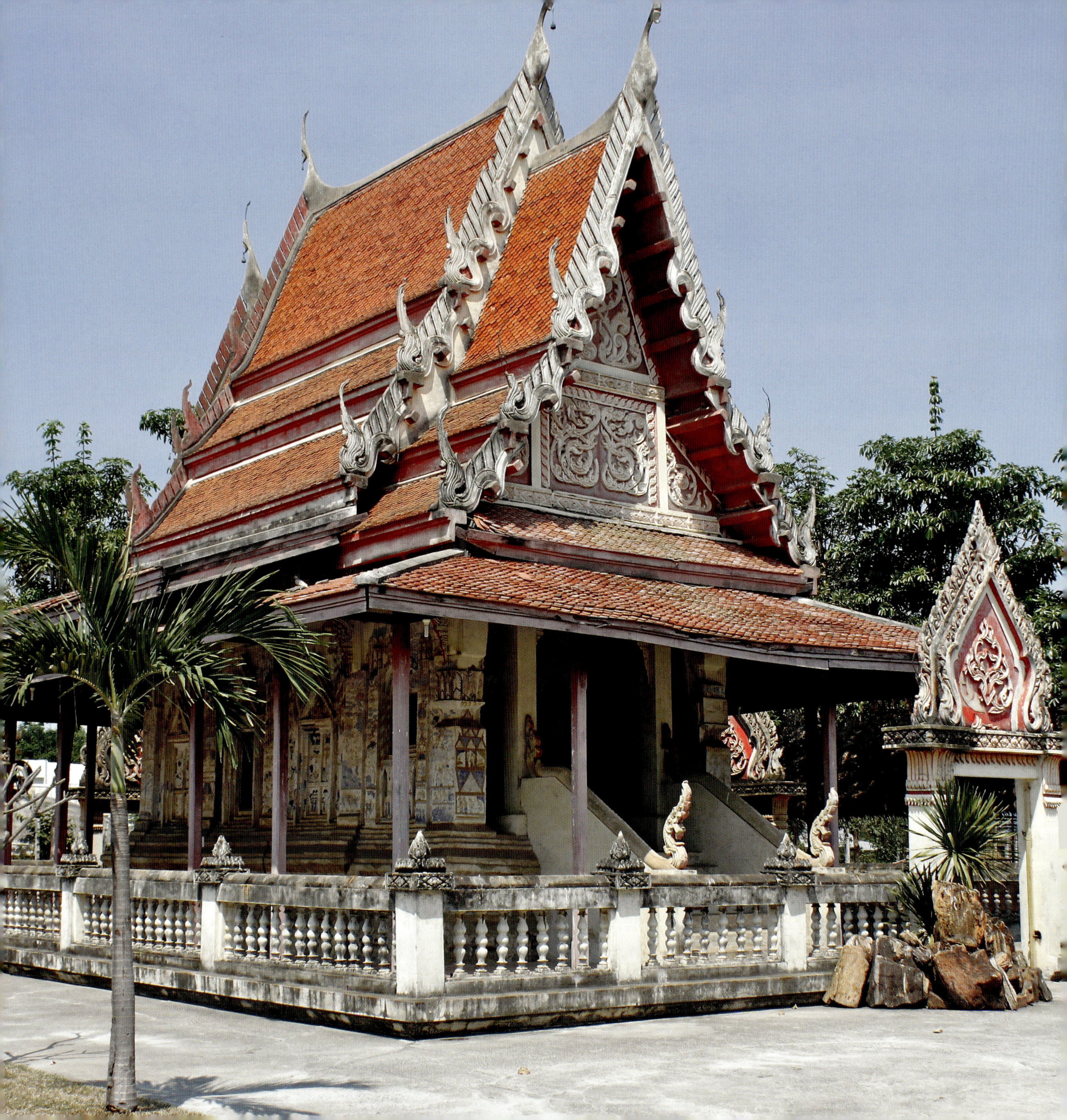

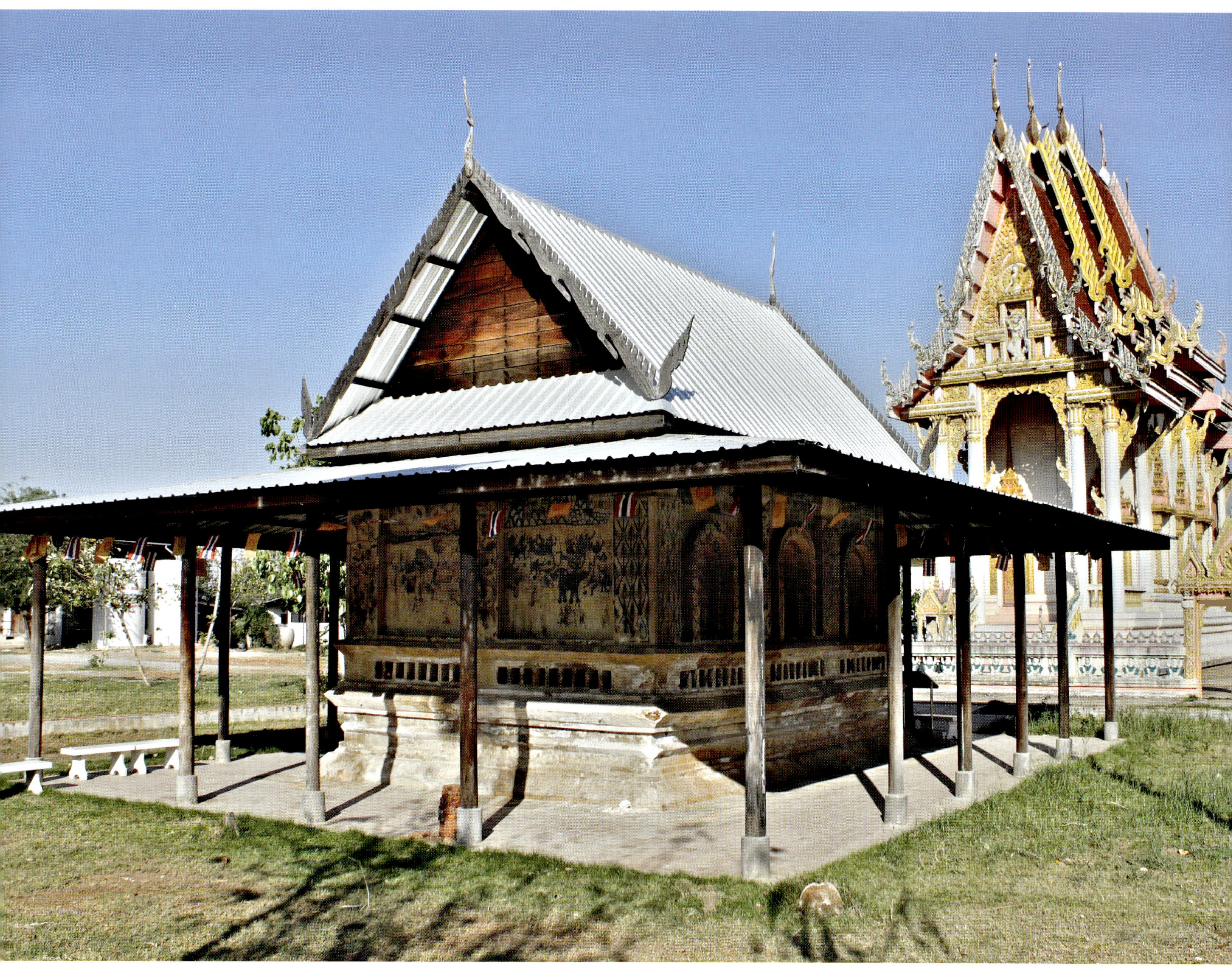

with a profile narrowing in the middle. Some have a gallery circling the exterior, from which the murals can be viewed. Most are three bays (or "rooms") long and two bays wide. The single entrance is reached by a stairway flanked by simple railings in the shape of a *naga* or, less frequently, a *singha* (a mythical lion) (figures 11 and 12). The *naga* is a serpent-like mythical animal that plays a central role in legends and beliefs throughout South and Southeast Asia. It is a particularly important motif in Lao folklore, weaving, and Buddhist iconography. Its form on Isan *sim* railings is simple and highly stylized, unlike the multiheaded cobra-like figure seen in Khmer or Khmer-influenced forms in many parts of Thailand.

Another important architectural feature found on many *sim* is a wide gabled roof extending outward to shelter the murals on the walls below. It sometimes includes one or two narrow tiers and often has *naga*-shaped finials. Roofs were originally made of wooden shingles, but many have been replaced by galvanized metal or orange Central-style glazed tiles. Unfortunately, there are instances of well-intentioned but insensitive renovations that have drastically changed a building's character. For example, Wat Chai Si's *sim* (seen in figure 8) now has a tall, steep Central-style roof. By contrast, Wat Sa Bua Kaeo's new roof (figure 10) is a stylistically compatible replacement even though its shingles are made of red ceramic in the Central Thai style, rather than of brown wood in the local style.[4]

NOTES

1. This explanation was given by Pairote as well as by monks in the monasteries we visited.

2. The Buddhist *Vinaya* (Book of Discipline) classifies *sim* into two types: water *sim* and land *sim*. This classification appears to reflect the concern in early Buddhism for finding an appropriately pure site for ordinations. Accordingly, ordinations could be held within a sanctified area of a monastery or, in the absence of such an area, in the middle of a body of water. Such a water *sim* could be a raft, boat, or a building surrounded by water. Nowadays, water *sim* are rare in Isan and, indeed, throughout Thailand. Much more common are land *sim*, which have ground-level stones (*bai sema*) at the corners and midpoints of each side, indicating the locations of *luk nimit*, boundary markers, buried below ground.

In Isan, land *sim* are further classified as either open or closed *sim*. Again, this classification seems to reflect the development of Buddhist material culture, as open *sim* are no longer constructed and the remaining examples are few. In this type of structure, only the back wall behind the main Buddha image extends up to the roof, while the lateral walls, constructed in a series of steps leading up to the back wall, are open. At some open *sim*, traces of murals can be found on the interior back walls, but they are in ruinous condition. Much more common are the closed *sim*, which are enclosed by four walls with a single entrance door at the front (east side). See Wiroj (1993).

3. Several Isan *sim* along the Mekong River are stylistically similar to some in Vientiane and may be related to the movement of people from the Lan Chang capital after its defeat by Siam in 1828. Earlier *sim* were constructed of wood, but few of these old buildings are still standing (Wiroj 1993).

4. The Siam Society lists on its website the names of individuals, companies, and agencies that contributed to the renovation. http://www.siam-society.org/heritage/watsrabua.html.

➤ **FIGURE 10.** *Sim* renovation with local roof style, but Central-style tiles. Wat Sa Bua Kaeo, Khon Kaen. สิมที่ได้รับการบูรณะ ประกอบหลังคาใหม่แบบท้องถิ่น แต่ใช้กระเบื้องแบบภาคกลาง วัดสระบัวแก้ว จังหวัดขอนแก่น

FOLLOWING PAGES

➤ **FIGURE 11.** *Naga* figures flanking stairway. Wat Sanuan Wari, Khon Kaen. บันไดนาค วัดสนวนวารี จังหวัดขอนแก่น

➤ **FIGURE 12.** *Singha* and human figures on stairway leading to entrance. Notice the borders surrounding the doorway and corners. Wat Sa Bua Kaeo, Khon Kaen. รูปปั้นสิงห์และมนุษย์ที่บันไดทางเข้า สังเกตเสาขนาบช่องประตูและบริเวณมุม วัดสระบัวแก้ว จังหวัดขอนแก่น

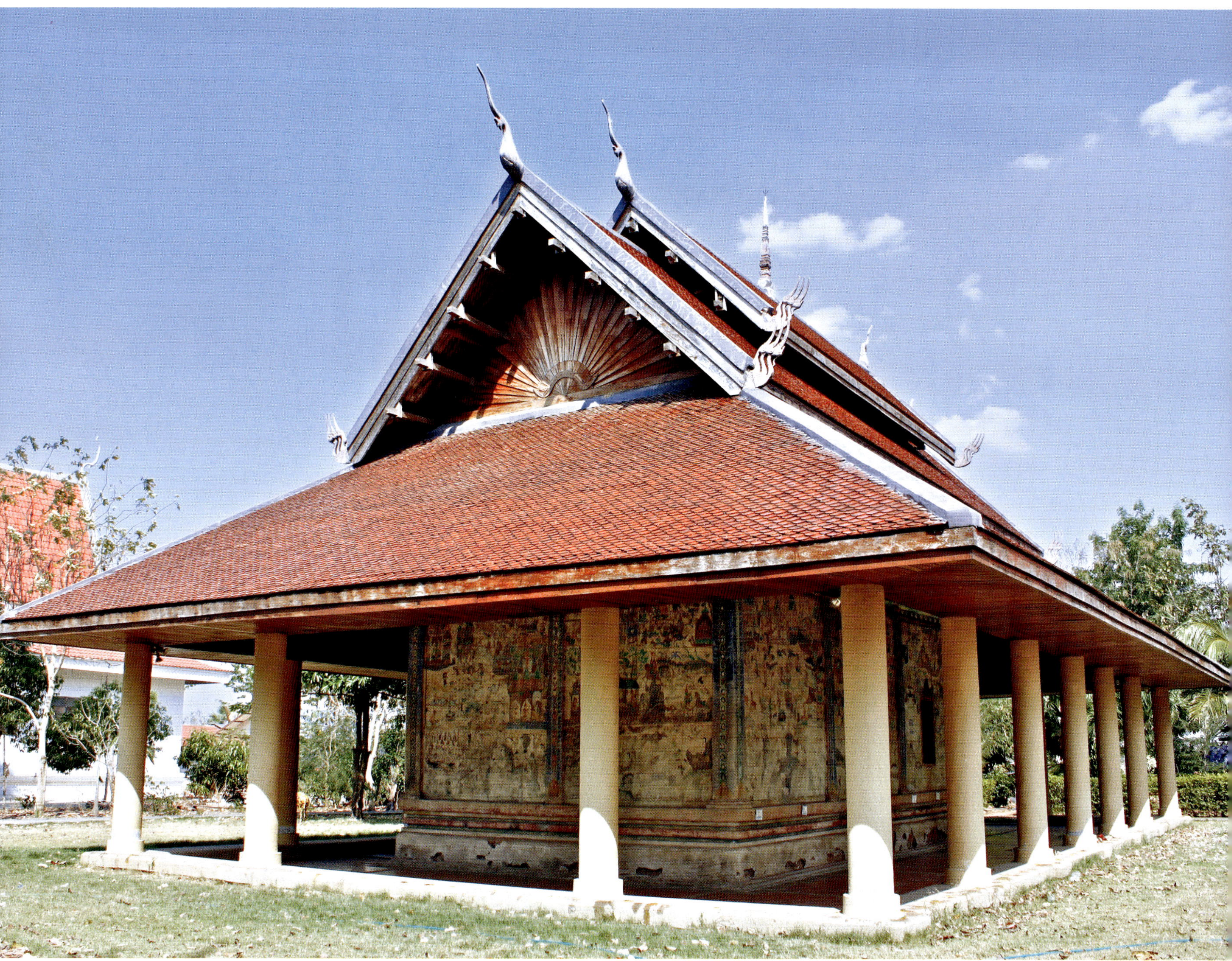

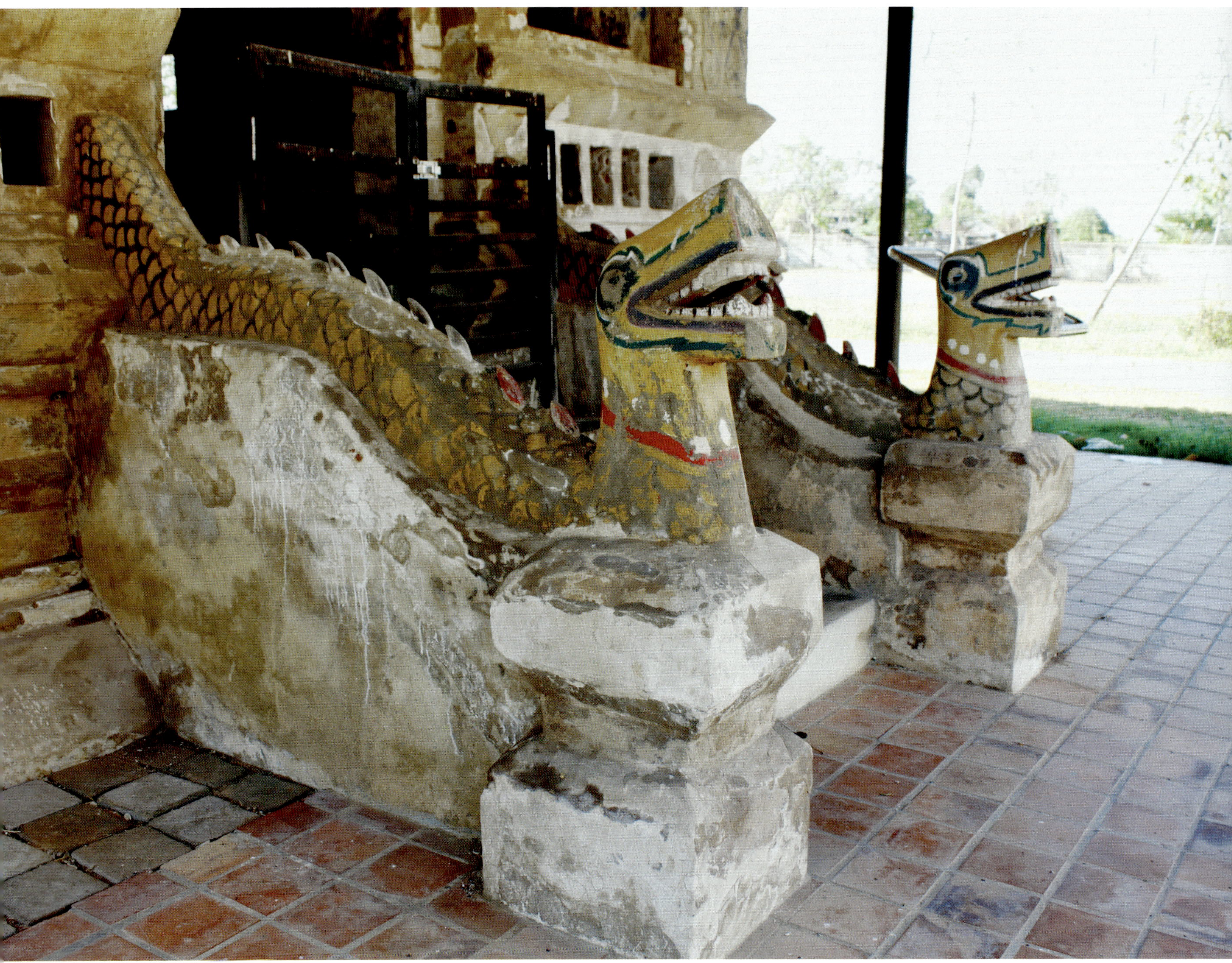

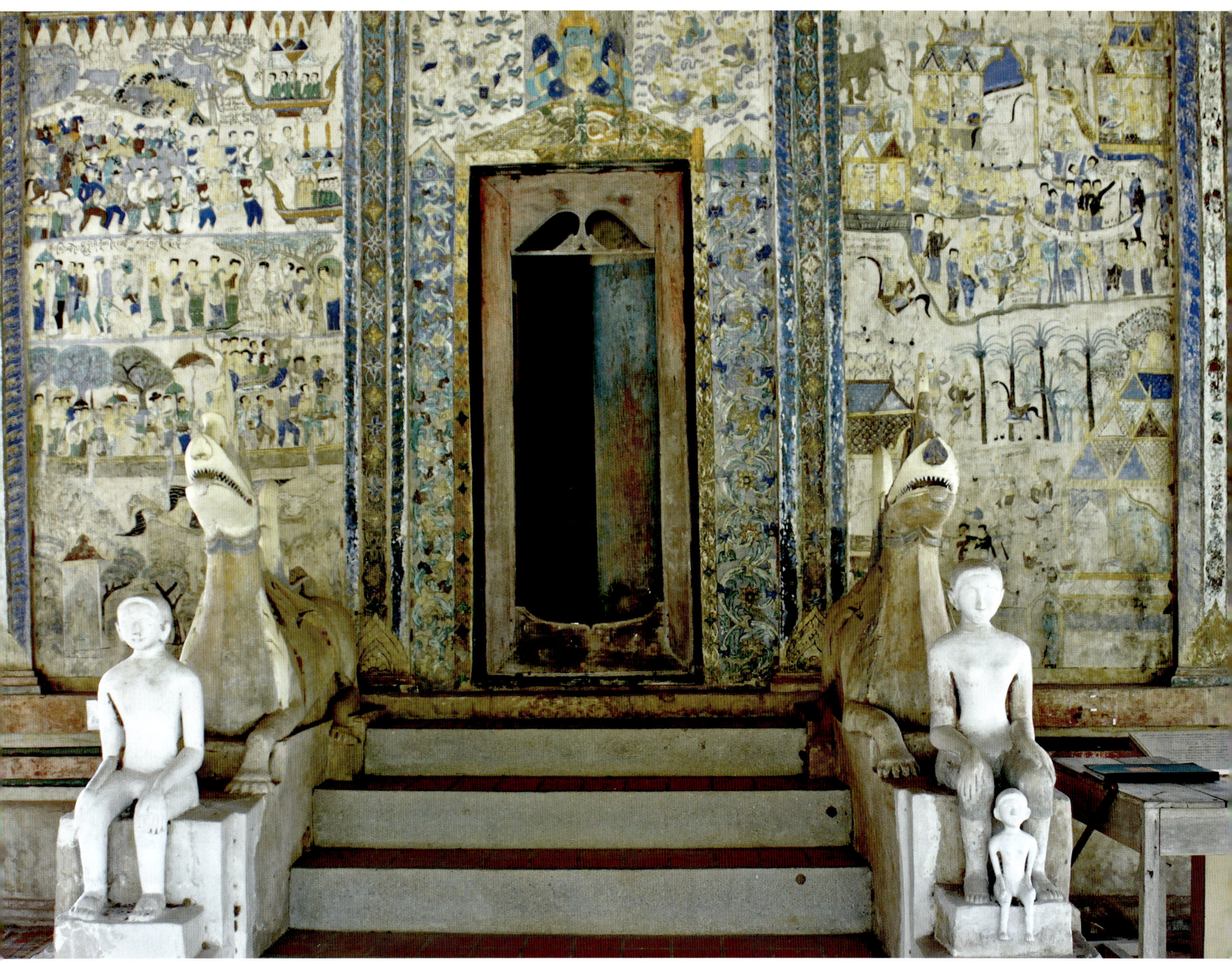

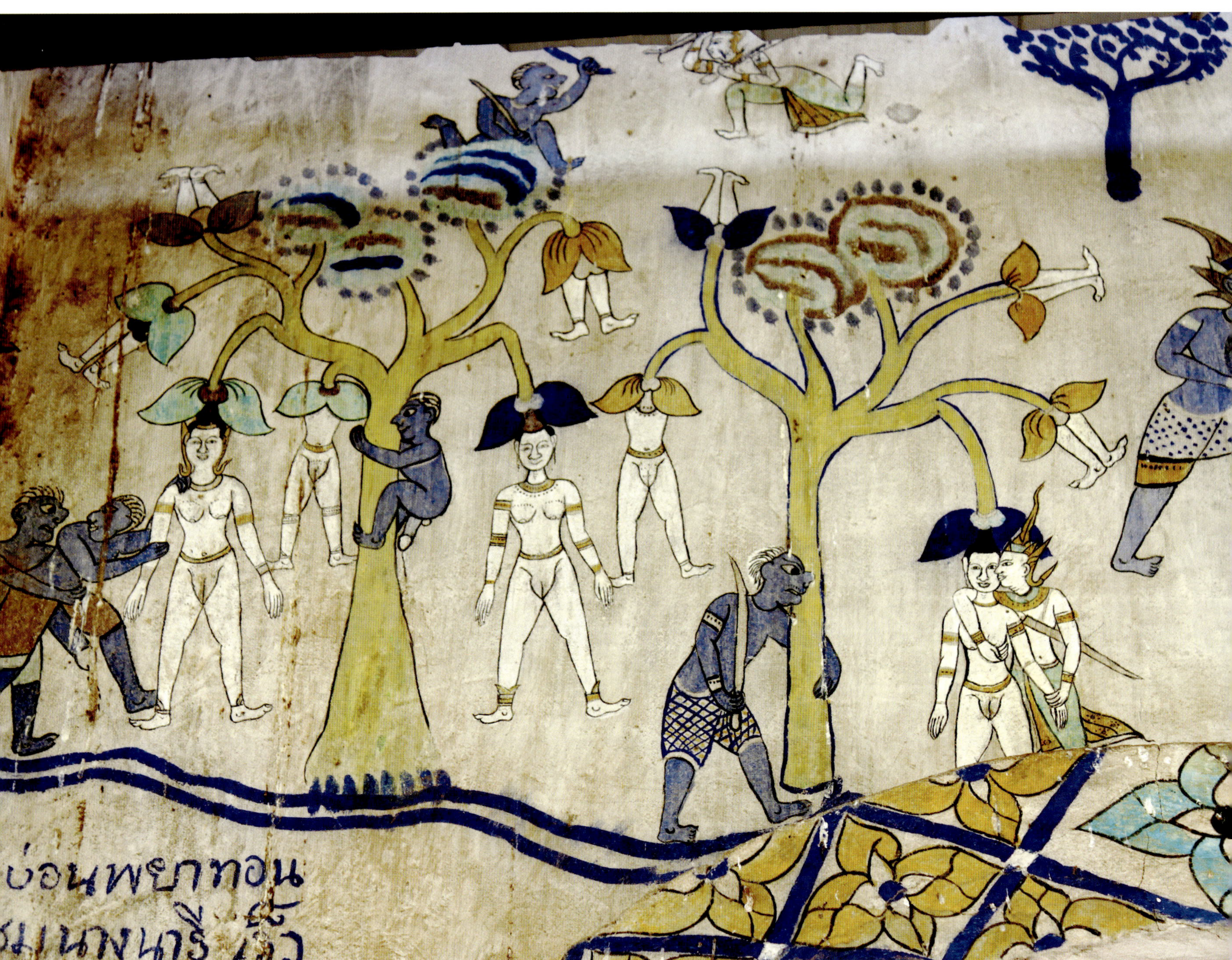
บ่อนพยาทอน
นนางนาริ์ เว้า

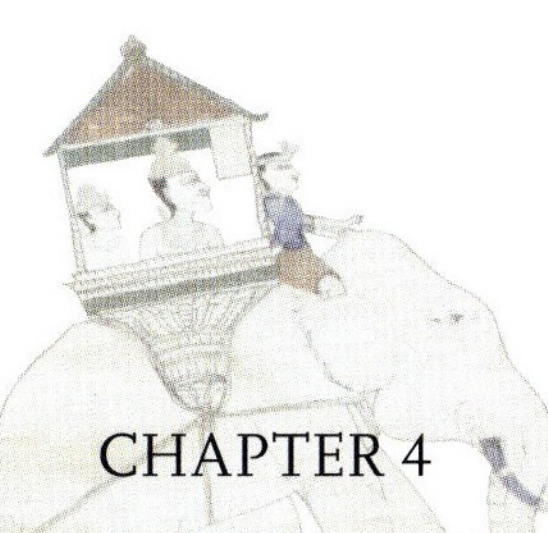

CHAPTER 4

THE ISAN HEARTLAND AS SEEN IN MURALS

Viewing a central Isan mural is like entering a peaceable kingdom densely laden with myriad forms of local plant and animal life—wild and domesticated, real and mythical, food source and friend. Banana, bamboo, banyan, *bodhi*, palm, papaya, jackfruit, tamarind, and other types of real and imaginary trees provide the background to many scenes. Jungle-dwelling deer, tigers, hogs, monkeys, peacocks, owls, and vultures are found alongside royal elephants and horses as well as village dogs, ducks, chickens, and water buffalo.

Extraordinary creatures derived from Hindu-Buddhist cosmology are present as well. They include the *naga*, mentioned above, a highly revered water serpent found throughout South and Southeast Asian mythology and particularly important to the Lao; the *kinnari*, a beguiling being that is half human and half bird; the *singha*, a stately lion-like creature that often serves as a door guardian; and the *khotchasi* (see figure 31, p. 39), a lion-like animal with elephant tusks and trunk.

Botanical species are no less wondrous, particularly the *nariphon* tree (figure 13), whose fruits are nubile maidens that emerge feet first from the flowers and sway delicately from its branches. Not surprisingly, they are plucked and consumed by some of the male characters in certain stories. This fruit is an essential motif in the Sin Sai epic, an important local legend summarized in chapter 5. (The motif is also common in Burmese murals, where the lady-fruit emerge fully clothed, while those in Isan are clad only in a few pieces of jewelry.)

Most compositions are tightly packed with details. Foliage, landscape elements, humans, and animals are drawn as flat, outlined figures with no concern for realistic proportion or scale. At most *wats*, the figures fill all available space; the notable exception is Wat Sanuan Wari, where simply drawn figures are loosely lined up against a light background.

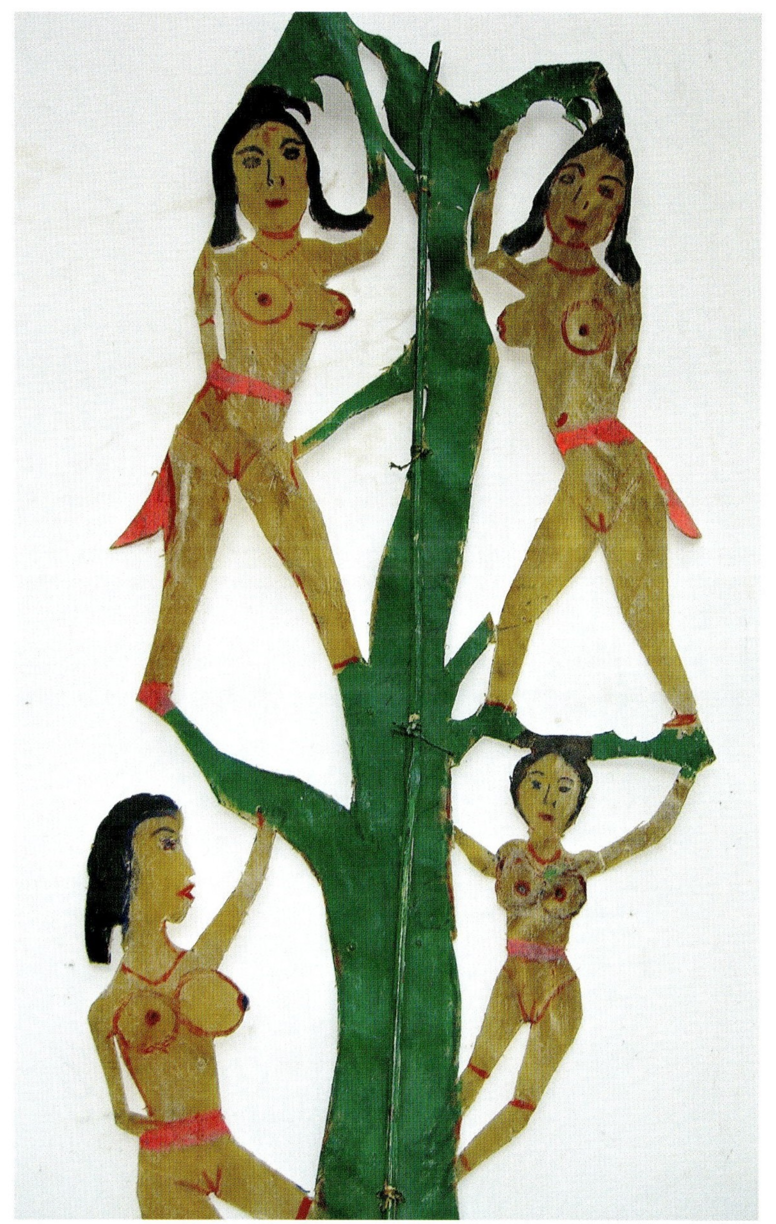

◀ **FIGURE 13.** *Nariphon* tree. Wat Sanuan Wari, Khon Kaen. ต้นนารีผล วัดสนวนวารี จังหวัดขอนแก่น

▶ **FIGURE 14.** *Nariphon* tree shadow puppet. ตัวหนังประโมทัยรูปนารีผล

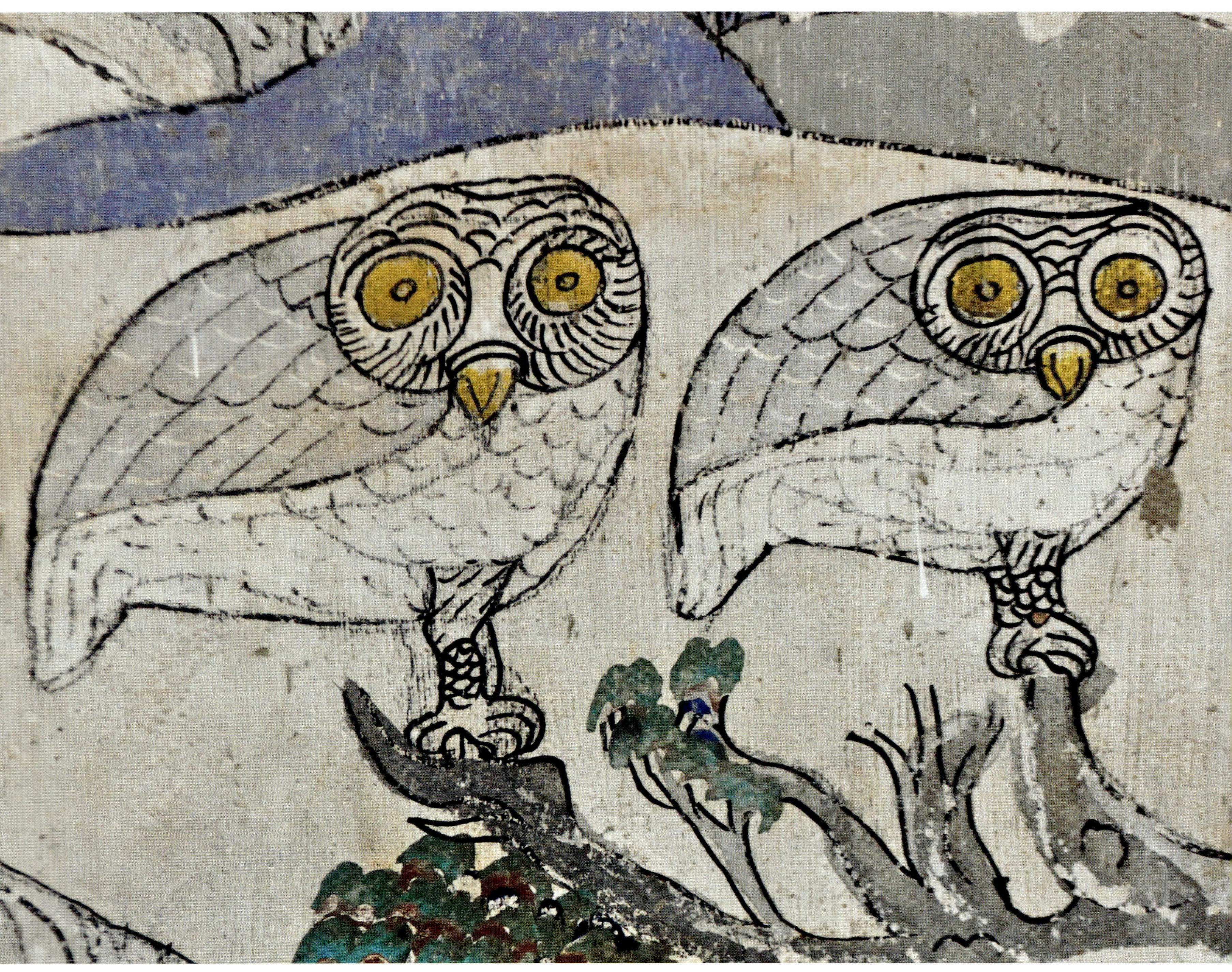

At all *wat*s, humans and animals are disproportionately large in comparison to their background. Horses and elephants resemble carousel figures ridden by toy soldiers; palaces look like doll houses; and forests are clusters of bonsai plants. Foliage is frequently painted in a range of soft brushstrokes resembling those of impressionistic works. Western artistic conventions describe unschooled artists as "naive" and "primitive," and such words immediately come to mind when one encounters this untamed, but gentle, ambiance. To focus on such pejorative terms, however, is to miss the point. To the painters, what was important was not creating a naturalistic representation of the subject, but rather a symbolic and iconographic representation, as seen through the eyes of the local people.

The abundance of fauna and flora depicted in a mural painting may be surprising, given the amount of deforestation that one notices in Isan nowadays. However, as late as 1960 much of the region was still heavily forested, and thus was home to many plant and animal species that are now found only in national parks. Paintings from virtually every temple include forests scenes that reveal intimate knowledge of assorted varieties of trees, with uniquely shaped canopies, limbs, and leaves—all inhabited by birds of various species (see figure 15, Wat Ban Yang). Isan muralists were surrounded by nature—probably to a greater extent than they would have preferred, as nature also connoted an "uncivilized" territory, that is, home to terrifying creatures. Among the most feared were the unpredictable spirits or ghosts (*phi*), sometimes depicted as short-tailed beings sauntering through the forest (figure 16, Wat Pa Rerai). Other frightening creatures included ferocious tigers, like the one seen attacking a man in figure 18, from Wat Ban Yang. Yet some of the tigers found in paintings resemble house cats and others even have human characteristics, like the smiling feline couple in figure 17, from Wat Sa Bua Kaeo. Whatever their species or status, most of the beings have a benign quality to them. Spiritually evolved characters

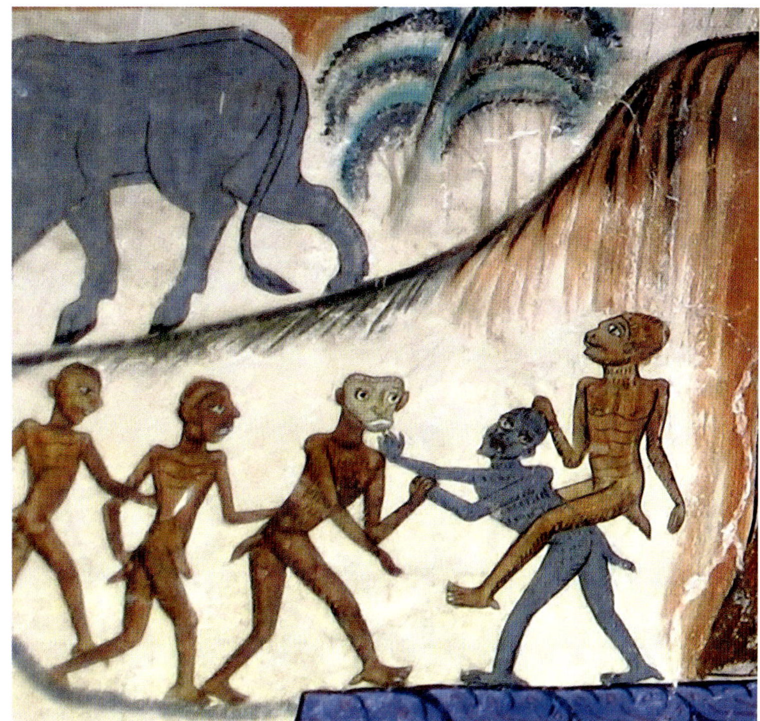

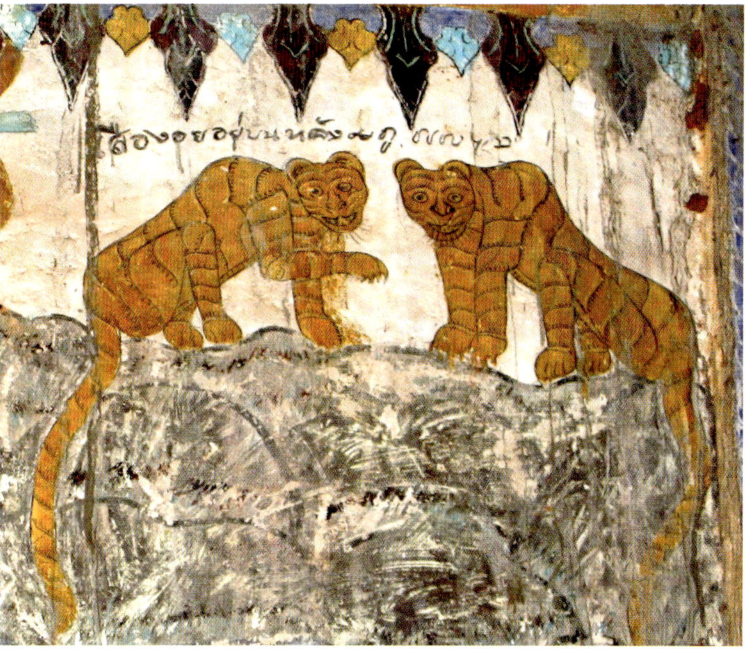

◀ **FIGURE 15.** Owl couple. Wat Ban Yang, Maha Sarakham. นกฮูกผัวเมีย วัดบ้านยาง จังหวัดมหาสารคาม

▶ **FIGURE 16.** *Phi* in forest. Wat Pa Rerai, Maha Sarakham. ผีในป่า วัดป่าเรไร จังหวัดมหาสารคาม

▶ **FIGURE 17.** Smiling tigers. Wat Sa Bua Kaeo, Khon Kaen. เสือยิ้ม วัดสระบัวแก้ว จังหวัดขอนแก่น

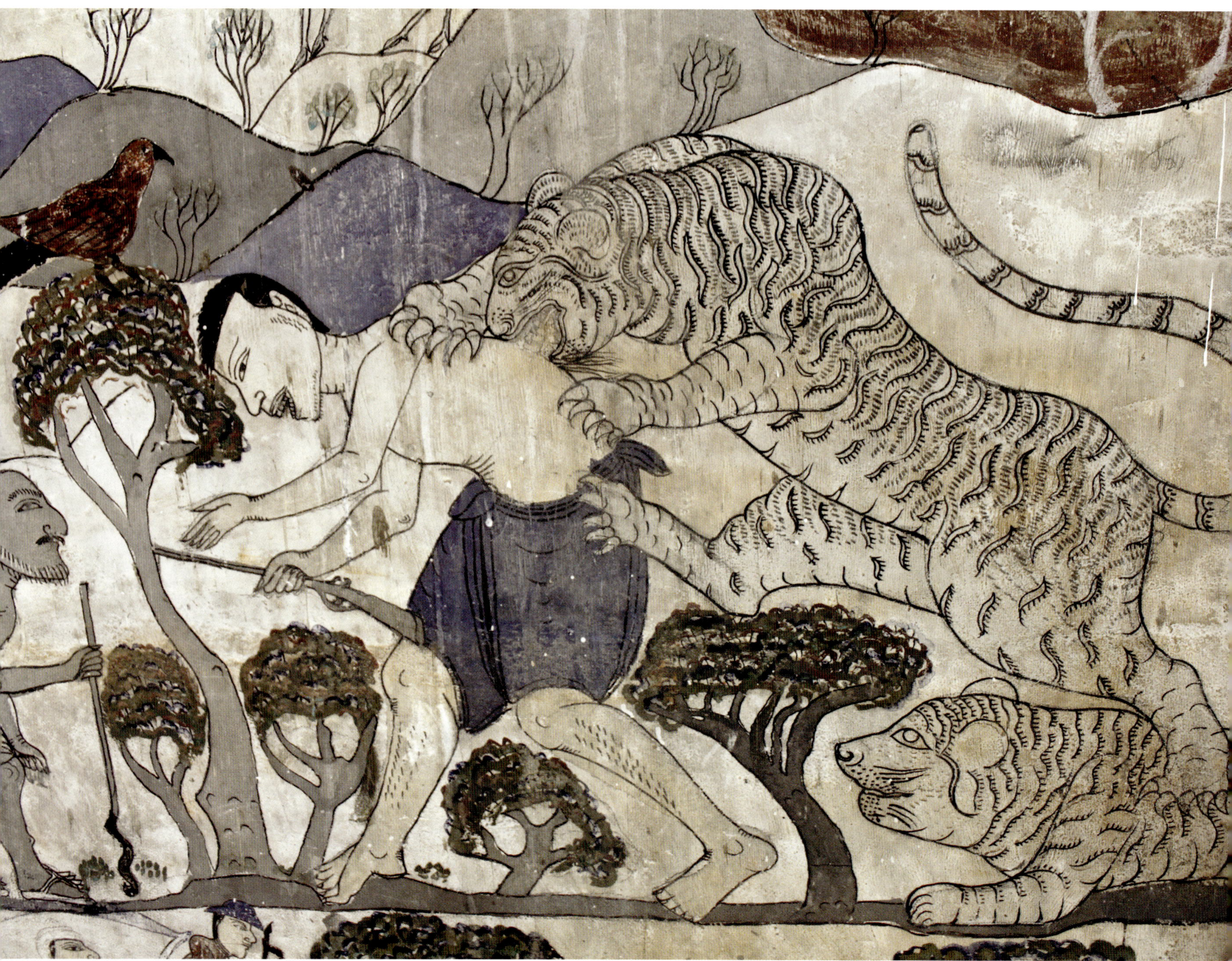

such as gods, heroes, and heroines (including *bodhisattva*s and their families) are especially sweet and gentle.

Even villains and demons are not entirely intimidating. For example, giants, despite their sturdy physiques, bulging eyes, and sharp teeth, are presented as symbols of craving and desire to be pitied rather than feared. Scenes depicting their battles with heroes are iconographic and stylized, with no evidence of blood or gore. For example, in figure 19, from Wat Sanuan Wari, the giant's dismembered body parts fill an entire wall, but rather than being graphic and gory, they are neat and tidy.

The murals thus have a storybook quality that is reinforced by the ubiquitous decorative borders, comprised of interwoven bands of stylized flower petals, found on a *sim*'s corners, doorways, and windows (see figure 47, p. 57).[1] These characteristics are unique to Isan heartland murals.

NOTES

1. These borders can be compared to the woven pieces of cotton that are used to wrap Buddhist manuscripts engraved on palm leaf (*pha ho khamphi*). Both serve as embellishments of sacred texts and delineations of their boundaries from the secular world.

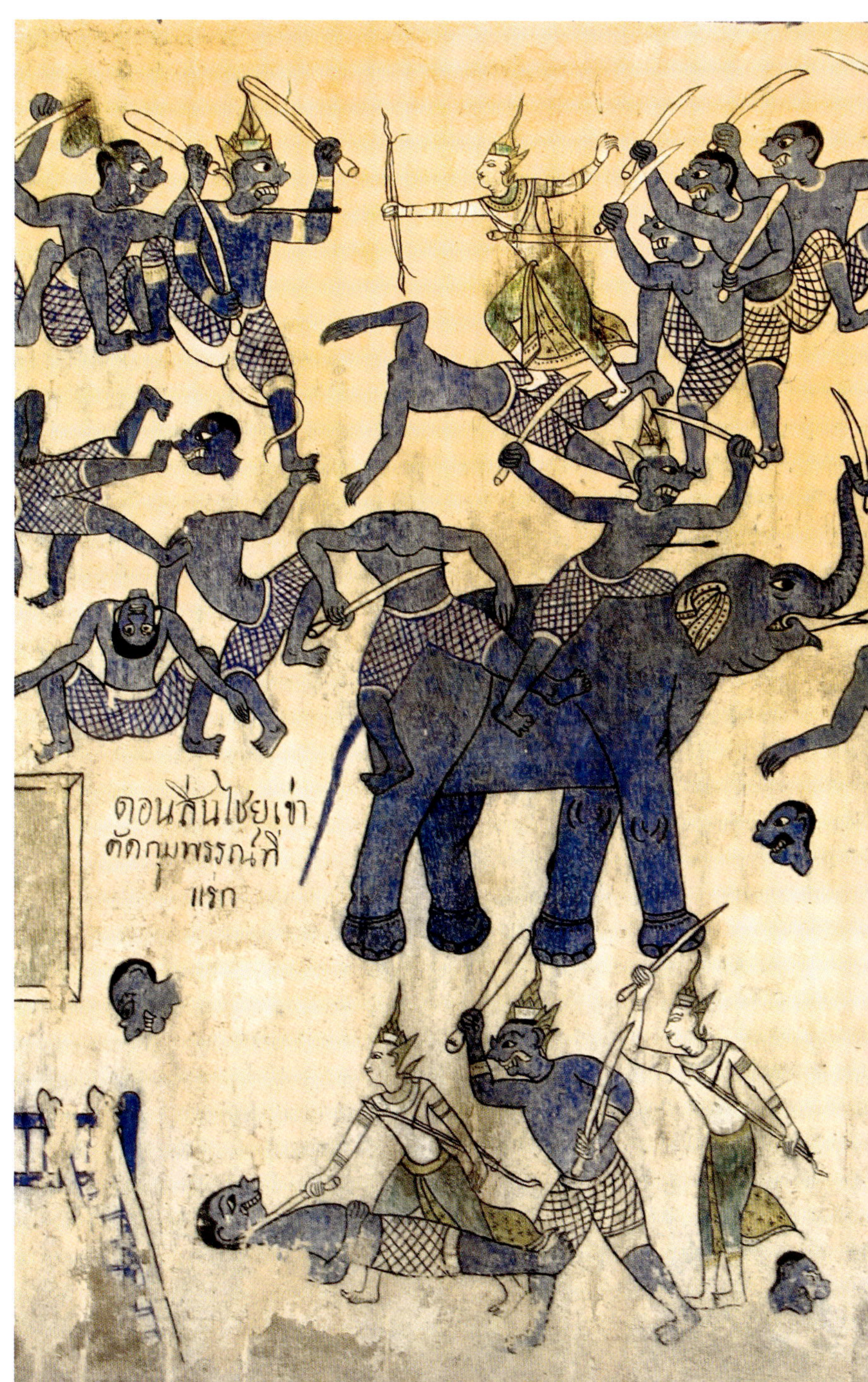

◀ **FIGURE 18.** Ferocious tiger attacking a man. Wat Ban Yang, Maha Sarakham. เสือดุโผน เข้ากัดคน วัดบ้านยาง จังหวัดมหาสารคาม

▶ **FIGURE 19.** Sin Sai story: heroes battling with giants. Wat Sanuan Wari, Khon Kaen. เรื่อง สินไช ตอนสินไชรบยักษ์ วัดสนวนวารี จังหวัดขอนแก่น

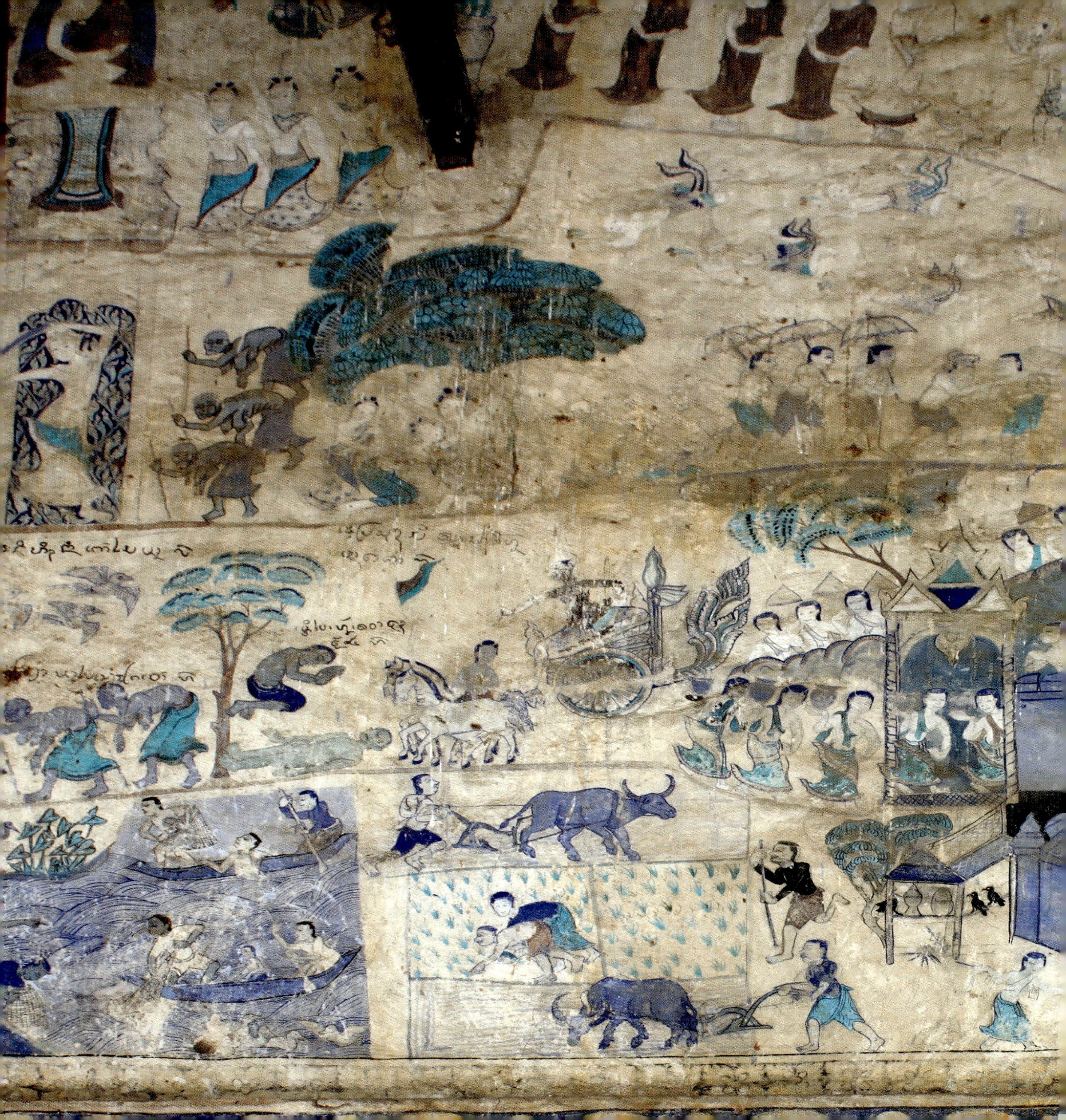

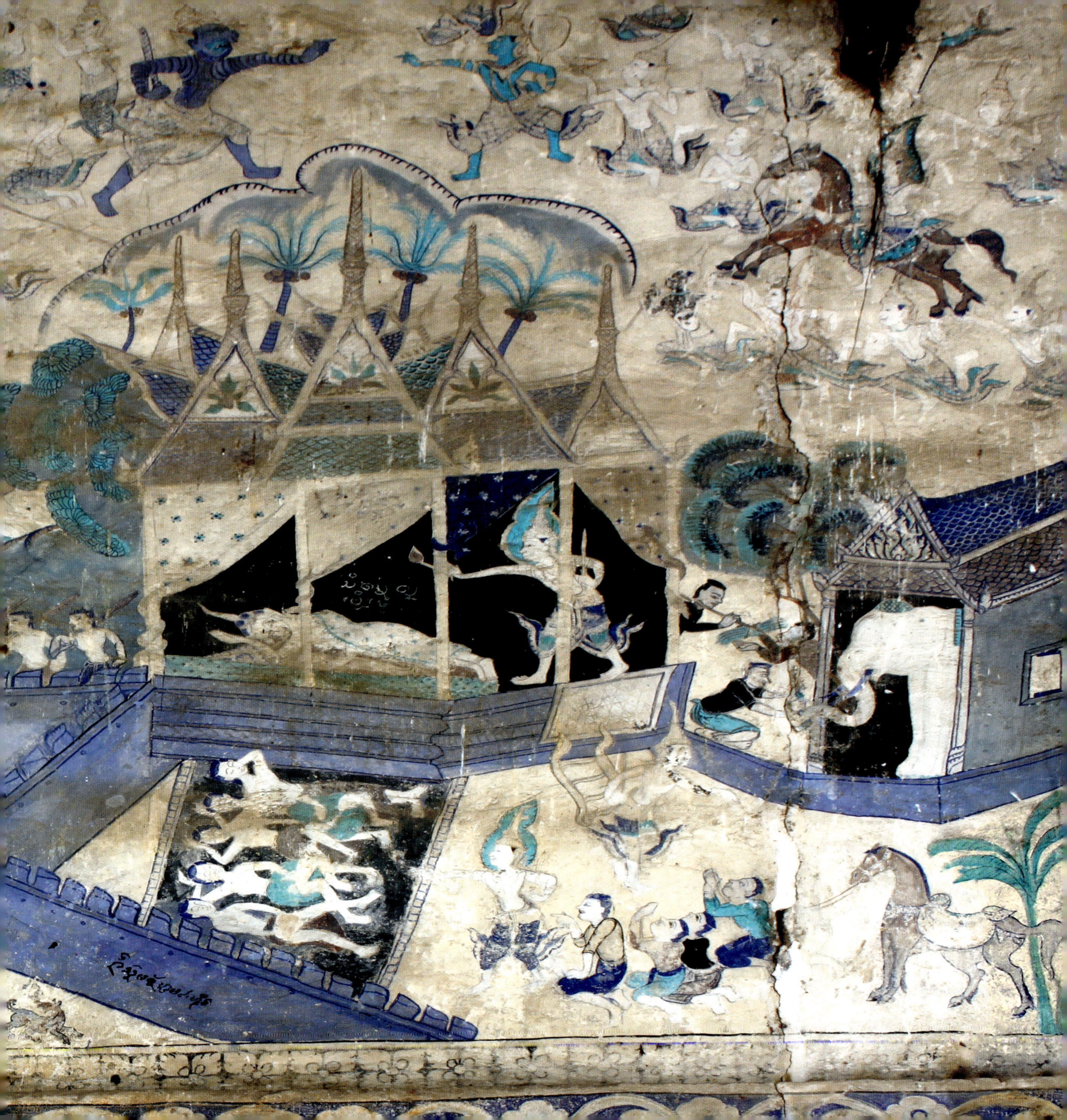

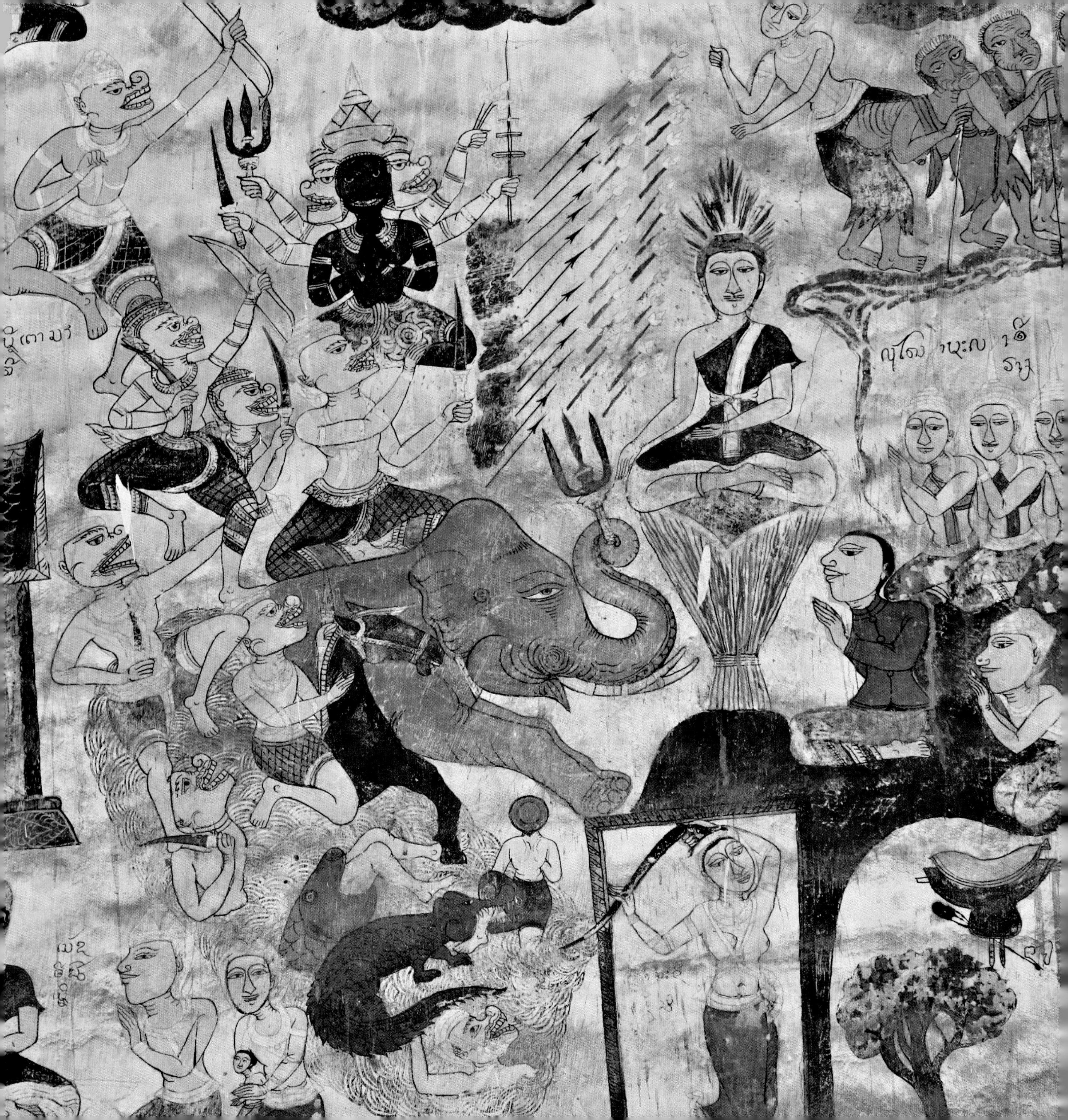
ลุไต ฯยะล ๑ ชิ รงฯ
ด(ตา)มงฯ
ดิฉบิຄ
ເຊะ ຄິ ຫຼ

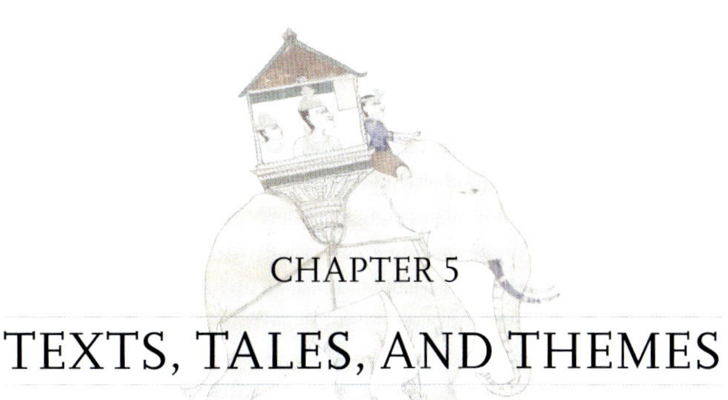

CHAPTER 5

TEXTS, TALES, AND THEMES

Isan artists drew inspiration for their work from sermons preached by local village monks as well as from tales told by traditional storytellers (Wajuppa and Macdonald 2004). The sermons were not abstract philosophical discourses, but rather engaging and even entertaining narratives that were part of an oral tradition, deeply embedded in the memories of the tellers and vividly recounted in a melodic verse form similar to the region's Lao *lam* singing. These narratives also comprised a written tradition, as they were transcribed on manuscripts made of palm leaf. The stories included key events in the life of the Buddha, accounts of his former lives, and local renditions of grand epics and legends known throughout Southeast Asia. While the texts, tales, and themes the artists chose to represent are generally the same as those in other parts of Thailand, their Isan tellings are often laced with local emphases and idiosyncrasies.

The Life of the Buddha

The Buddha's biography, as found in written versions in Thailand, includes an extensive series of episodes, including his miraculous birth from his mother's side, prognostications given by his royal family's soothsayer, excursions outside the palace, departure, quest for enlightenment, interactions with relatives, visit to Tavatimsa Heaven, performance of miracles, and more.[1] The specific episodes are depicted not only in

murals but also in wood carvings and stucco reliefs throughout Thailand. They vary from one *wat* to another and often reflect the preferences of local abbots and patrons. While artists in many parts of the country generally depicted ten or more episodes, Isan heartland painters usually chose only three: the Buddha-to-be's departure from the palace[2]; his victory over Mara (a demonic-looking personification of delusion) prior to attaining enlightenment; and his passing away (which includes his *parinirvana*, or final extinction). These events are in many ways not only the most essential to the Buddha's spiritual quest, but they also have the greatest emotional impact on the viewer.

In the first of these three events, the Great Departure, as seen in figure 20 from Wat Photharam, the future Buddha pauses to take a final gaze at his consort Yasodhara and newborn son Rahula sleeping peacefully in the middle of the night. Next to them is a cluster of dozing concubines sprawling on the bedding, their garments disheveled. One can imagine that villagers would have empathized with the young father about to leave his family for the sake of his spiritual search. On the other hand, one could view the future Buddha as propelled to pursue his quest by the repulsive sight of the palace concubines.

In the next event, the victory over Mara, the Buddha-to-be is seated in meditation under the *bodhi* tree with legs crossed, left hand on his lap, right hand on right knee with fingers touching or nearly touching the earth, as seen in figure 21 from Wat Ban Yang. This scene might be called the defining moment in the Buddhist narrative; the posture associated with it, *mara vijaya* (victory over Mara), is the one most commonly depicted in sculpture and painting throughout Southeast Asia. Below the future Buddha stands the earth goddess, Nang Thorani, wringing from her hair a mighty stream of water that sweeps away Mara's warrior demons. The stream comes from the water of donation that the Buddha-to-be had poured onto the earth each time he performed an act of generosity during his past lives. In Isan murals, as in those throughout Thailand, the water flows toward the left (from the viewer's

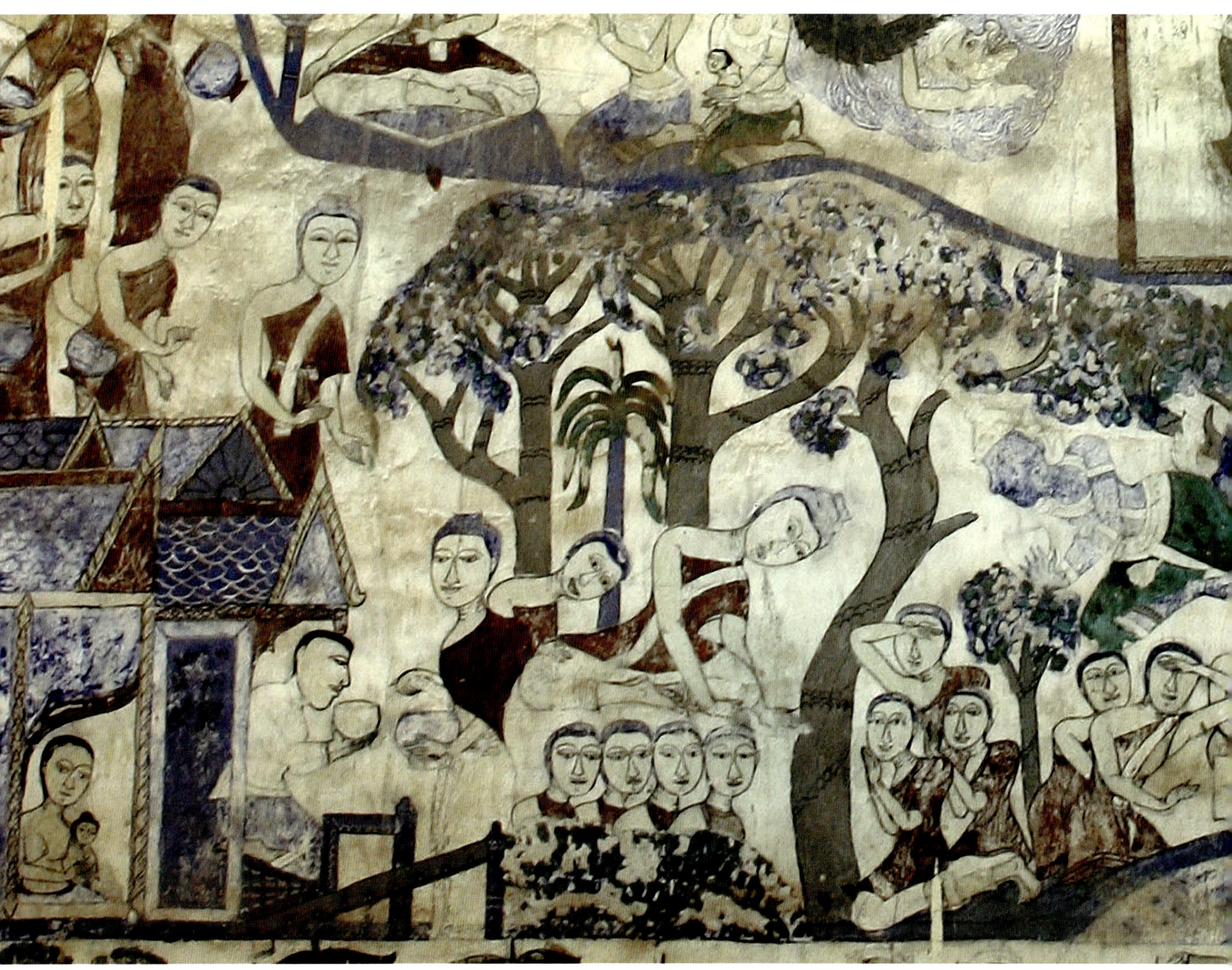

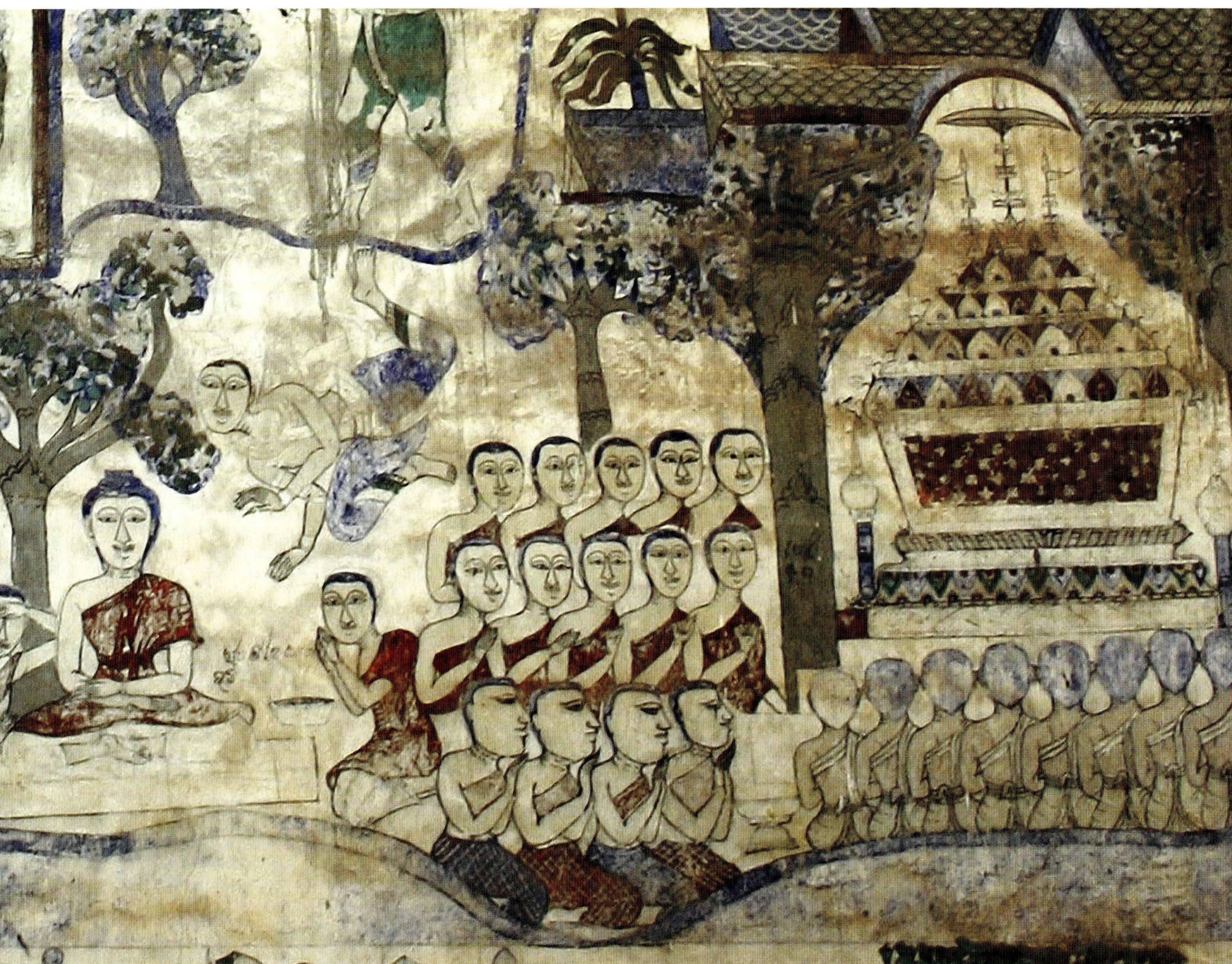

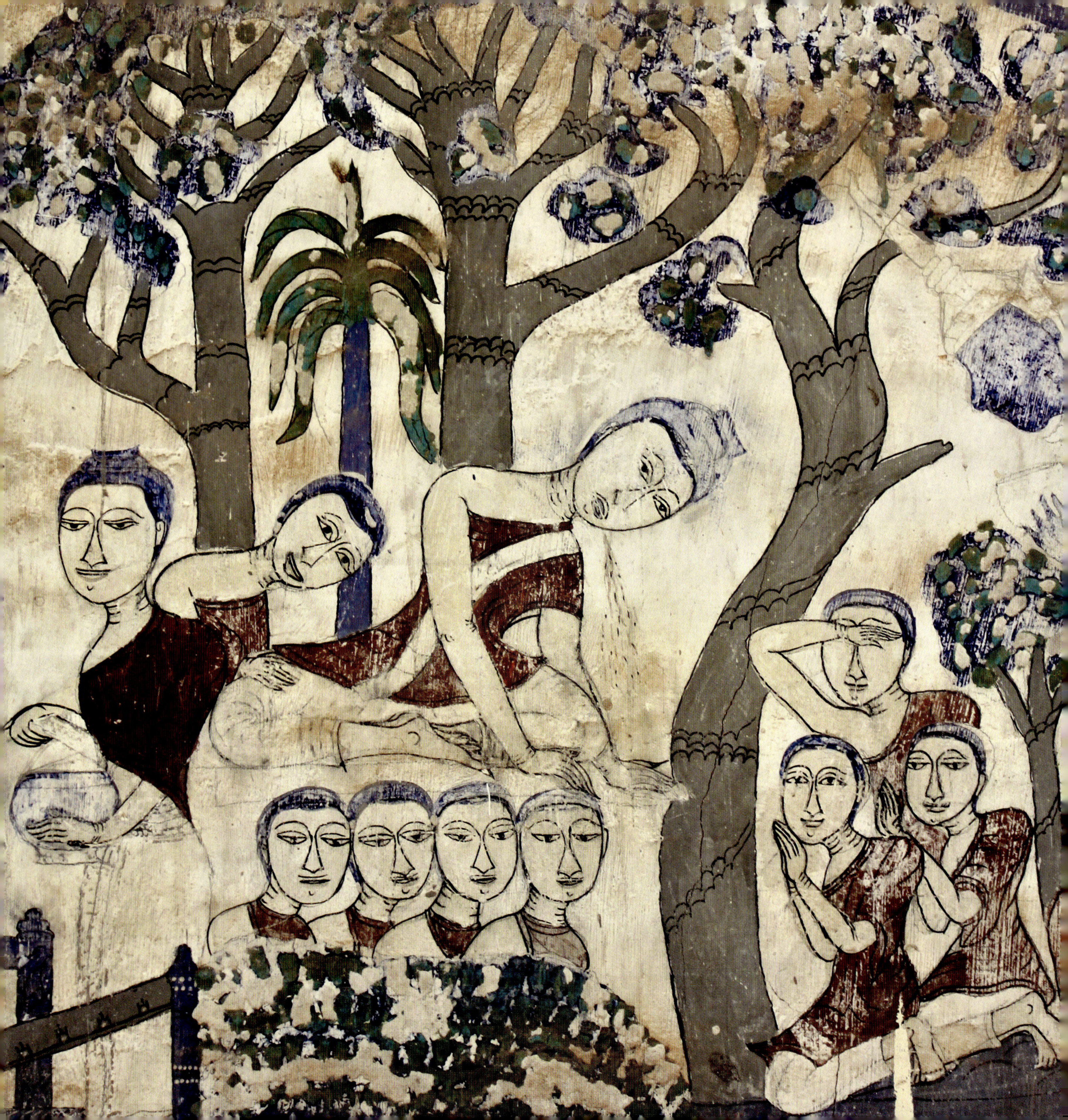

perspective), engulfing the demons, who are devoured by giant fish, or in some cases, crocodiles.

Finally, the third event, the Buddha's death, is often portrayed with particular poignancy throughout Thailand for it represents the deepest internal conflict that Buddhists feel upon the death of someone they have loved and respected: on the one hand, grief and on the other, the need to let go of their attachment to the deceased. A particularly sensitive depiction of the series of events leading to the Buddha's passage from the mundane world into nirvana appears at Wat Ban Yang (figure 22). On the far left we see a householder unknowingly bestowing upon the future Buddha an offering of food that would ultimately cause his sickness and demise. According to traditional accounts, the Buddha died of food poisoning, having eaten spoiled curry made of either pork or mushrooms. Next, we see a most unique rendition of the illness leading to the Buddha's death. The mural portrays in realistic terms his stomach distress and vomiting (figure 23). Southeast Asian Buddhist artists are usually reluctant to show the revered Great Teacher undergoing any kind of suffering, and this painting is thus a rare and sympathetic portrait.[3]

Moving to the right, we see the reaction to the Buddha's death, as monks sit in a scattered array of postures and angles that reveal their individual expressions of grief; they cover their eyes as they weep, overcome with woe. Then, on the far right, for the funeral they turn and line up in identical poses as the collective Sangha (figure 24) to allow their beloved teacher to pass into nirvana. Moreover, the artist presents the monks in an unusual series of perspectives, as we see them first from the front, then from the side, and finally from behind as they face the cremation pyre. The total composition is a masterpiece in its interplay of varying postures and perspectives to convey both human emotions and higher teachings.

The life of the Buddha, however, is just one of many stories depicted in Isan heartland murals. Several other tales generally play a greater role in local teachings and rituals, and occupy a greater amount of mural space than does the Buddha's biography. These include stories

◄ **FIGURE 23.** Detail of the Buddha's sickness. Wat Ban Yang, Maha Sarakham. อาการอาพาธของพระพุทธเจ้า วัดบ้านยาง จังหวัดมหาสารคาม

► **FIGURE 24.** Detail of the Buddha's cremation. Wat Ban Yang, Maha Sarakham. ถวายพระเพลิงพระพุทธสรีระศพ วัดบ้านยาง จังหวัดมหาสารคาม

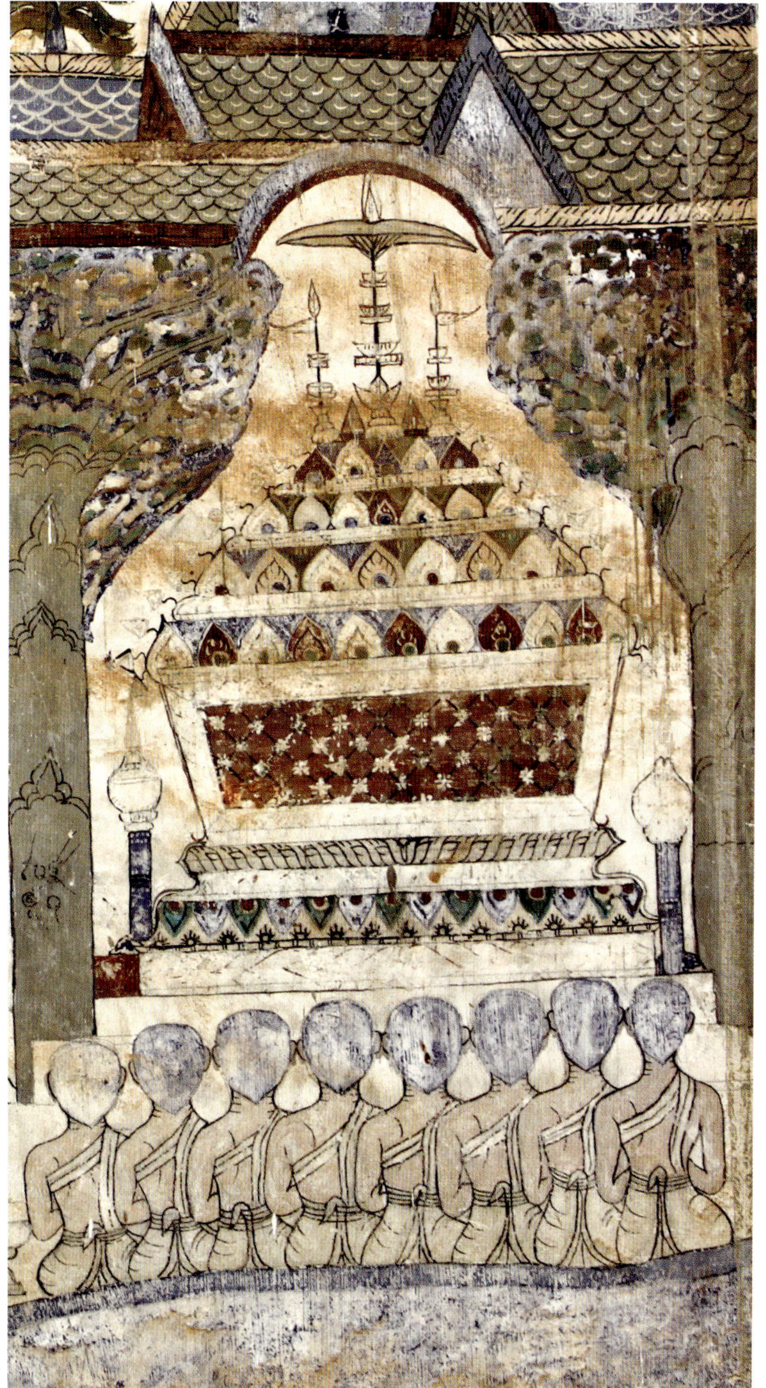

of the Buddha's previous lives, in which he practiced good deeds and thereby accumulated the requisites necessary for him to be born as the *bodhisattva* Gotama. It is these stories that serve as teachings and models of ideal behavior for the faithful.

Past Lives of the Buddha

Because the basic Buddhist ideas concern karma and rebirth, stories of the Buddha's previous lives are important themes in art and literature. The Theravada tradition includes a collection of 547 or sometimes 550 life stories, known as *Jataka*s, each of which recounts a meritorious act performed by the Buddha-to-be during a specific reincarnation. In Thailand and Laos the best known by far are the last ten, known as the *Thotsachat*, each of which exemplifies one of the ten ultimate Buddhist values (*parami*) that the Buddha accomplished in the ten lives before his incarnation as Gotama. These values are equanimity, loving-kindness, determination, truthfulness, patience, energy, wisdom, renunciation, morality, and generosity. Of the ten stories, the final one, *Vessantara* (Thai: *Phra Wetsandon*; Lao: *Pha Wet*), exemplifying generosity, is best known and is emphasized in rituals, paintings, and sermons throughout the country and especially in the northeast.[4]

In fact, at most Isan heartland *sim*, *Vessantara* is the only *Jataka* depicted. The story recounts the unparalleled generosity of Prince Vessantara, or Pha Wet as he is known in Isan, who is willing to give everything that is asked of him. This quality first becomes apparent when he is approached by a group of Brahmans from a neighboring drought-ridden kingdom. They ask for his kingdom's auspicious white elephant, whose presence ensures adequate rainfall, and Pha Wet gives it without hesitation, as seen in figure 25 from the interior of Wat Sanuan Wari.

His people are incensed at this act and the consequences that the loss of the elephant will have on their livelihood. As a result, Pha Wet is banished to the forest, where his wife Matsi and their young son and daughter join him. On the way to the forest he continues his acts of generosity, giving away his royal carriage and the stately steeds that pull it (figure 26, from the same *wat*).

Pha Wet's foil is the Brahman Chuchok. He is portrayed as dark-skinned, ungainly, crude, and avaricious; thus, he represents the antithesis of the fair-skinned, graceful, spiritually refined, and generous future Buddha. Pha Wet eventually gives Chuchok everything he asks for, including his young son and daughter. Fortunately, deities disguised as the children's parents descend from heaven to take care of them while they are separated from their parents. Pha Wet's final act is to give his beloved wife Matsi to the god Indra disguised as a Brahman. As soon as Pha Wet performs this act, Indra reveals his identity and returns Matsi to him. In the end, the prince is reunited with his entire family and his citizens. Having perfected the virtue of generosity, he is invited back to the kingdom by his parents as well as by throngs of royal attendants, musicians, dancers, and subjects (figure 28, from Wat Ban Lan).

This story is in many ways the most important one in Theravada Buddhist Southeast Asia and Sri Lanka. It exemplifies generosity, which can also be construed as non-attachment, the ultimate Buddhist value. Listening to the *Jataka*'s recitation is considered a way of making sufficient merit to enable one to be reborn during the era of the next Buddha, Maitreya, and thereby have a better opportunity to attain nirvana (Brereton 1995). Traditionally, the story was recited in most parts of the country at the end of the Buddhist rains retreat, but this practice has waned considerably in recent decades. In Isan it was and still is recited annually at virtually every *wat* between the months of February and April as a component in the year's biggest merit-making occasion, which entails elaborate preparations and rituals lasting several days. Since most of the temple murals in Isan focus on the *Vessantara* story, we will devote much of chapter 5 to this event and its depiction.

> **FIGURE 25.** *Vessantara Jataka*: donation of elephant. Wat Sanuan Wari, Khon Kaen. *เวสสันดร ชาดก* ตอนพระเวสสันดรทรงบริจาคช้างปัจจัยนาคเป็นทาน วัดสนวนวารี จังหวัดขอนแก่น

FOLLOWING PAGES

> **FIGURE 26.** *Vessantara Jataka*: donation of horses. Wat Sanuan Wari, Khon Kaen. *เวสสันดร ชาดก* ตอนทรงบริจาคม้า วัดสนวนวารี จังหวัดขอนแก่น

> **FIGURE 27.** *Pha Lam Sadok*: the infant Nang Sida is floated down the river on a raft. Wat Sa Bua Kaeo, Khon Kaen. *พะลามชาดก* ตอนทารกนางสีดาถูกนำไปลอยแพ วัดสระบัวแก้ว จังหวัดขอนแก่น

> **FIGURE 28.** Three-panel wall depicting Pha Wet's donation of Matsi and her return to him (left panel), followed by their journey back to the royal city. Wat Ban Lan, Khon Kaen. ผนังสามช่อง เล่าเรื่องพระเวสสันดรทรงบริจาคนางมัทรี และพระอินทร์ถวายนางคืน (ช่องซ้าย) กับภาพ สี่กษัตริย์นิวัติพระนคร วัดบ้านลาน จังหวัดขอนแก่น

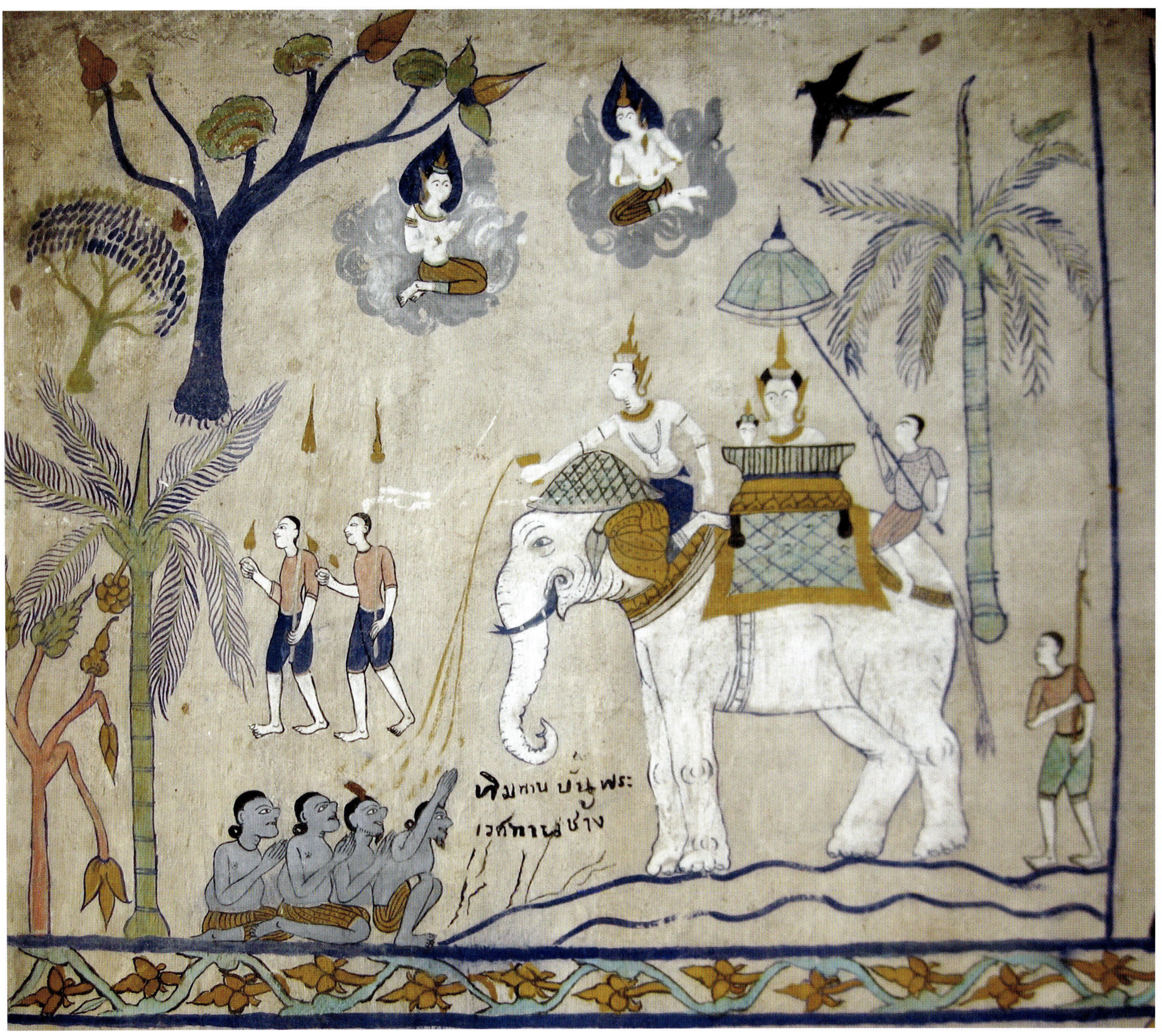
เวสสันดร บำเพ็ญพระ
เวสสันดานช้าง

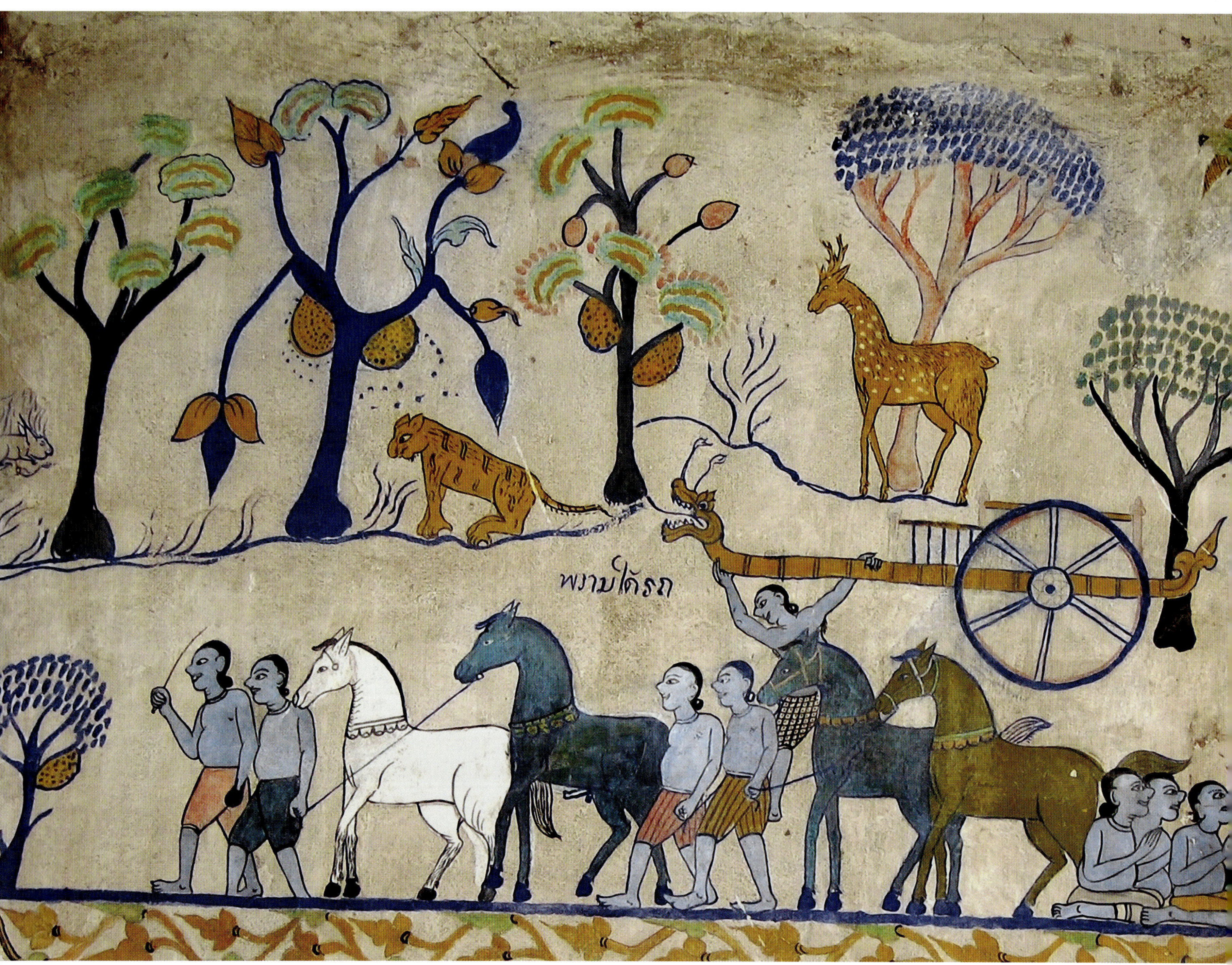
พญาบโครถ

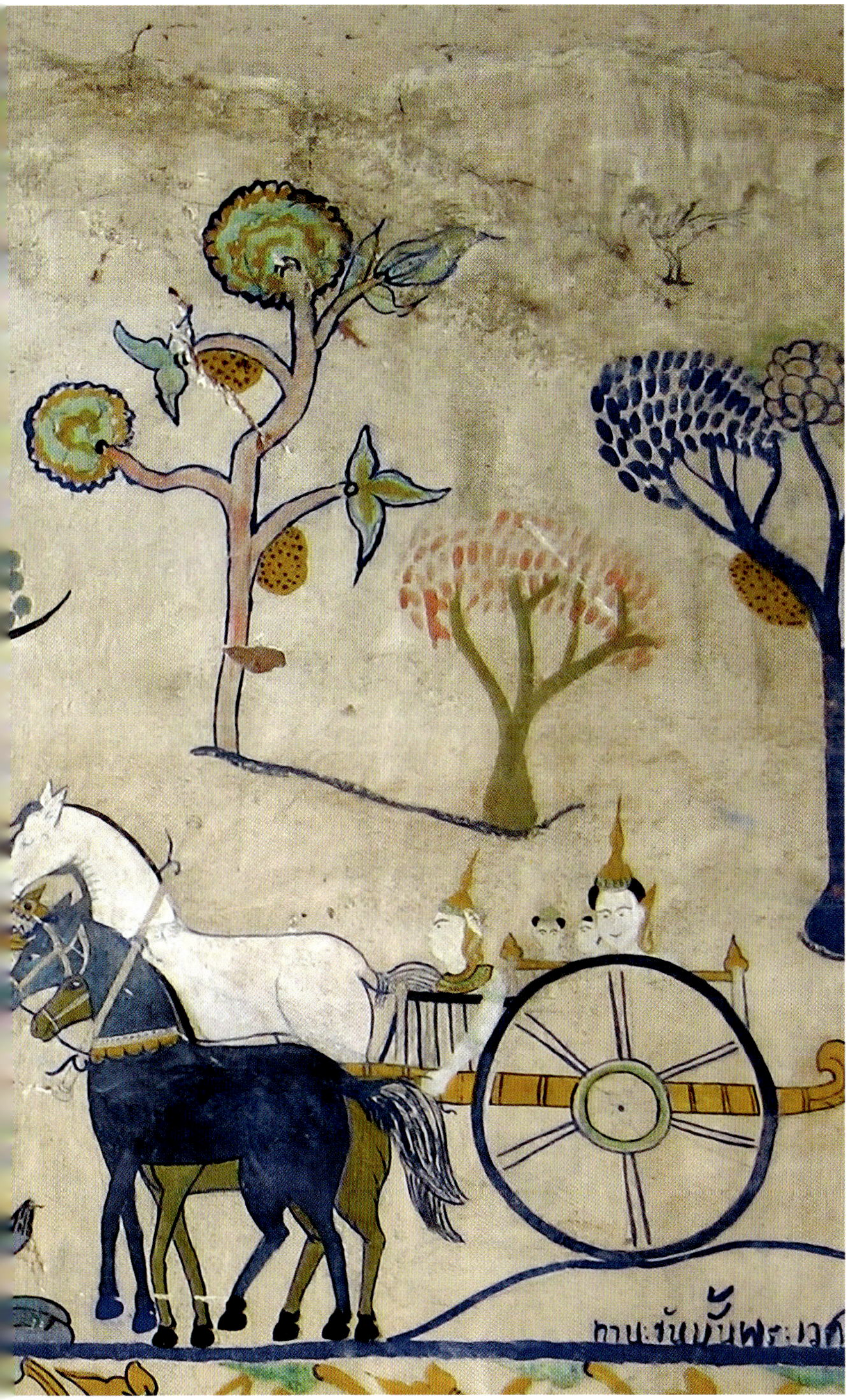

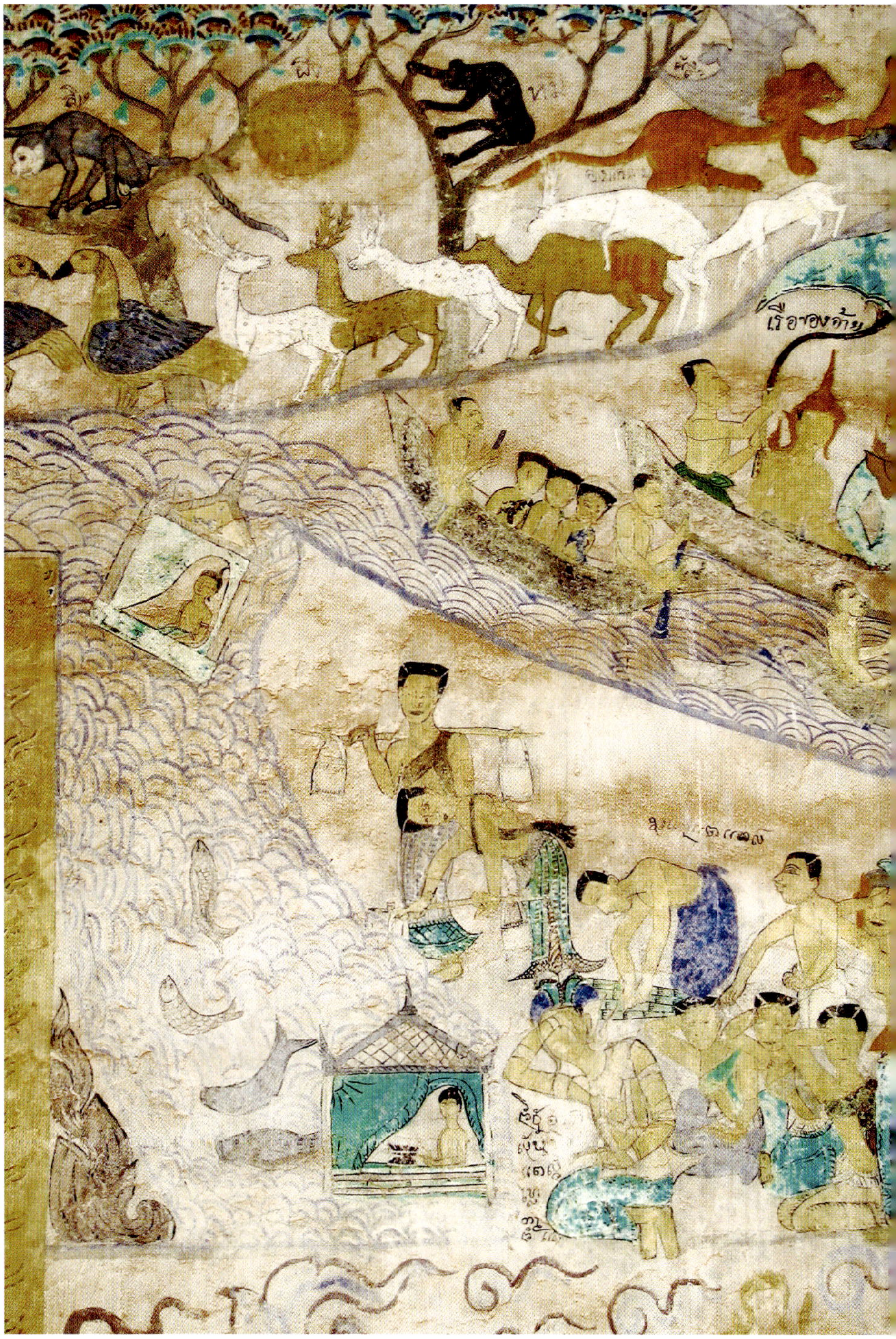

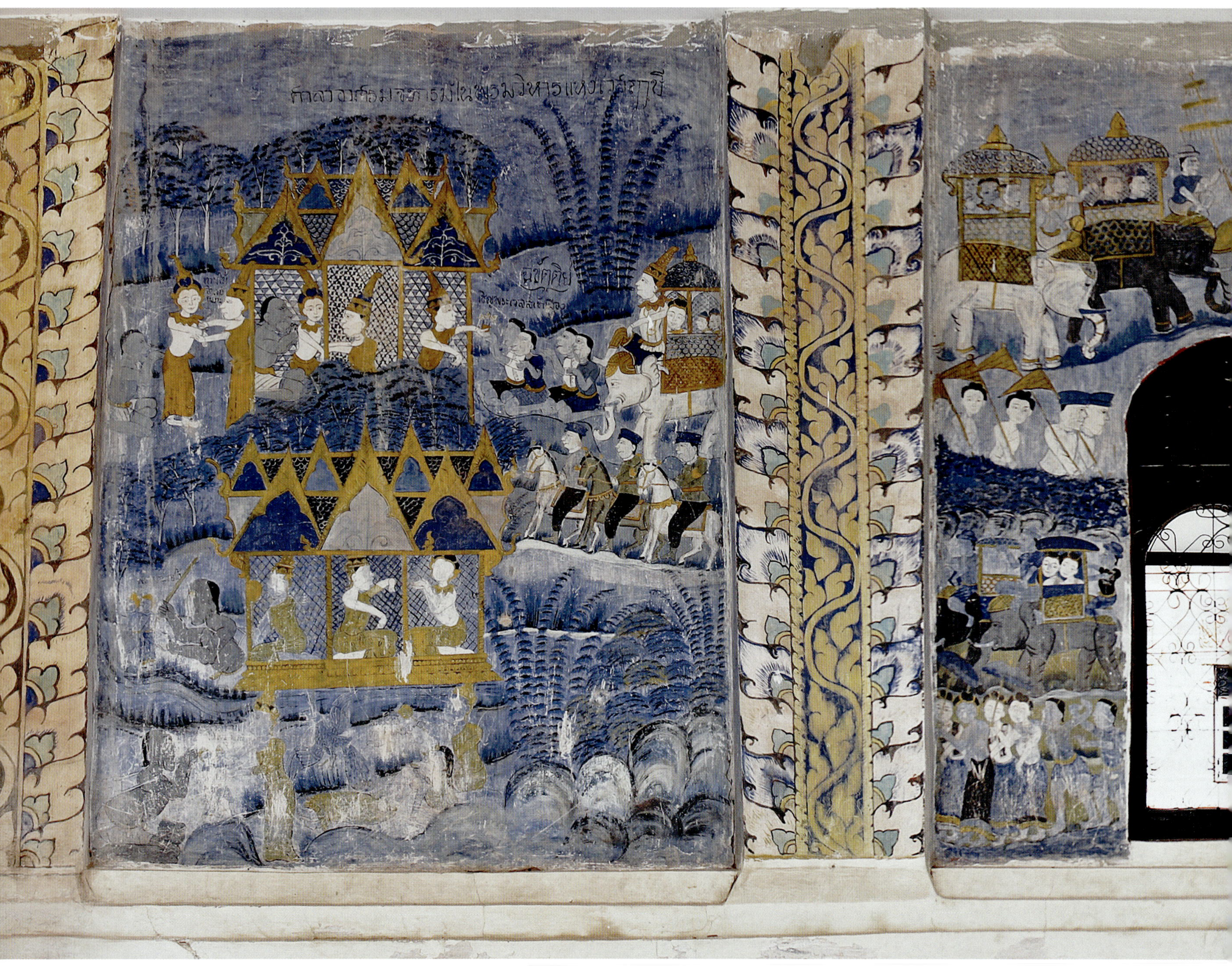

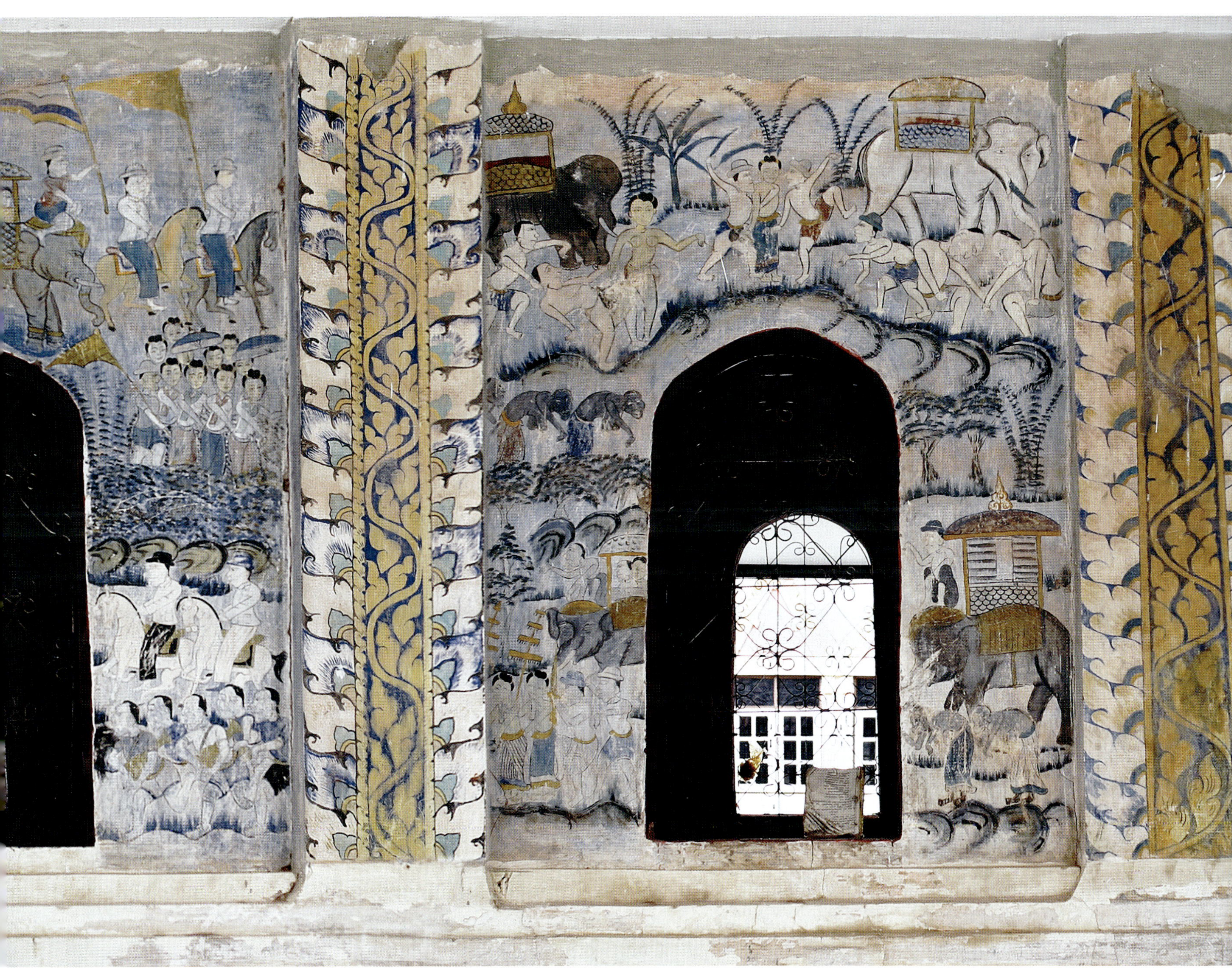

The Rama Epic

The Indian epic, the *Ramayana*, and its local variant tellings are famous throughout South and Southeast Asia. In the Central Thai *Ramakian*, which exists in several versions, Phra Ram (an incarnation of the Hindu deity Vishnu), after a palace intrigue, is exiled to the forest accompanied by his brother Phra Lak and his wife Nang Sida. The latter is captured by the ten-headed demon Thotsakan and eventually rescued by Phra Ram with the help of a band of monkeys led by their general, Hanuman.

In Isan, along with the *Ramakian*, at least two Lao tellings of the epic are known: *Pha Lak Pha Lam* and the *Pha Lam Sadok* (*Rama Jataka*). It is these variant versions, rather than the *Ramakian*, that are depicted on Isan heartland murals. The Lao versions of the epic differ from the *Ramakian* in numerous ways. The most significant difference is that they are Buddhist, rather than Hindu, stories. That is to say, unlike the *Ramakian*, where the hero Phra Ram is an incarnation of the Hindu deity Vishnu,

Pha Lam in the Lao story is a *bodhisattva*, or Buddha-to-be. Moreover, Phra Lak (or Pha Lak, as he is known in Isan) is not just his brother, but his twin.

Another distinction is that in the Lao version the monkey general Hanuman is Pha Lam's son, conceived when the latter assumed simian form (because of having eaten a certain kind of fruit) then had a liaison with a female monkey. Moreover, an important motif in the Lao tellings is that Thotsakan (known therein as Hapmanasun) is actually the father of Nang Sida. She was conceived when the demon seduced Nang Susada, one of Indra's wives, by tricking her into believing that he was the god himself. Nang Susada, furious upon learning of the deception, takes rebirth as her own daughter, Nang Sida, so that she can avenge Hapmanasun's betrayal. Immediately after her birth, she attempts to kill the giant, but her effort is thwarted and she is sent down a river on a raft. As the raft floats away it is spotted by a hermit, who takes pity on the baby and adopts her. This is one of the key scenes in the murals portraying this story (figure 27, from Wat Sa Bua Kaeo).

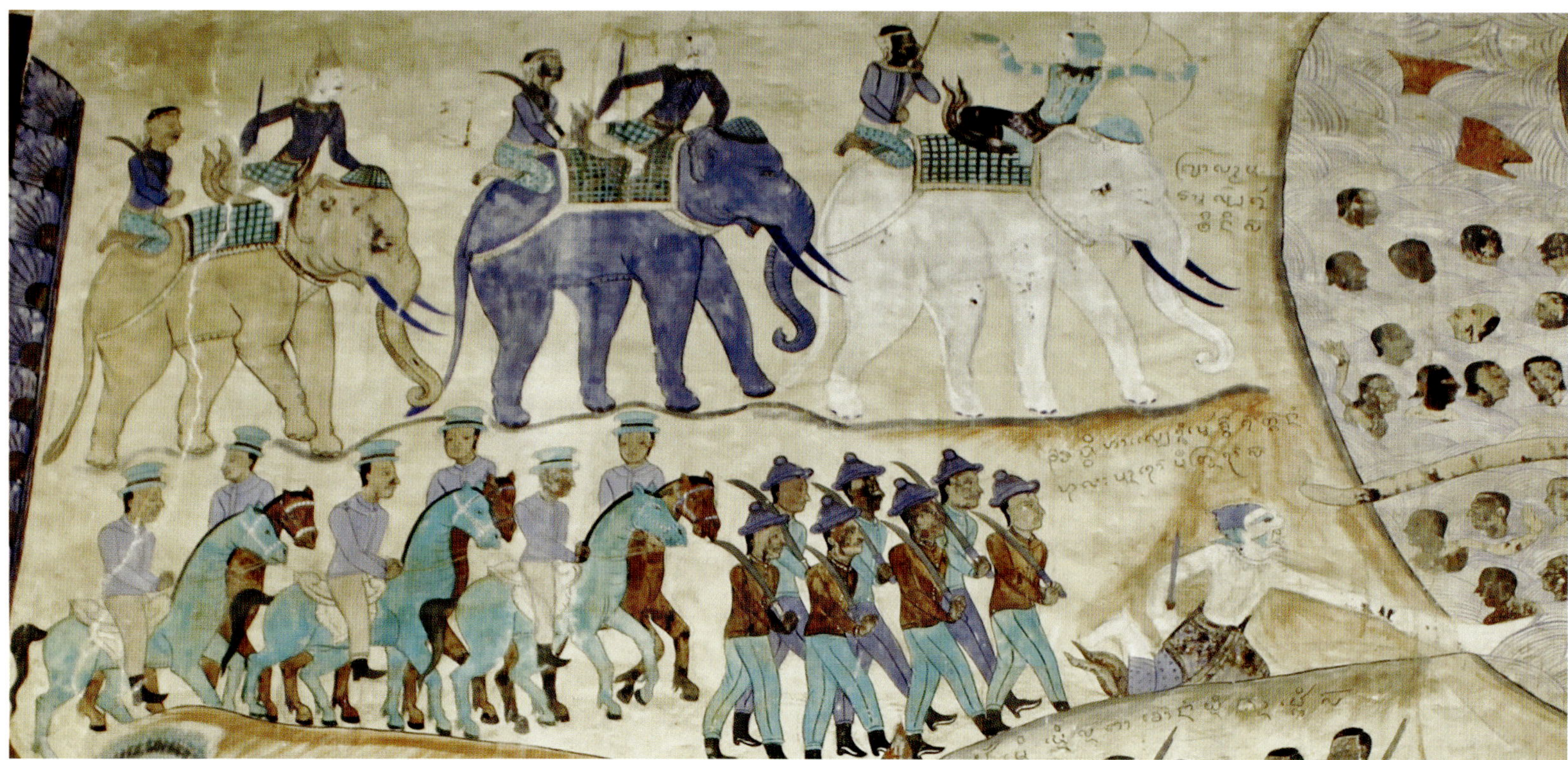

The Lao Thotsakan (Hapmanasun) is a much more multifaceted character than his Central Thai counterpart. Unaware that Nang Sida is his daughter, he abducts her because he is passionately in love with her. Moreover, he is embarrassed about an earlier incident in which he failed to win her in a contest arranged by her stepfather requiring participants to lift a magic arrow, which Pha Lam was able to do with ease. Disappointed and humiliated, Hapmanasun becomes obsessed with making Nang Sida his wife.

Like the Lao characters, the Lao plot is also more complex than the Central Thai version, with a multitude of folkloric twists and turns (many of them erotic) not found in the *Ramakian*, including supernatural transformations, episodes involving Pha Lam's numerous earlier wives, and his efforts to avoid war, which are spurned by Hapmanasun. The ending is similar, however, in that Pha Lam defeats the giant and is eventually reunited with Nang Sida.

The Sin Sai Story

The Sin Sai story, part of a local collection of fifty *Jataka*s, is very popular among the Lao people. To Central Thai it is known as *Sang Sinchai*, a play written by King Rama II. As with the canonical *Jataka*s, its main character is an incarnation of the future Buddha. The earliest written version appears to date from the middle of the eighteenth century C.E., when a poetic version was composed in Vientiane (Chob 2007, 1–3). Not only is the story depicted on the exterior of several Isan *sim*, it is also reenacted in the region's vigorous shadow theater, *nang pramothai*.

Like the Rama epic, the Sin Sai story involves the abduction of a beautiful woman—in this case Nang Chantha—by a *yak* (giant), Kumphan, who has fallen in love with her. And, like the Rama epic, it is full of extraordinary events and characters whose heroic actions and sexual prowess are aided by their magical powers.

◄ **FIGURE 29.** Scene from *Pha Lam Sadok*. Wat Sa Bua Kaeo, Khon Kaen. ตอนหนึ่งจากเรื่อง *พะลามชาดก* วัดสระบัวแก้ว จังหวัดขอนแก่น

► **FIGURE 30.** Isan shadow puppet representing Sang Thong. Notice that the conch component of his body is relatively small in this example. หุ่นหนังประโมทัย ตัวสังข์ทอง สังเกต ส่วนที่เป็นหอยสังข์บนตัวหนัง ซึ่งมีขนาดค่อนข้างเล็กเมื่อเทียบกับหุ่นสังข์ทองทั่วไป

However, in the Sin Sai story, as contrasted with *Pha Lak Pha Lam*, it is not the abducted woman's husband but her brother, King Kusarat, who initially goes to find her. After searching far and wide, the distraught king is unable to locate her but maintains his resolve to free her.

Over the years that follow, King Kusarat marries eight women and fathers nine sons. Three of the sons are born with unusual physical characteristics and supernatural powers. As we see in figure 31 from Wat Sanuan Wari, Sin Sai holds a sword and a bow and arrow; Siho is a *khotchasi* (a mythical lion-like animal with elephant tusks and trunk); and Sang Thong has a body that is part human, part conch. The other six sons are ordinary

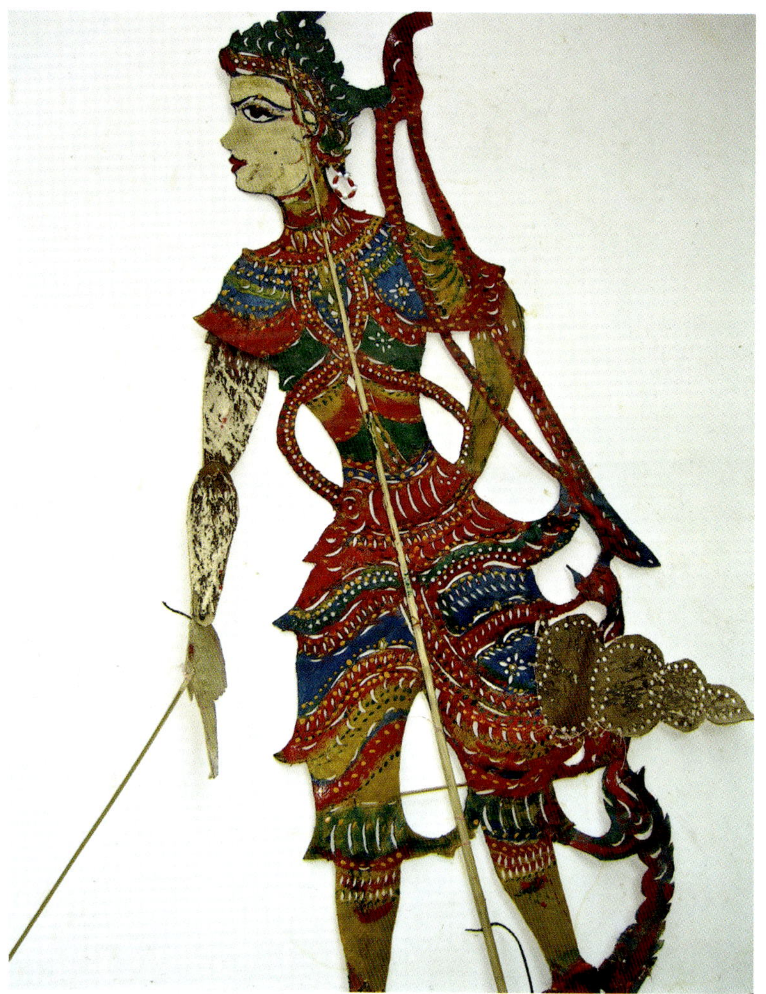

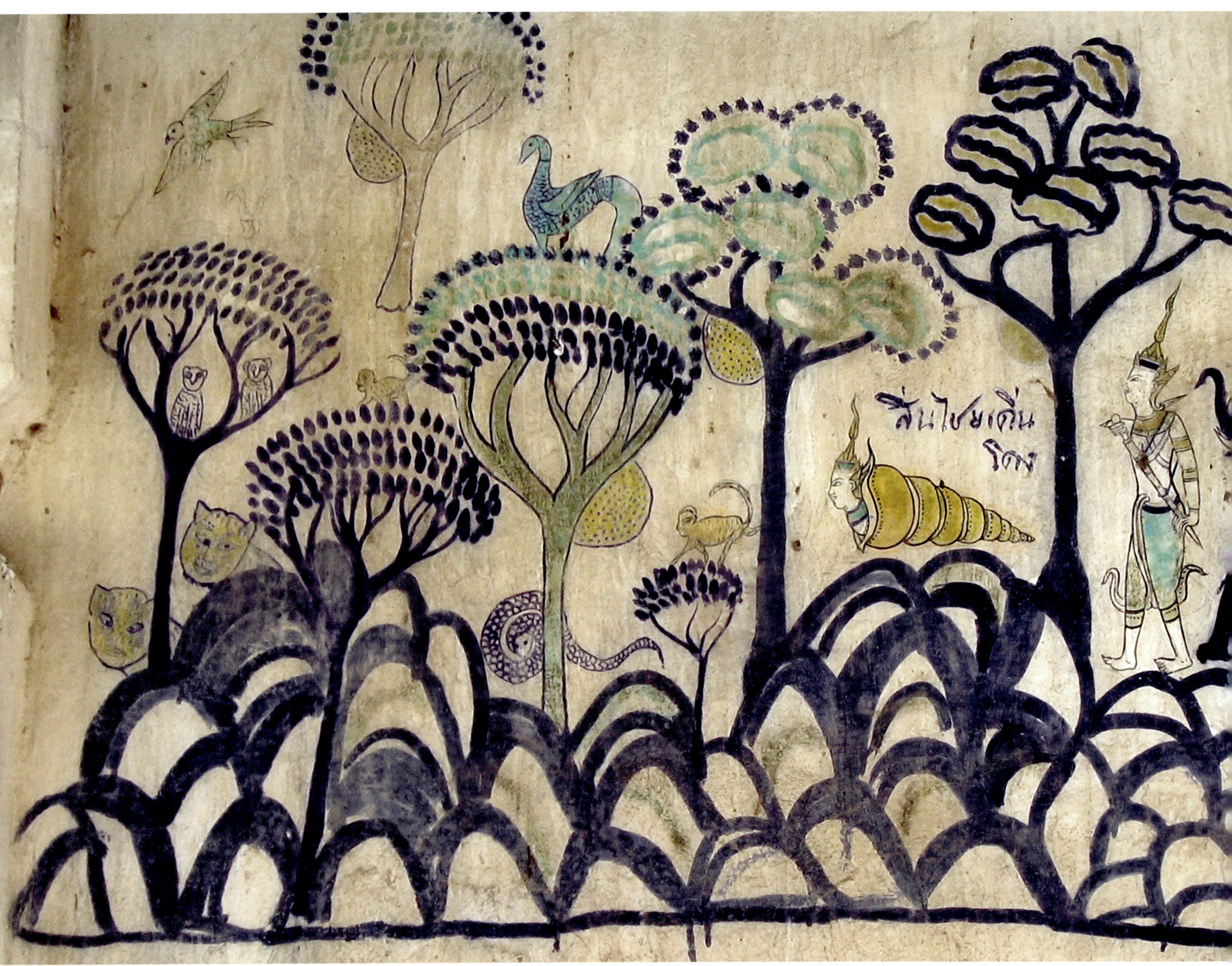
สินไซยเคลื่น
โดง

males, whose mothers, after hearing a prediction that the throne will be inherited by a son with special features and powers, conspire to have Sang Thong, Sin Sai, and Siho banished to the forest, along with their mothers.

Years later, when the six ordinary sons have grown up, the king sends them to search for their aunt. Entering the forest, they come upon Sang Thong, Sin Sai, and Siho, and after talking together they realize that they are all brothers. The six princes from the royal city persuade the others to accompany them in the search for their aunt. Sang Thong, Sin Sai, and Siho lead the way. The other six, having never entered the forest, are full of fear; at the same time they have also schemed to have their magical siblings killed by having them go first. The three leaders reach the *yak*'s dwelling, and in a long series of battles Kumphan is killed and regenerated numerous times, and Sang Thong transforms himself into various forms, including a boat, in order to allow his brother to pursue the demon. In the end, Sin Sai is finally able to kill Kumphan (figure 19, p. 21). Nang Chantha, who has fallen in love with the giant after having lived with him for many years, grieves at his death and reluctantly agrees to return to her brother's kingdom.

Phra Malai and Hell Scenes

The Phra Malai story, which is told in numerous different versions throughout Thailand, concerns an *arhat*, or spiritually evolved being, whose supernatural powers enable him to fly to the Buddhist hells and heavens (Brereton 1995). On visiting the hells, he uses his magical skills to relieve the hell beings' sufferings and agrees to relay their requests to their relatives in the human realm to make merit for them. Returning to the human realm, as he walks his alms round one morning he is given eight lotus blossoms by a poor man. Upon receiving the lotuses, Phra Malai decides to present them as an offering at the Chulamani Chedi in Tavatimsa Heaven, where the Buddha's hair relic is enshrined.

Flying to this abode, he meets Indra, the presiding deity, with whom he converses as a series of lesser deities, each surrounded by larger

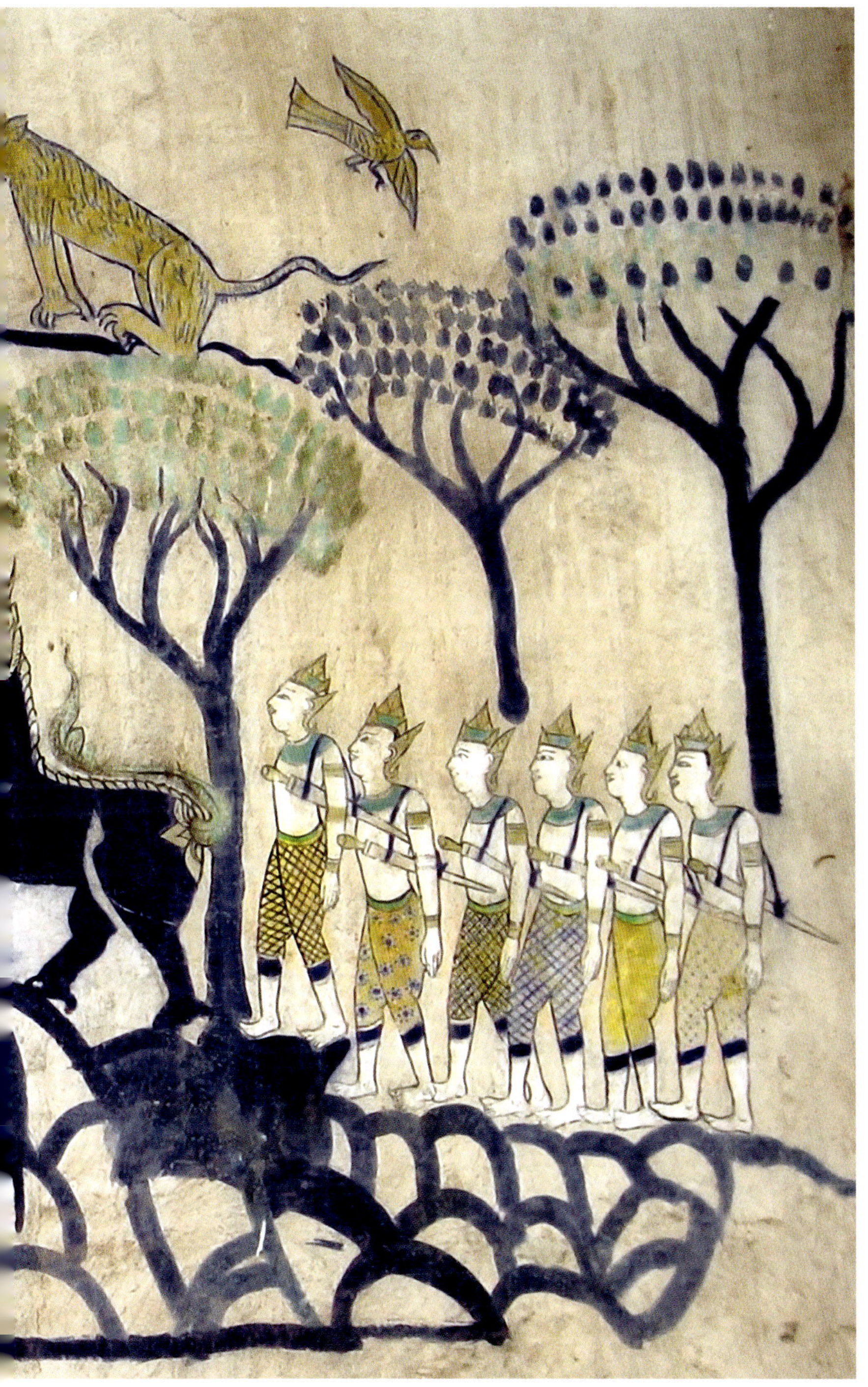

◀ **FIGURE 31.** Sang Thong, Sin Sai, Siho, and the six ordinary brothers, Wat Sanuan Wari, Khon Kaen. สังข์ทอง สินไซ สีโห และพี่ชายทั้งหก วัดสนวนวารี จังหวัดขอนแก่น

and larger retinues of celestial beings, arrive to worship the *chedi*. In each case, Indra describes the acts of *dana* (giving) that the deity had performed in a previous life, resulting in divine rebirth. Eventually the *bodhisattva* Maitreya arrives to pay reverence, and asks Phra Malai about those in the human realm, especially their merit-making activities. Phra Malai lists their diverse acts, which are all motivated by their desire to be reborn at the time when Maitreya is the Buddha. Those who hear him preach will be able to attain nirvana, an accomplishment that is considered most difficult, according to Theravada teachings. Maitreya then gives the *arhat* a message to take back to the human realm: those who wish to be born at that time should follow the Five Precepts (to refrain from killing, taking what is not given, lying, taking intoxicants, and sexual misconduct). They should also practice generosity and listen to the entire *Vessantara Jataka* recitation in one day and one night after presenting one thousand each of various offerings, such as sticky rice balls and lotuses of various colors.

The scenes most often depicted in Isan heartland murals are of Phra Malai hovering above the suffering hell beings, who appear as grotesque forms with human bodies and the heads of animals. They are sometimes depicted boiling in pots of hot oil or climbing thorn trees with vicious dogs snarling below.[5] Phra Malai is also seen conversing with Indra alongside the Chulamani Chedi. At some *wats* these two incidents are combined into a single mural, usually painted on the back (west) or left (south) exterior wall. At Wat Ban Yang they are combined along with still another scene: Phra Malai's conversations with people in the human realm (figure 32).

Moreover, at many *wats* hell scenes occur without the figure of Phra Malai. A popular location is the front (east) wall, to the left of the door as one enters, probably because the paintings here are immediately visible to anyone entering the *sim* or walking around it. A striking example is at Wat Chai Si, in a tightly packed collage of suffering beings being tortured by oversized birds, hell wardens, and dogs (figure 33). Another is the exterior west wall at Wat Sanuan Wari, where the murals include captions describing specific local interpretations of the law of karma (figure 34). Along with the standard thorn tree we see a male creature, with a human body and buffalo head, with his scrotum secured in a clamp, the traditional method of castration. Below is a caption that reads, "the consequence of castrating water buffalo."[6]

Other topics, including the *Thotsachat* and Buddhist riddles, are occasionally found on Isan heartland *sim*. However, the texts, tales, and themes described above are the most common, suggesting that they were the favorite subjects of sermons and that they had the greatest impact on the ways in which Buddhism was understood and practiced locally.

NOTES

1. See Swearer (2004, 122–129) for an account of the narrative. The story is also known through oral renditions and mural paintings.

2. The scene as found at Wat Photharam and Wat Pa Rerai includes the future Buddha gazing at his wife, newborn child, and concubines; the Buddha departing on his horse; and the cutting of his hair to become an ascetic. His earlier encounter with the four sights (and old man, a sick man, a corpse, and an ascetic) is also included in abbreviated form.

3. After completing the writing of this book, we were surprised to find a similar scene in Battambang, Cambodia, at Wat Hemanaram, which was established in the 1970s (Roveda and Yem 2009, 164).

4. For a quick synopsis of the story accompanied by photos of Isan *pha pha wet* scrolls, see Gittinger and Lefferts (1992: 124–29). See also Cone and Gombrich (1977) for a more detailed translation from the Pali. The numerous Thai and Lao manuscript versions that exist differ from each other in small, but sometimes significant, ways.

5. Many of the tortures, such as being forced to climb thorn trees while being attacked by birds and dogs (the karmic result of adultery), are described in various tellings of the Phra Malai story.

6. The traditional method of castrating a water buffalo was to restrain it physically, clamp the scrotum by its neck between two flat bamboo strips, and pound the testicles with a heavy stone or metal bar. The buffalo would scream in pain and moan for hours following the procedure. See http://www.bar.gov.ph/bardigest/2003/julsep03_carabaocast.asp.

FACING PAGE

▶ **FIGURE 32.** *Phra Malai*. Wat Ban Yang, Maha Sarakham. พระมาลัย วัดบ้านยาง จังหวัดมหาสารคาม

FOLLOWING PAGES

▶ **FIGURE 33.** Hell scene. Wat Chai Si, Khon Kaen. นรกภูมิ วัดไชยศรี จังหวัดขอนแก่น

▶ **FIGURE 34.** Hell scene. Wat Sanuan Wari, Khon Kaen. นรกภูมิ วัดสนวนวารี จังหวัดขอนแก่น

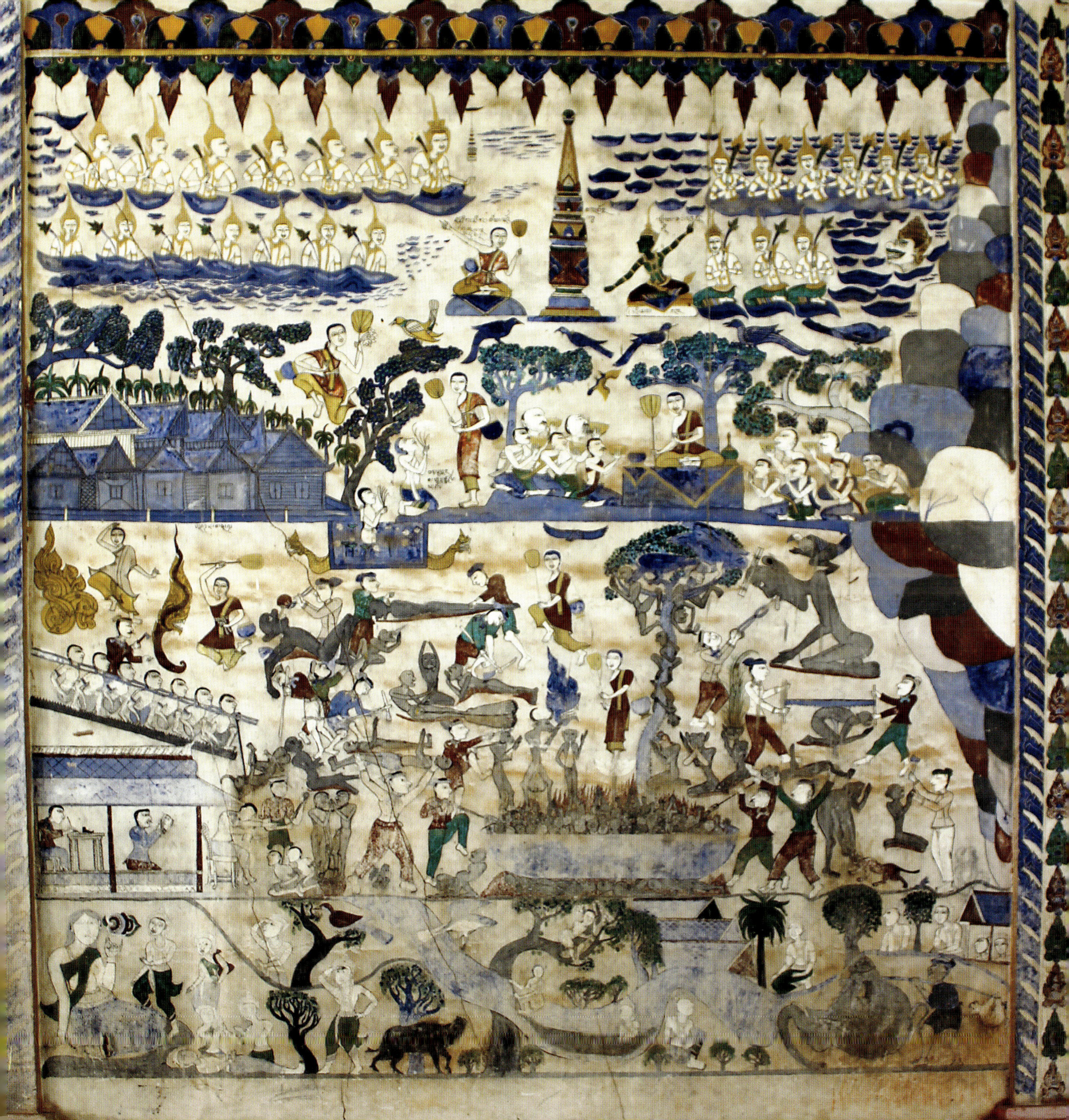

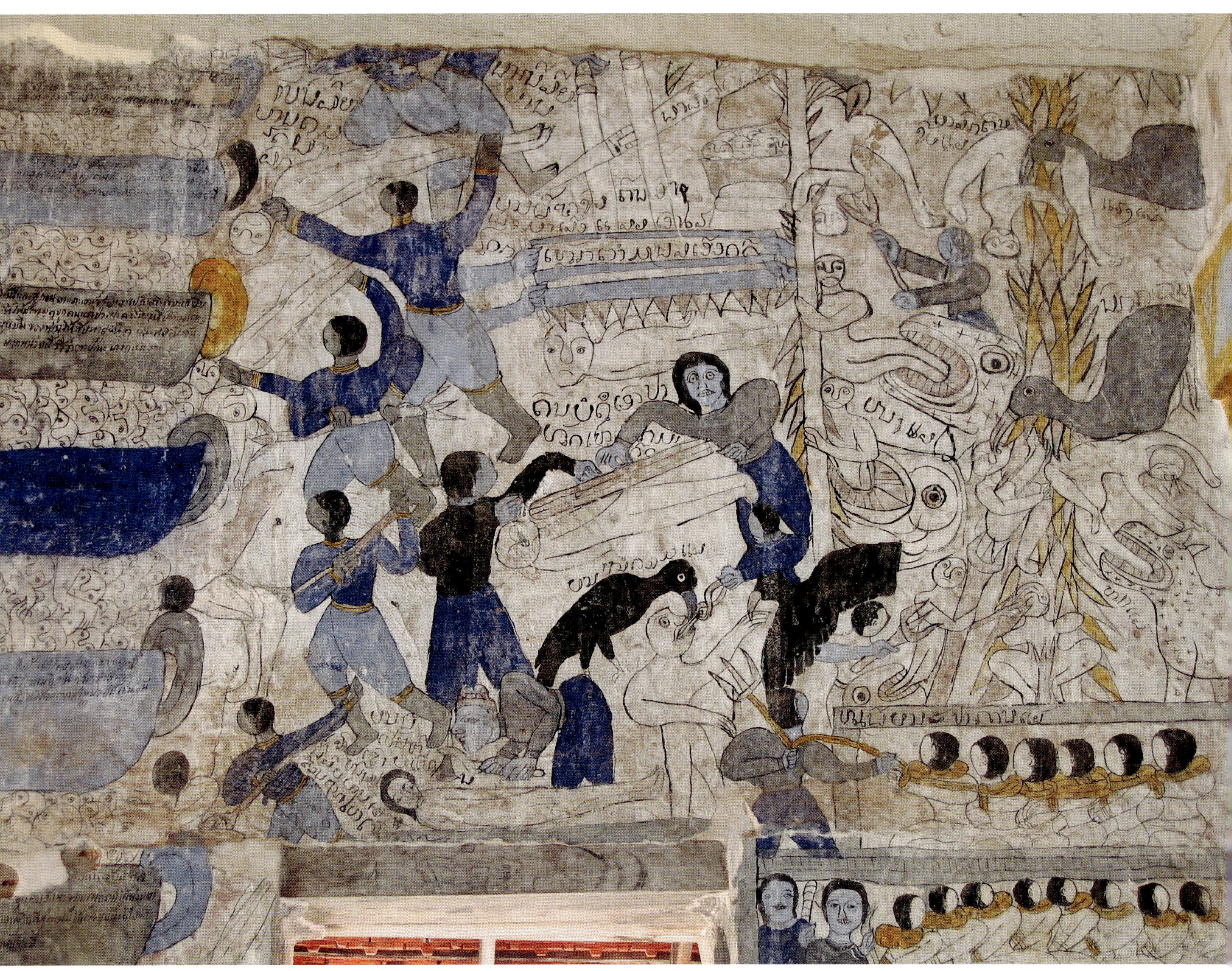

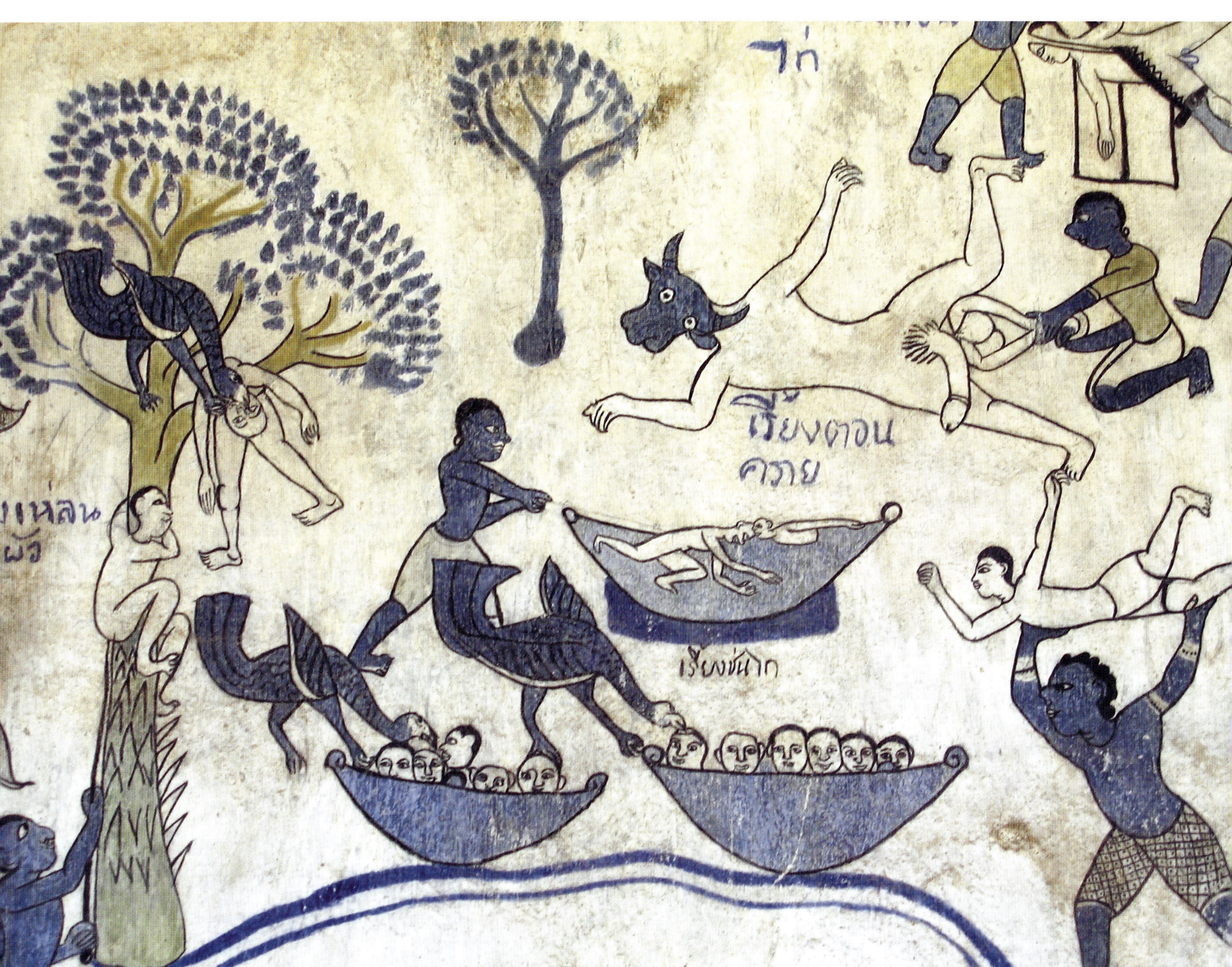
ไก่
เรี้ยงตอน
ควาย
เรี้ยงข่น้าก
เหล่น
ผัว

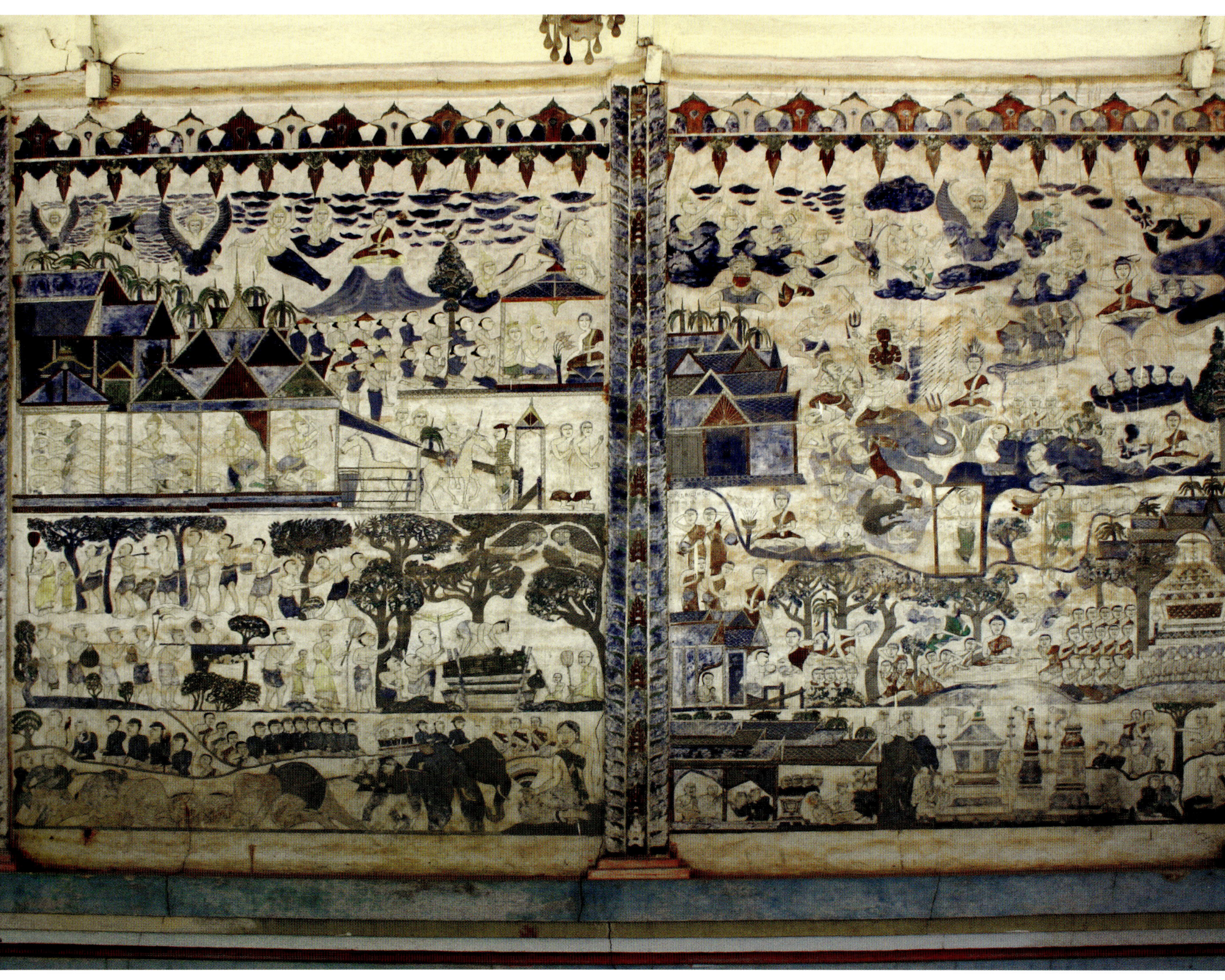

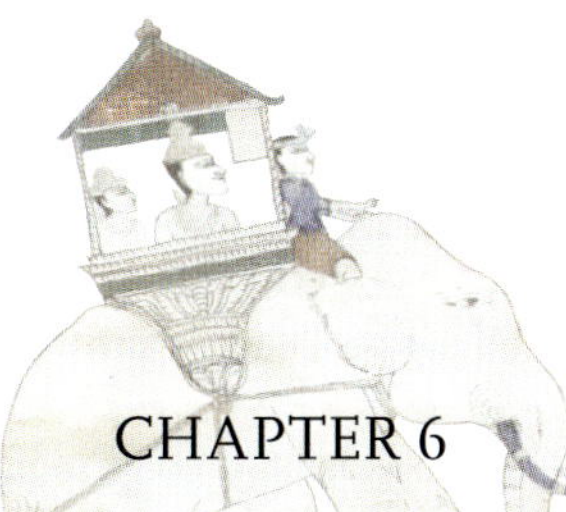

CHAPTER 6

COMPOSITION, CHARACTERS, AND POSTURES

At first glance, an Isan heartland mural is difficult to "read" and appears to lack compositional coherence. Most walls are divided into a series of registers or rows, each comprised of human figures and animals moving in a direction opposite to those in the registers immediately above and below (figure 35). Moreover, there is little sense of proportion between the various figures and the landscape. However, for the murals' creators and their intended audience, who were familiar with the story, this is not a problem—naturalistic portrayal is irrelevant compared with the narrative and iconographic elements needed to identify the characters and events. For example, Pha Wet can be identified by the hermit's rosary he sometimes holds (figure 36) and his gesture of pouring water as he gives away his possessions (figure 25 above), Sin Sai by the sword or bow and arrow he carries, and Phra Malai by his monk's robes and fan (*talapat*).

Another difficulty for the first-time viewer might be distinguishing males from females, as spiritually evolved figures of both genders have slender forms, ornate garments, and sweet facial features. In Isan, as in the rest of Thailand—and indeed in all of Southeast Asia—a typology of posture and color governs the drawing of mural figures and helps to identify them. Females and highly evolved males, such as the Buddha and deities, are always seen in full or nearly full face, rendering them tranquil and sublime. Males, especially heroic types, are usually seen in profile, which gives them a sense of energy and movement. An important difference, however, is that the lead characters in the Isan heartland group do not assume the *lakhon* (dance-drama) postures and hand gestures seen in Central Thai murals.[1]

In all parts of Thailand, whether the figures are shown in profile or full face, the shoulders and torso are drawn parallel to the picture plane, while the midriff is twisted so that it appears nearly in profile, and the

knees and feet face forward (sideways to the viewer). This convention is shared by shadow puppet figures throughout Southeast Asia, as seen in the Isan puppets in figure 37.

The color of a figure's complexion and the relative degree of coarseness versus refinement of his or her facial features are additional indicators of status and identity. The god Indra is usually green, and spiritually evolved beings—such as the Buddha, *bodhisattva*s, and certain deities—are light skinned, in sharp contrast to their antagonists, such as the swarthy, coarse-featured Chuchok or the bug-eyed giants Thotsakan and Kumphan. The handsome Chuchok in figure 65 is an exception.

As in shadow theater, background features consist of miniature rather than realistically sized vegetal and architectural elements. Were they drawn to scale, they would take too much space from the characters. Isan heartland murals, except for those at Wat Ban Lan, have a distinct white or off-white background that resembles shadow play screens and, as mentioned earlier, Isan does in fact have a local form of shadow play. However, research suggests that shadow theater is a relatively new phenomenon in the region, introduced in the 1920s and reaching its height of popularity just before World War II (Brereton and Somroay 2007). Thus the white background seen in this group of paintings was most likely the result of practical concerns rather than the influence of shadow theater. Applying a pale wash to the walls and then filling in the composition took much less time and resources than having to apply the dark background colors used in the Central Region. Moreover, the white background helped in the small interior space of the *sim*, which otherwise would have been extremely dark. Pragmatism is also evident in the skillful use of the limited colors that were available: artists, using a palette that consisted mainly of indigo and reddish brown obtained from natural pigments, were able to create a remarkable range of subtle hues and textures.

In terms of composition, Isan heartland murals are freer, more spontaneous, and less predictable than those in Central or Southern Thailand. Each *sim* is unique in terms of the location of stories and

◀ **FIGURE 35.** Wall at Wat Ban Yang. Notice the division of space into horizontal registers.
ผนังวัดบ้านยาง สังเกตวิธีแบ่งพื้นที่ของฉากตามแนวนอน

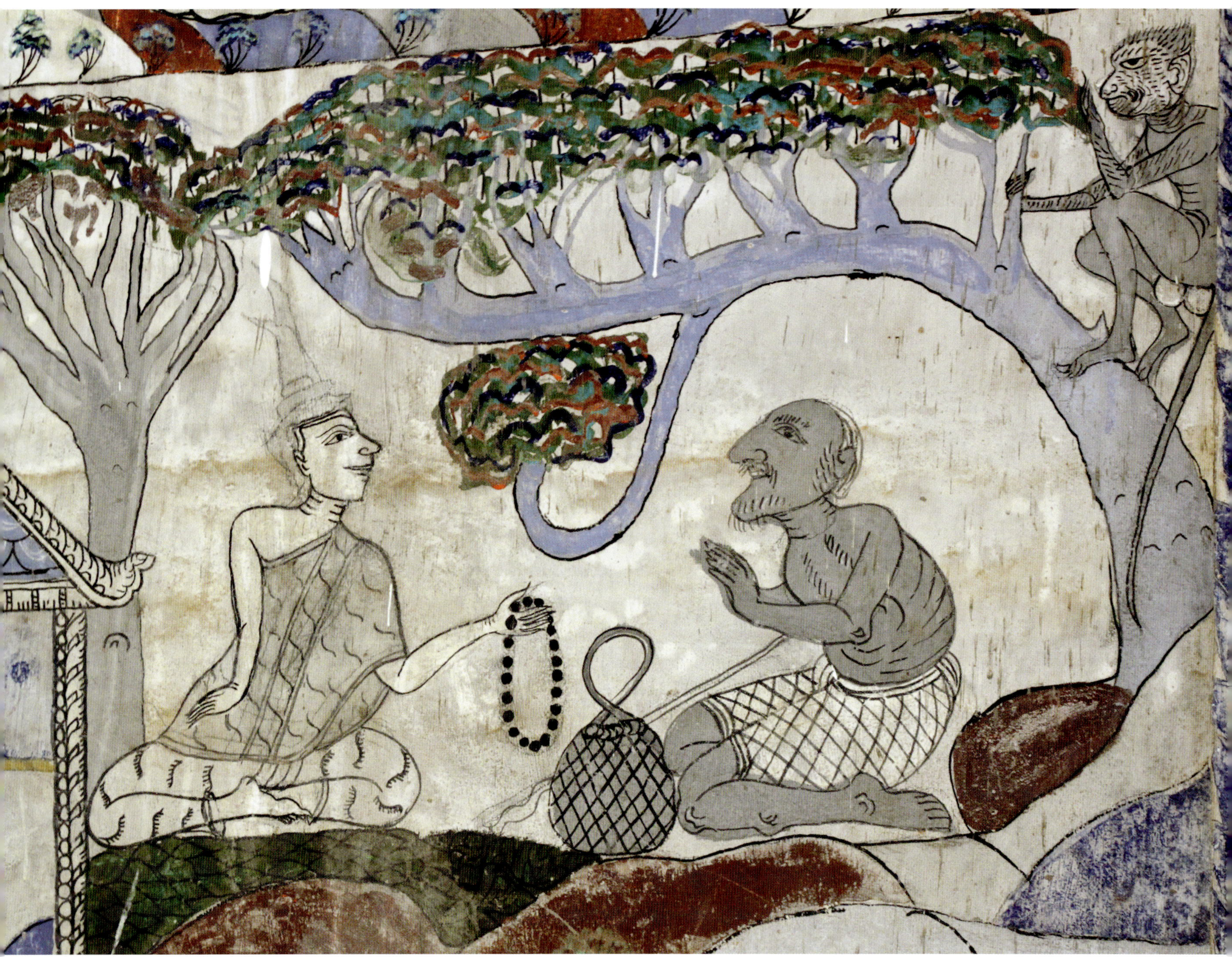

themes, the places where those stories begin, the individual renderings of certain characters, and the artistic skill involved. Yet, at the same time, Isan heartland painters shared a perspective of the Buddhist cosmos that differed significantly from that of painters in and around Bangkok. These differences can best be understood by comparing the ways in which narratives are depicted in Central Thai murals and those in the Isan heartland.

The narrative scenes in murals from the Central Region and the South are organized into a spatial hierarchy with celestial beings at the very top of the walls, high-born humans in the middle, and servants and other lower-class humans at the bottom or in out-of-the-way places, such as in doorways or corners. There the common folk, depicted as country bumpkins, are relegated to genre scenes found only on the

periphery, positions befitting "the dregs," to use the Thai technical term for these figures in art.[2]

Isan heartland murals are radically different in that the landscape they portray is a democratic one, in which commoners and their activities occupy all levels of the composition. They are the work of ordinary local people whose gaze was self-reflective rather than hierarchical.

Moreover, Isan heartland murals depict not only local Buddhist stories, but also the participation of the Buddhist faithful in the reenactment of these stories. Figures of ordinary people are found at all levels of the murals and their participation in the rituals is an integral part of the composition.

Another important difference is that in Central and Southern Region murals, scenes are arranged according to where they occur. For example, a forest background may contain several different scenes that take place in the forest, but are not necessarily in sequence. In addition, scenes are separated by zigzagged lines, walls, fences, or buildings such as palaces or pavilions. The sequence of events is unclear from the composition unless one knows the story. In the Isan heartland, by contrast, the murals are organized into horizontal registers separated by wavy lines.

◀ **FIGURE 36.** Pha Wet, left, holds an ascetic's rosary. Wat Ban Yang, Maha Sarakham. ฤๅษีถือประคำบอกทางไปเขาวงกตแก่ชูชก วัดบ้านยาง จังหวัดมหาสารคาม

▾ **FIGURE 37.** Isan shadow puppets at a performance, Khon Kaen. การเชิดหนังประโมทัย จังหวัดขอนแก่น

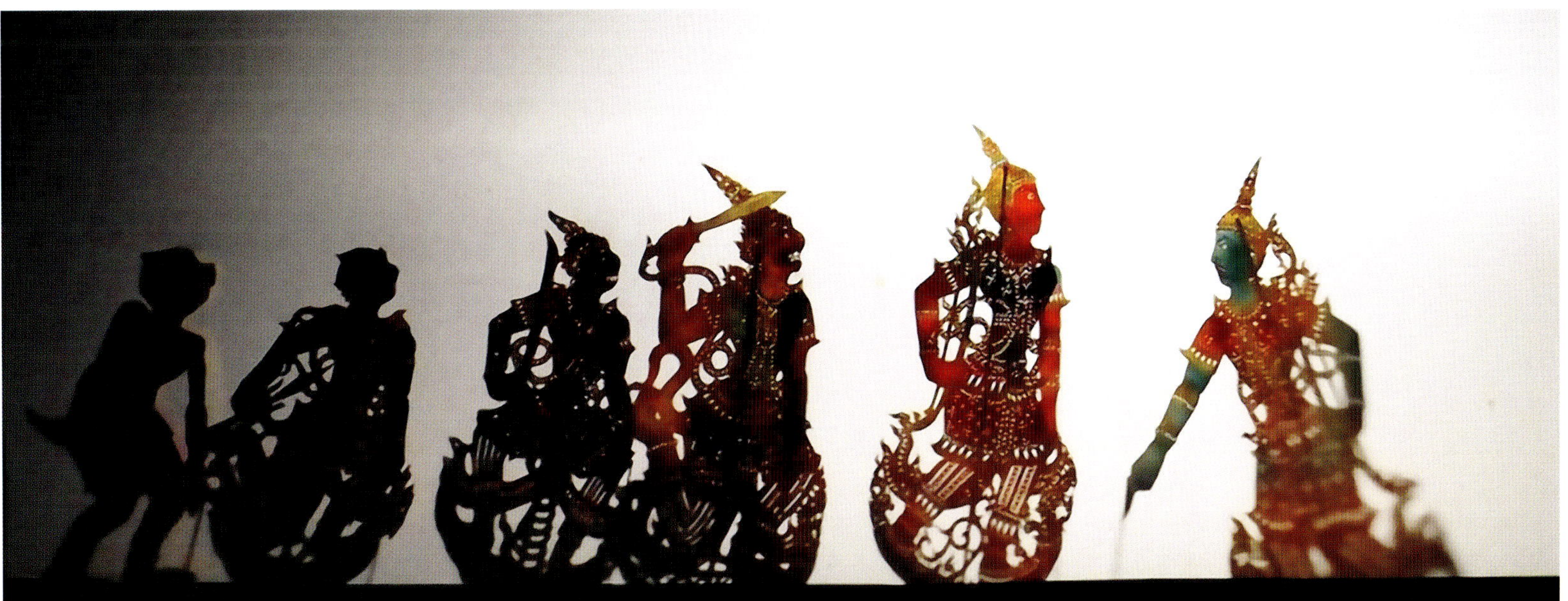

In trying to understand the composition of a mural, the relationship between one register and another is initially puzzling. While a mural's component parts can be identified, fitting them together into a comprehensible whole is at first difficult. The key lies in looking beyond a single mural and seeing instead the movement of the registers around the exterior of the *sim*. In doing so, it is helpful to call to mind the horizontal cloth scrolls (*pha pha wet*) on which are painted scenes from each chapter of the *Vessantara Jataka*. The similarities between murals and scrolls are obvious in the interior of Wat Sanuan Wari, where the murals give the appearance of a scroll that has been hung on the walls. (See figures 7, above, and 38.)

Scrolls like this are an integral element in Bun Pha Wet festival processions, as part of the ritual of inviting Pha Wet to return to the city after his long exile in the forest. (See figures 40 and 41, processions of Bun Pha Wet celebrants in Khon Kaen.) When the procession reaches the *wat*, the scrolls are hung around the interior of the preaching hall, where the story is recited later.

The scrolls and murals resemble each other iconographically and stylistically. Both replicate the movement of the congregation during Bun Pha Wet processions. As was mentioned earlier, virtually every Isan *wat* holds an annual festival at some time between February and April. Over a period of one day and one night, monks take turns reciting the thirteen chapters of the *Vessantara Jataka* in the local Lao language and the region's distinctive traditional *lam* singing style. The recitation of this all-important story is preceded by the recitation of a local version of *Phra Malai*, the tale of the *arhat* who travels to the Buddhist hells and Tavatimsa Heaven, bringing back Maitreya's admonitions to listen to the recitation of the *Jataka*. In this way local Buddhists fulfill one of the requirements prescribed by the future Buddha Maitreya to Phra Malai. Hoping to be reborn during Maitreya's time on earth as the next Buddha, they follow his instructions.[3]

The scrolls' final scene depicts Pha Wet's triumphant procession back to the capital. At the same time it reflects local practice: figure after figure—musicians, palace officials, and merrymakers—dance, play music, drink local brew, and flirt with abandon. Murals are filled with similar scenes, and both reflect the actual celebration of the Bun Pha Wet festival in thousands of *wat*s throughout the region. In this way the murals, the scrolls, and the ritual reenactment of this Buddhist story reiterate its significance to the lives of the local people and their belief system.

NOTES

1. The term refers to the elaborate system of dance positions to convey emotions and events. There is a strong correspondence between Central Thai classical dance-drama postures and mural figures. References to these connections can be found in *Buddhaisawan Chapel* (1983, 38). Moreover, murals at many Isan *wat*s outside the heartland area also follow these Central Region conventions.

2. This is also true in the Ubon Ratchathani area, which was greatly influenced by Bangkok. According to *Wat Yai Intharam* (1982, 30), "the Thai technical term for these figures in art is *kak* ('the dregs') . . . Some are crudely drawn and in general they lack the care taken over drawing the hieratic or 'priestly' (Thai: *phra*) figures."

3. Suriya et al. (1992) see this as a way of ensuring adequate rainfall for the forthcoming agricultural season, as it has parallels with Prince Vessantara's return to the kingdom mounted on his auspicious rain-bringing elephant. Lefferts (2004), on the other hand, sees it as a participatory reenactment of the *Vessantara Jataka*.

> **FIGURE 38.** *Pha pha wet* scroll used in Bun Pha Wet festivals. Wat Ban Lan, Khon Kaen. ม้วนผ้าผะเหวด ใช้ในงานฉลองบุญผะเหวด วัดบ้านลาน จังหวัดขอนแก่น

FOLLOWING PAGES

> **FIGURE 39.** Procession scene. Wat Photharam, Maha Sarakham. ฉากขบวนแห่ วัดโพธาราม จังหวัดมหาสารคาม

> **FIGURE 40.** Procession of celebrants at Bun Pha Wet festival. Khon Kaen, 1984. ขบวนฉลองบุญผะเหวด จังหวัดขอนแก่น พ.ศ. 2527

> **FIGURE 41.** Women in *wat* at Bun Phra Wet festival. Khon Kaen, 2009. ผู้หญิงในวัด ช่วงงานบุญผะเหวด จังหวัดขอนแก่น พ.ศ. 2552

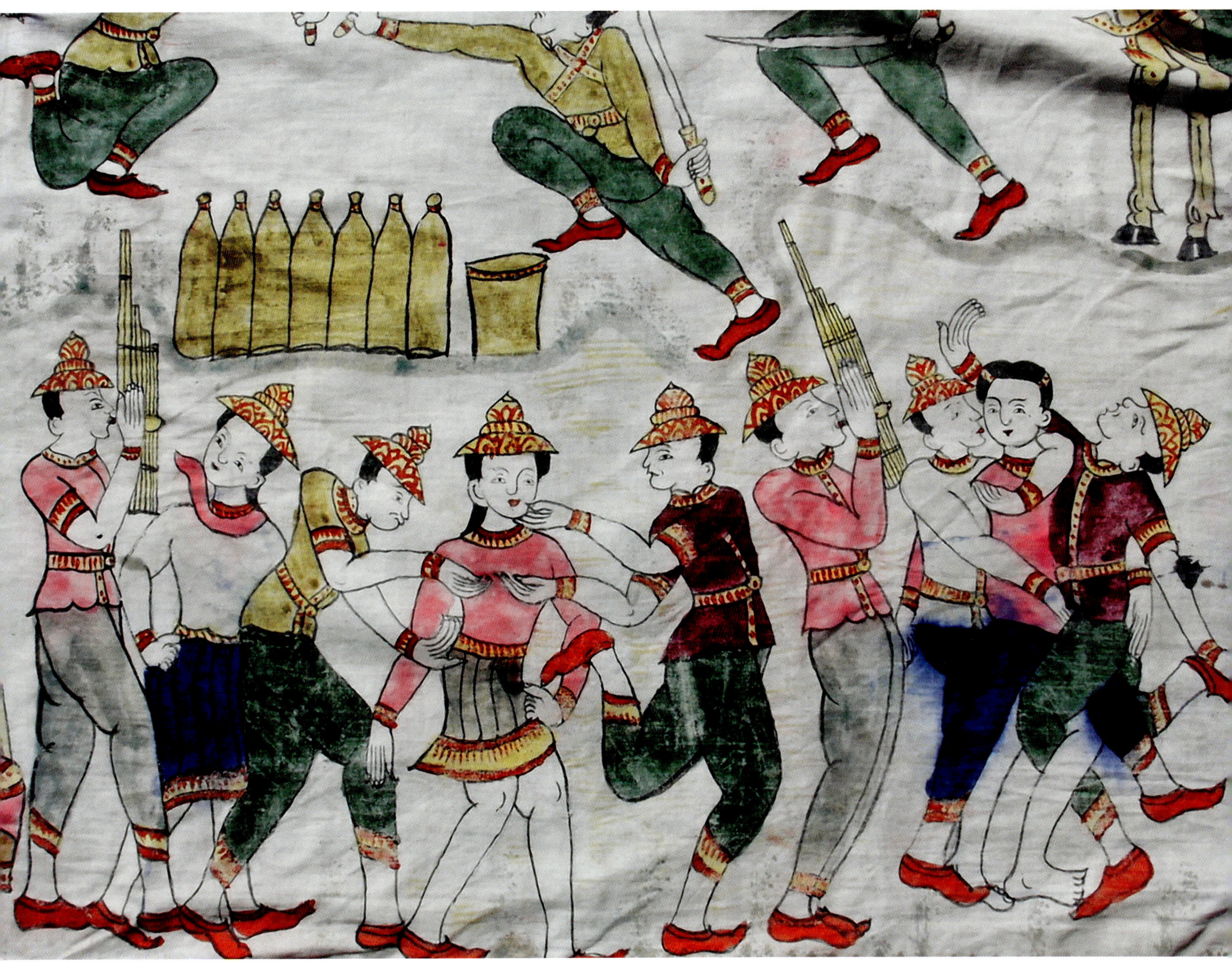

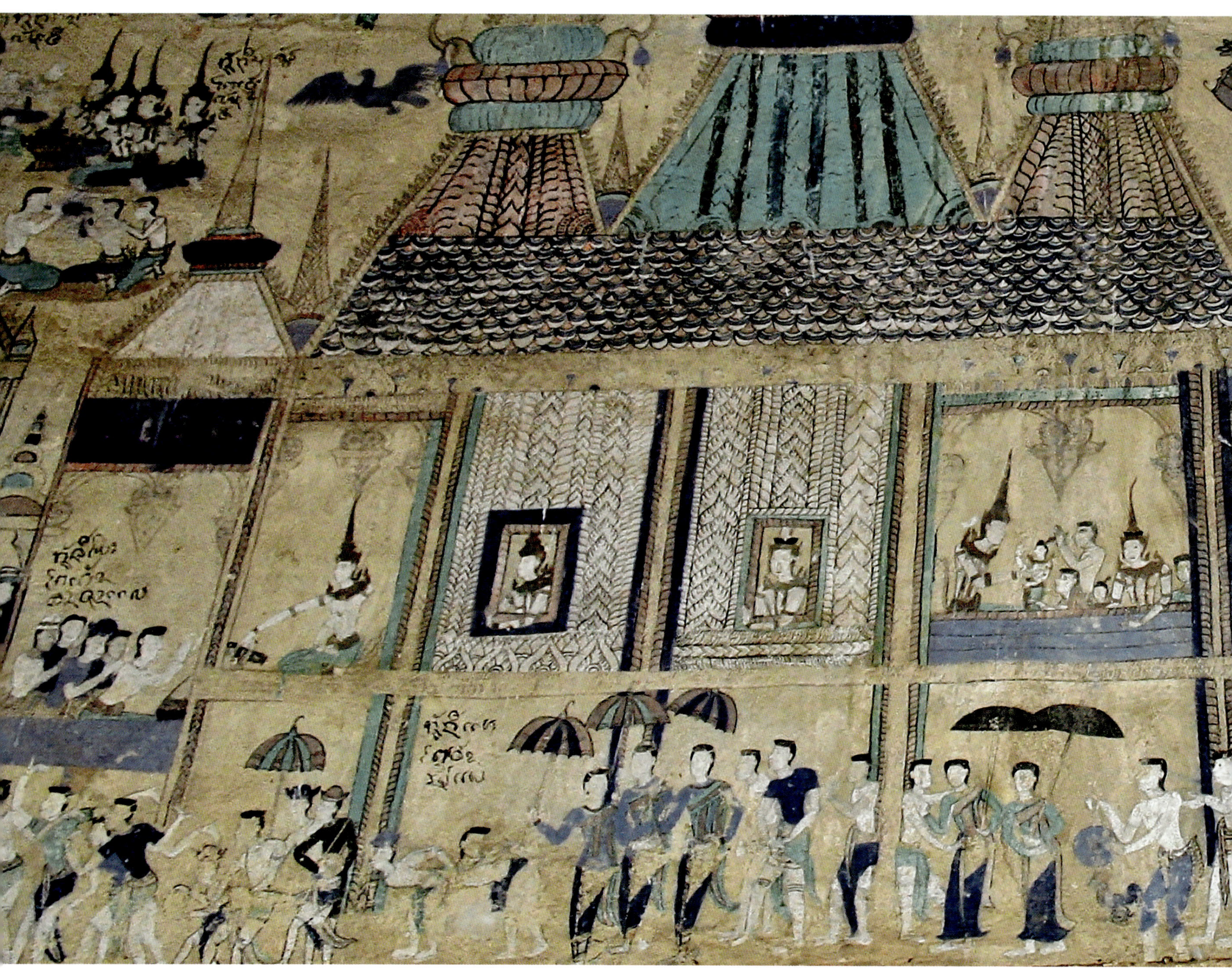

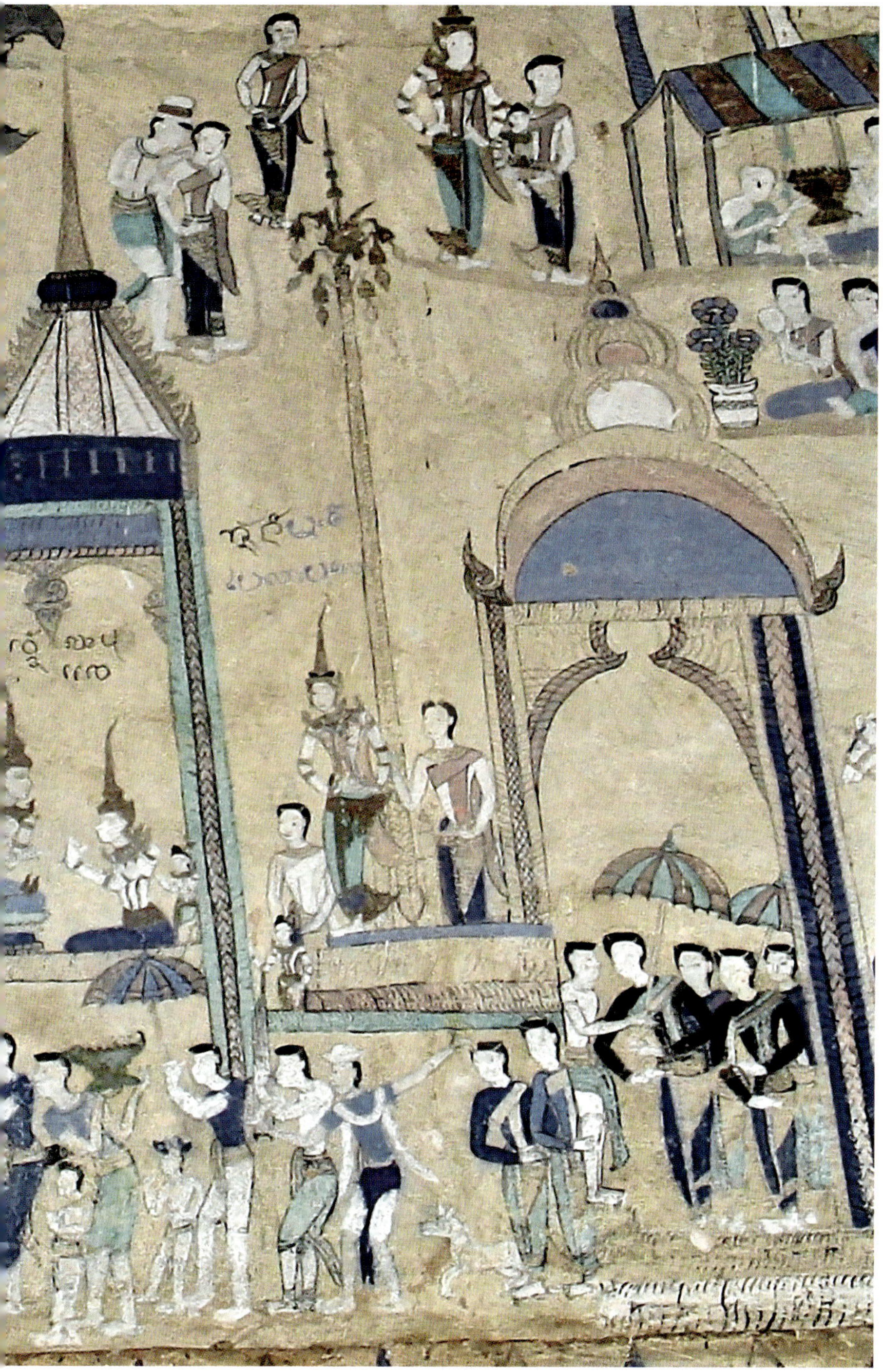

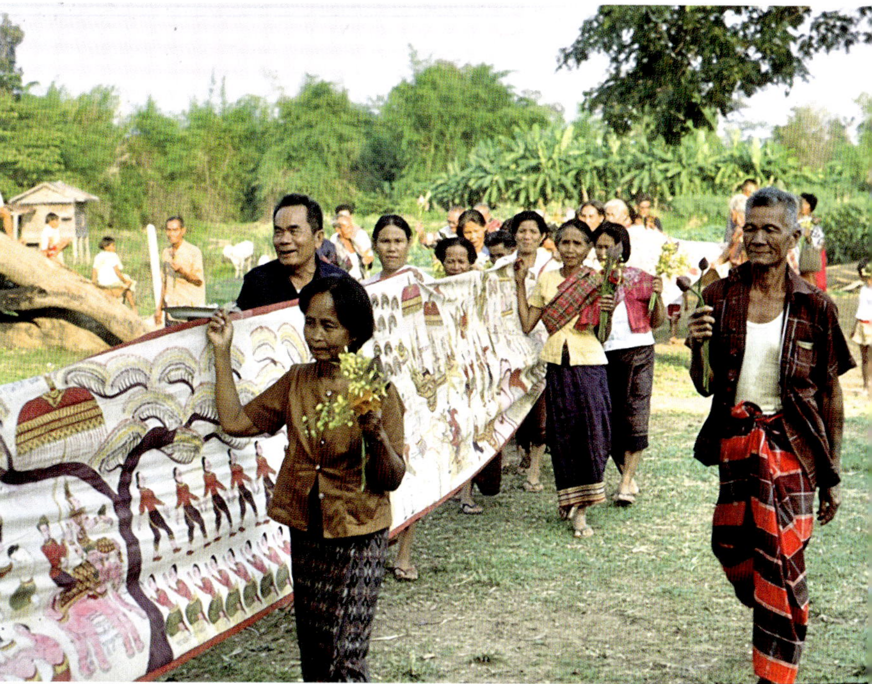

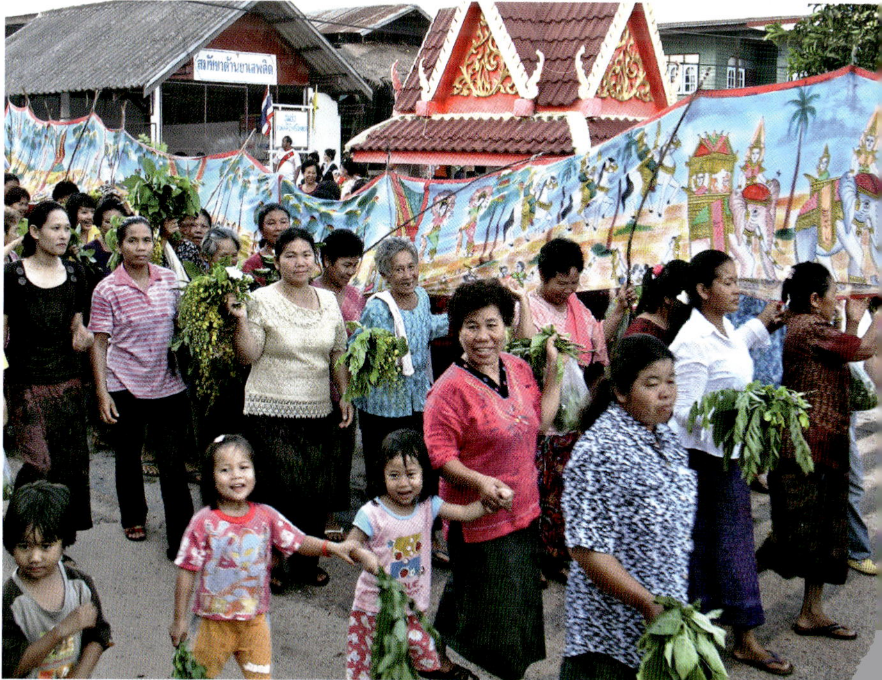

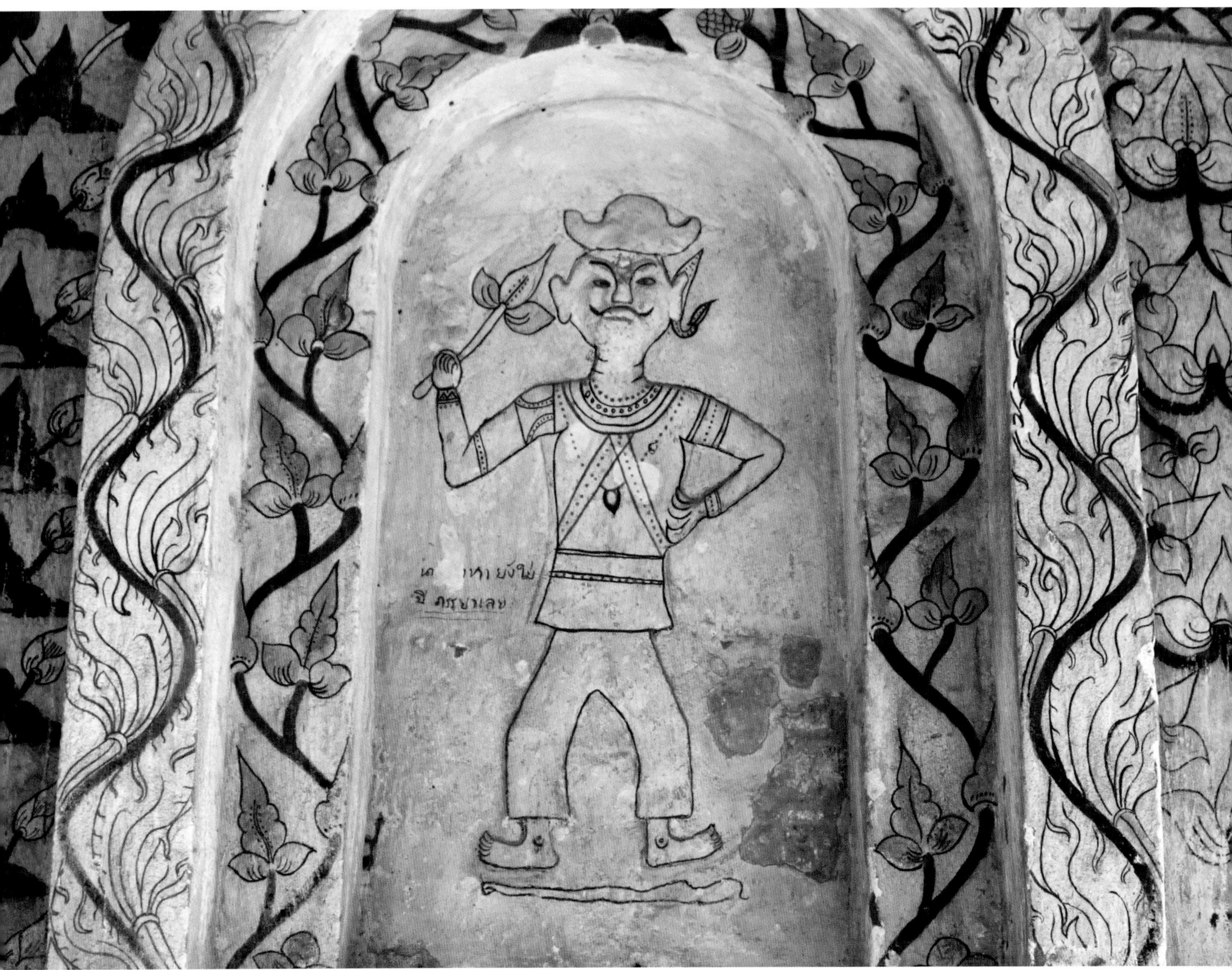

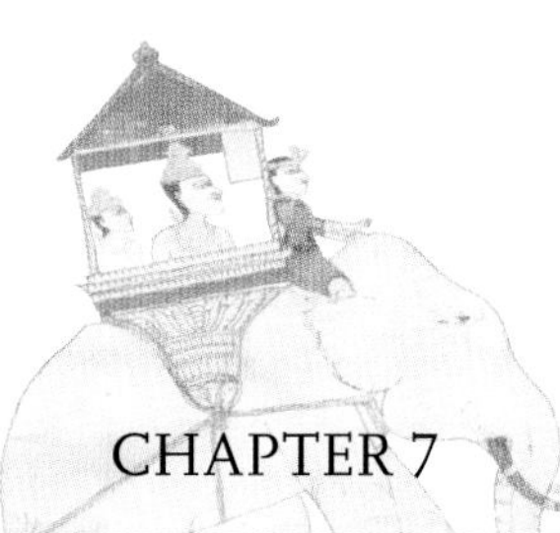

CHAPTER 7

ARTISTS AND SPONSORS, TOOLS, AND TECHNIQUES

Little is known about Isan heartland muralists because their names were seldom recorded. Those who are remembered are known only by their first names (usually nicknames) and titles, indicating that they included both laypeople and monks.[1] The lay artists most likely had spent some time in the monkhood as either fully ordained monks or novices, since this was the usual practice for males at the time. Boys received their education at monastery schools often after having been ordained as novices, and most young adult males entered the monkhood for periods of time ranging from several days to several years. In this way, most laymen were former monks with a background rich in Buddhist stories.

One remarkable exception to the general lack of documentation of artists is the self-portrait and autograph of Nai Yuak depicted on the external south wall of Wat Sanuan Wari, in which the artist is standing in a jaunty pose, barefoot but wearing a hat and holding a flower (figure 42). Nai Yuak's painting style, as seen in both his self-portrait and his murals, is distinctive. It is an extreme example of the Isan heartland style: clearly outlined figures are simply drawn and carefully placed in linear compositions against an off-white background.

In comparing murals from different monasteries, one sees creations emanating from a stunning diversity in vision, conception, and composition. Wat Sa Bua Kaeo's walls are crammed with countless small figures enacting narrative scenes and local customs (figure 43), while Wat Ban Lan has a more relaxed, expansive feel with fewer scenes and larger compositions (figure 44). At Wat Chai Si, colossal, roughly sketched, energetic figures meander beyond the walls around corners onto redented window frames and pilasters (figures 45 and 46). At Wat Sanuan Wari, by contrast, figures are clearly outlined and evenly spaced (figures 7, 31, 34).

Despite such differences, all these murals have enough in common to warrant classifying them into a style. One of these common themes is the division of wall space into horizontal registers or panels that loosely circle the perimeter of the *sim*. Still another is the predominant use of blue.

As for the pigments used, before chemical dyes and paints were available, artists blended their colors from natural dyes extracted from things like plants, shells, soil, and animal parts. The deep rich blue seen so frequently in murals and farmers' shirts came from the indigo plant, while yellow came from the gamboge tree, reddish brown from ochre mixed with tree gum, various shades of green from numerous plant stems and leaves, black from soot, and white from pulverized shells found in the Mekong River (Pairote 1989, 264). Brushes were made from certain tree roots that were pounded, shredded, and shaped at the tip. Preparing the walls, particularly in the Isan heartland, began with applying stucco over the brick walls and then covering them with a wash of white or a light color. The artist would next sketch out the scene, and then fill it in with color.

Sponsorship was generally a community effort, and villagers contributed as much as they could—either in cash, kind, or labor. A rare insight into the contributions of donors is on the walls of Wat Udom Pracharat in Kalasin, in a list of twenty-five individuals who contributed a total of twenty-seven baht for the murals. This extraordinary list provides a valuable record of both the dynamics of communal support and the value of the Thai baht when the building was completed in 1938.

NOTES

1. Pairote (1989, 264), Sumali (2006, 22–25), Tirapong (1994, abstract).

◀ **FIGURE 42.** Artist's self-portrait. Note the decorative bands of floral chains around the false window. Wat Sanuan Wari, Khon Kaen. รูปเหมือนศิลปิน สังเกตลายเครือเถาประดับกรอบ ซุ้มหน้าต่างหลอก วัดสนวนวารี จังหวัดขอนแก่น

FOLLOWING PAGE

▶ **FIGURE 43.** Dense composition filled with figures. Wat Sa Bua Kaeo, Khon Kaen. รูปวาดที่มีองค์ประกอบหนาแน่นด้วยภาพบุคคลจำนวนมาก วัดสระบัวแก้ว จังหวัดขอนแก่น

▶ **FIGURE 44.** Loose composition. Wat Ban Lan, Khon Kaen. รูปวาดที่มีองค์ประกอบหลวม ๆ วัดบ้านลาน จังหวัดขอนแก่น

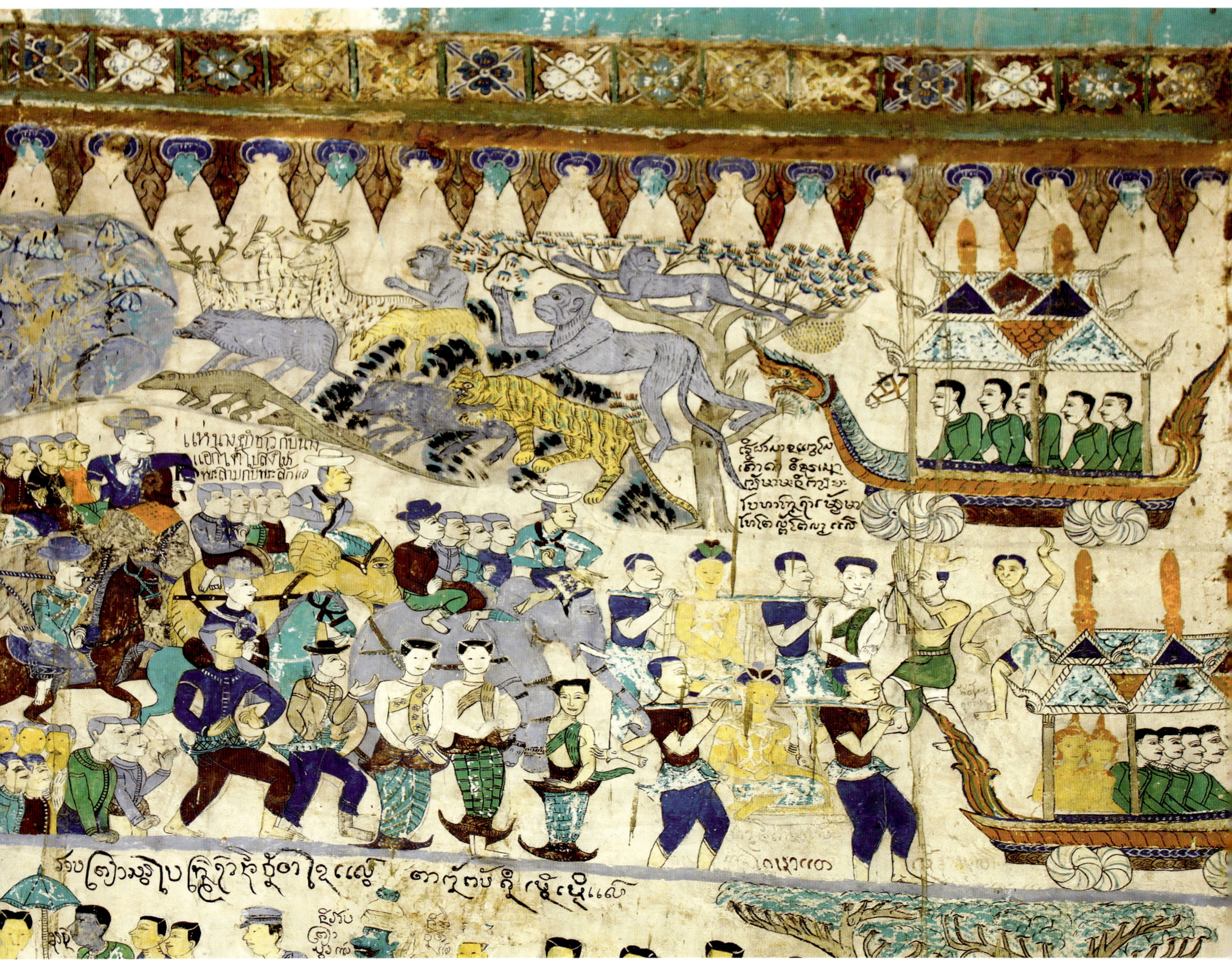

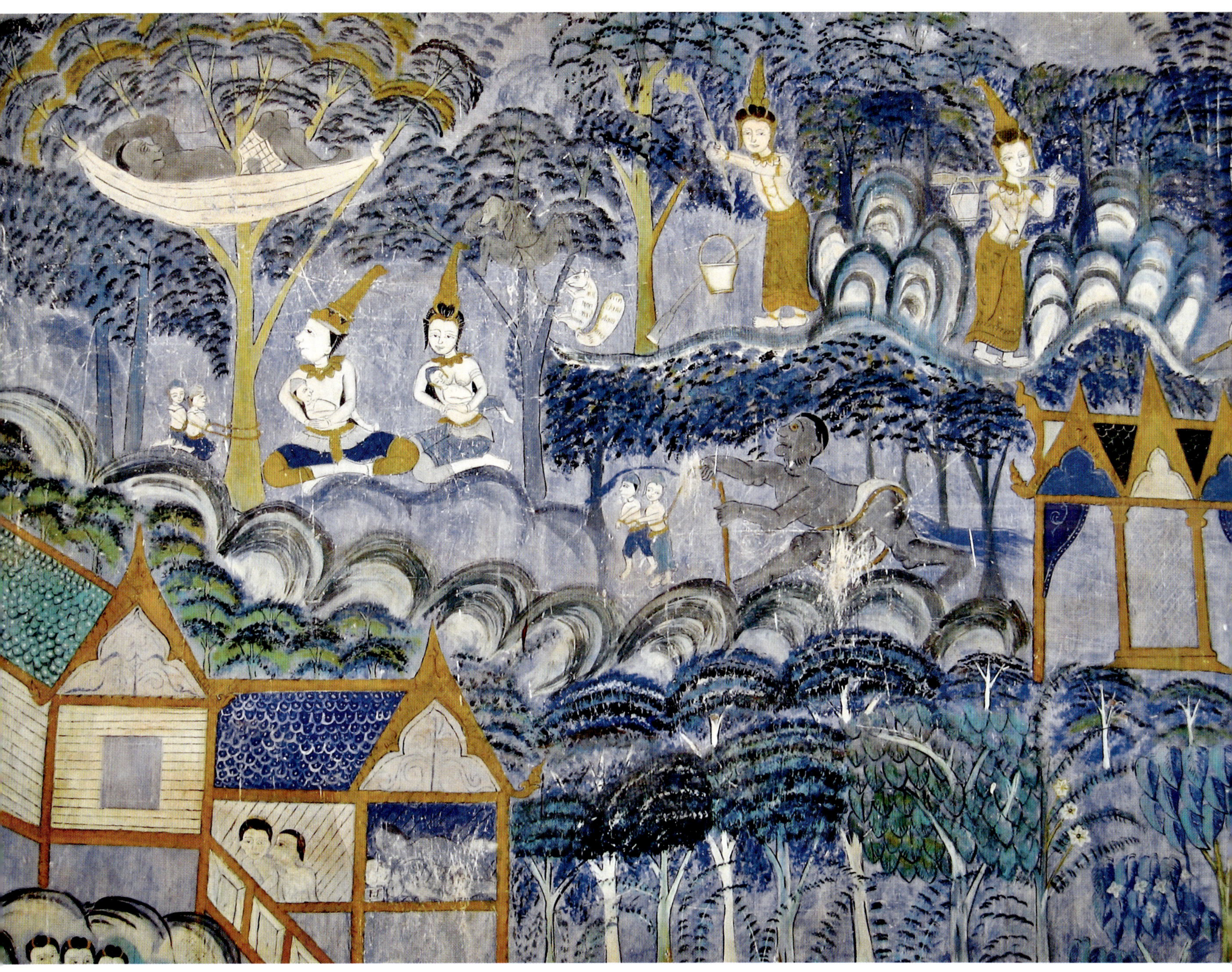

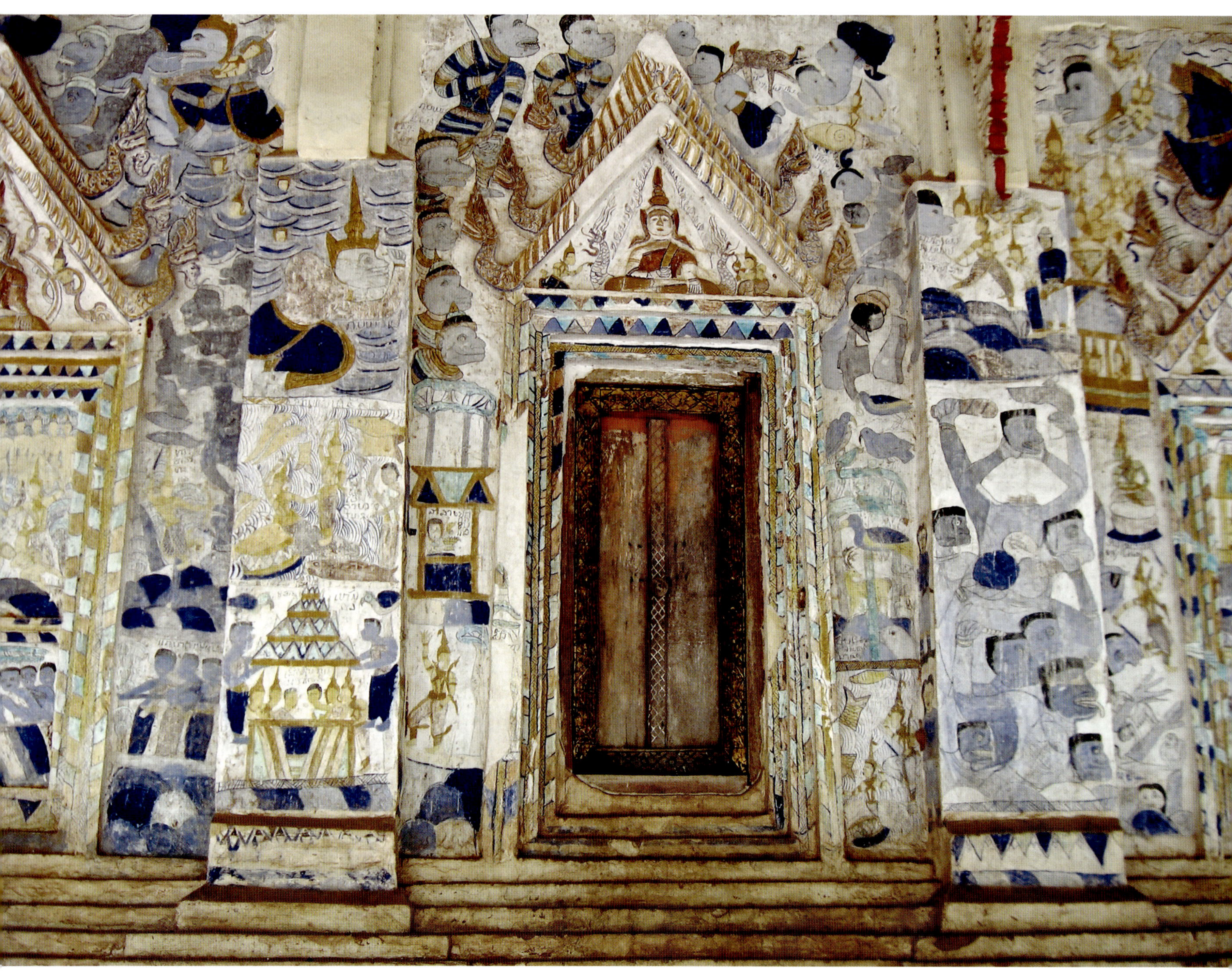

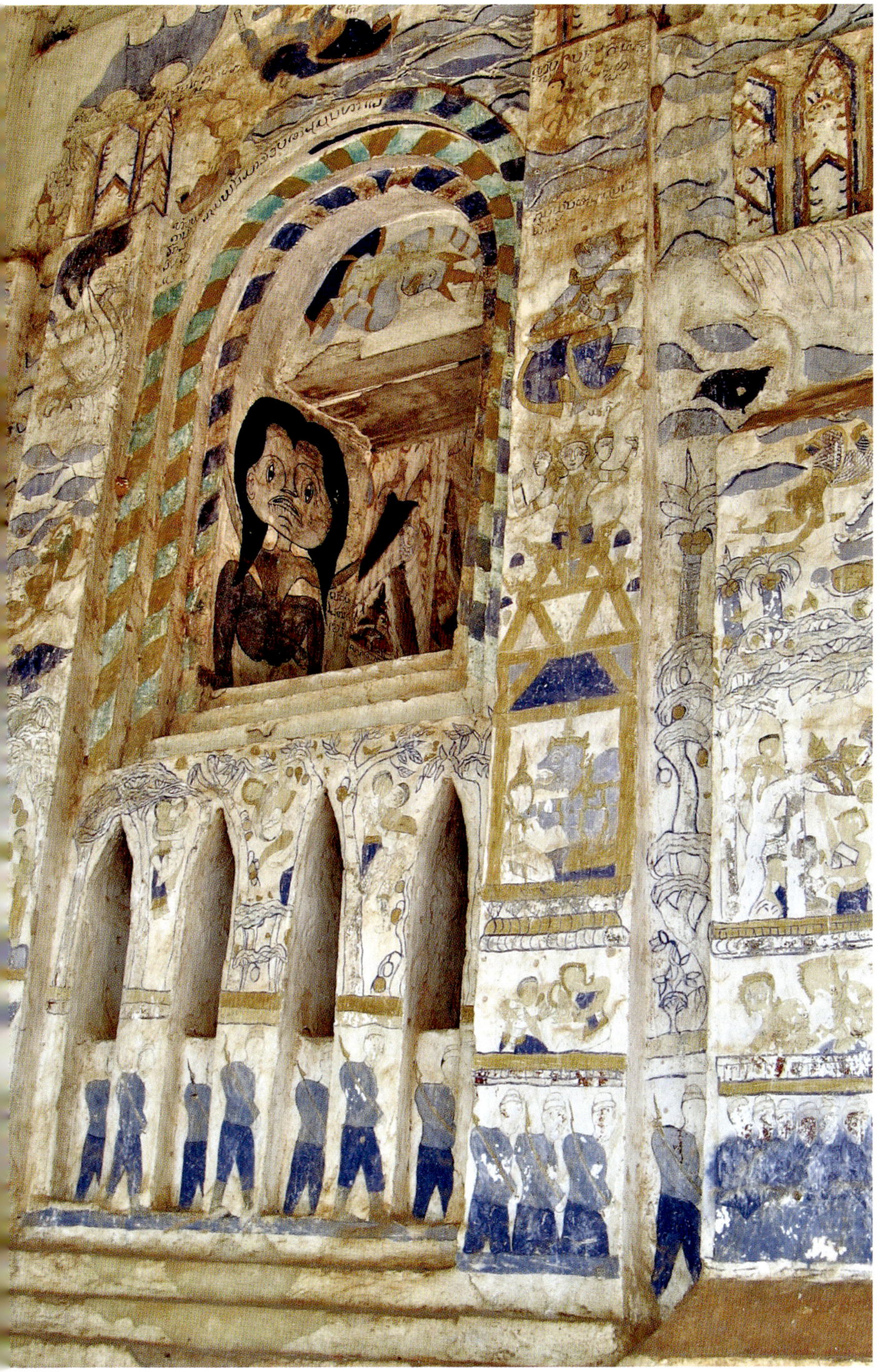

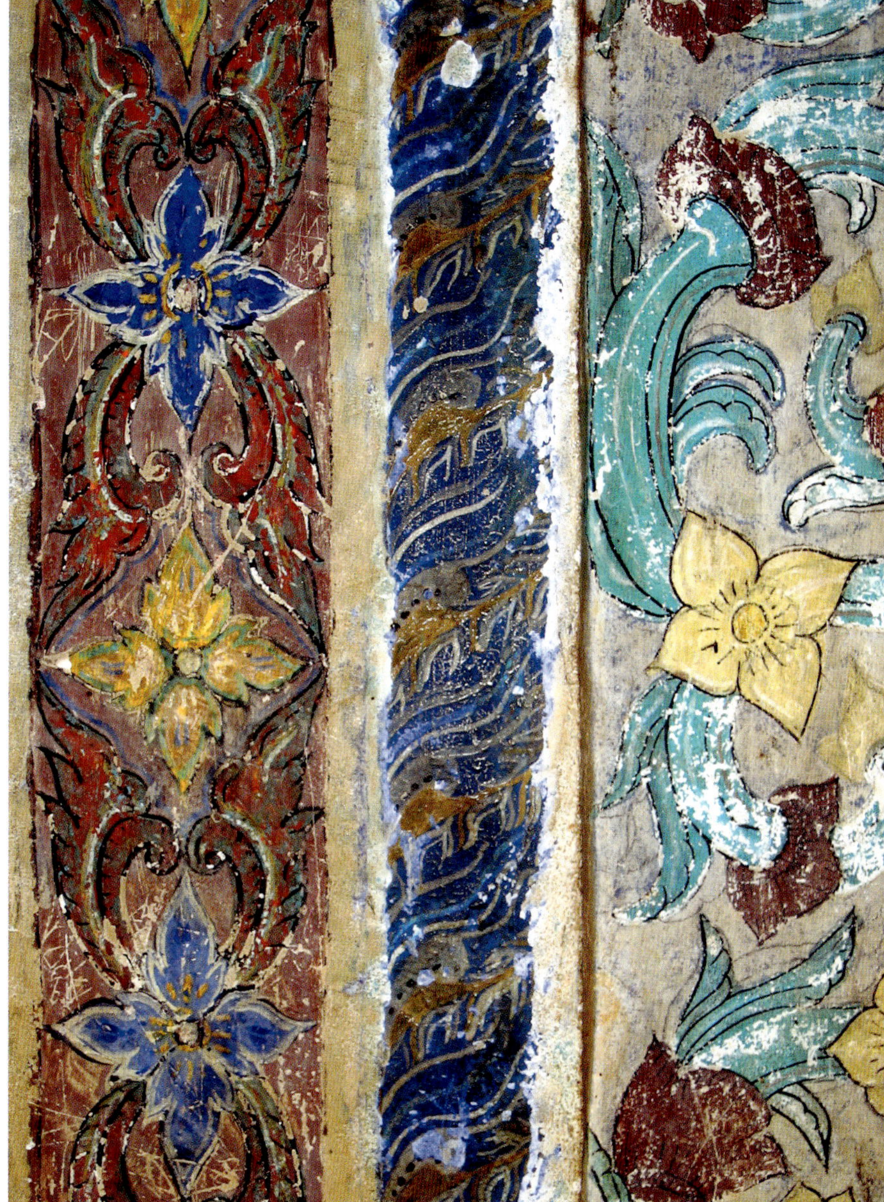

◀ **FIGURES 45 AND 46.** Wat Chai Si's murals covering the external walls, including corners and niches. Khon Kaen. จิตรกรรมฝาผนังของวัดไชยศรีจะวาดเต็มพื้นที่ว่างทั้งหมดบนผนัง

▲ **FIGURE 47.** Border detail. Wat Sa Bua Kaeo, Khon Kaen. รายละเอียดของกรอบ วัดสระบัวแก้ว จังหวัดขอนแก่น

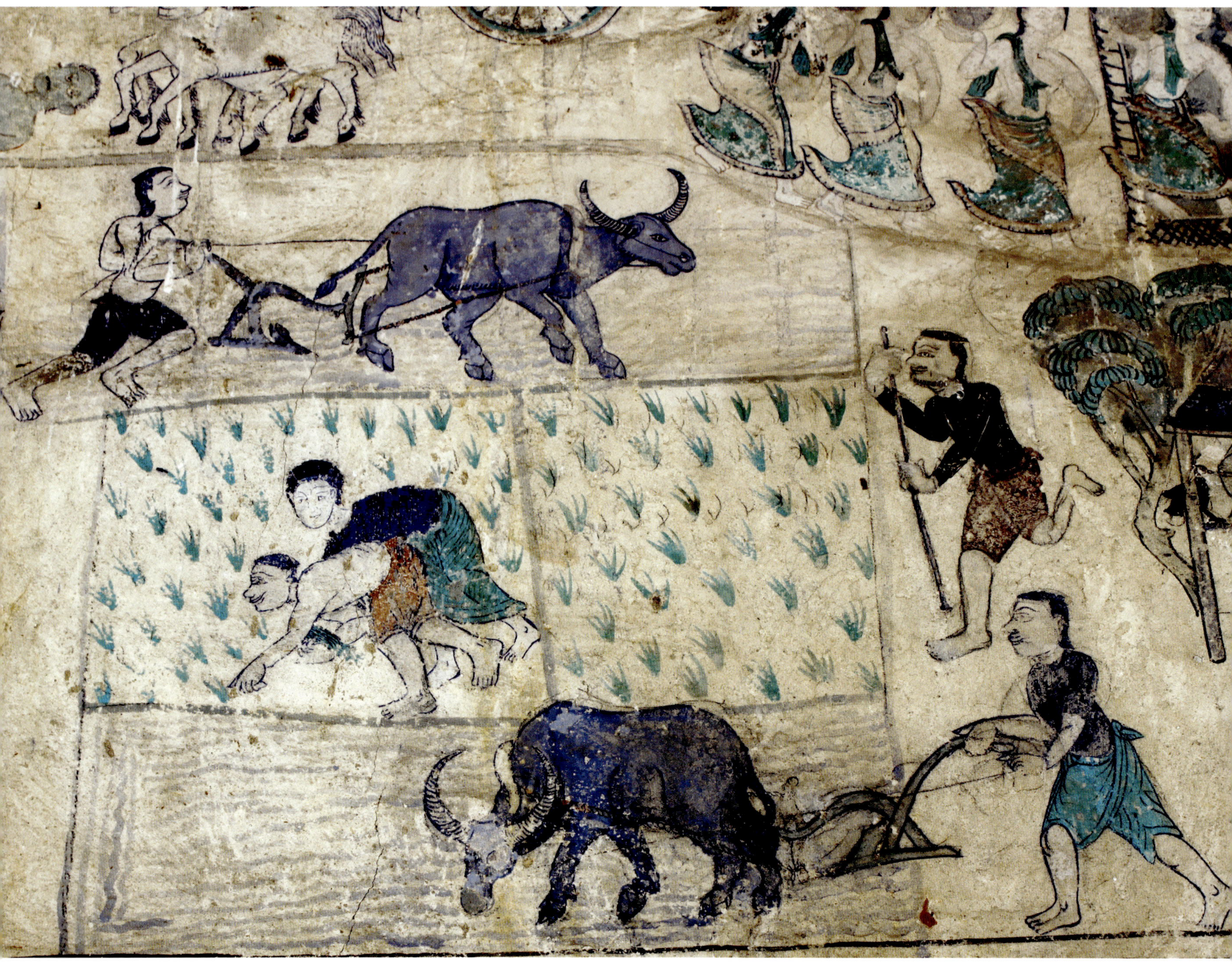

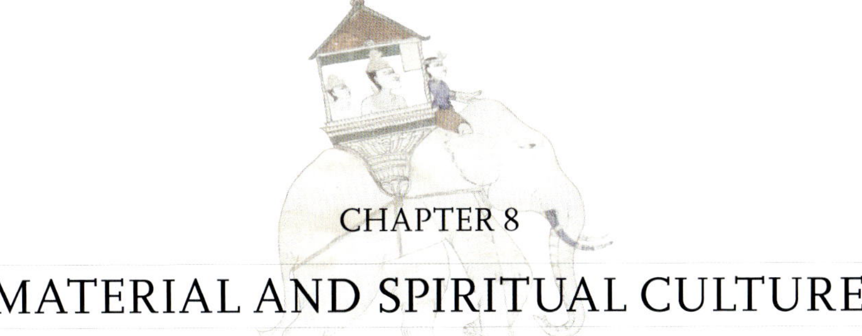

CHAPTER 8

MATERIAL AND SPIRITUAL CULTURE

Artists in the Isan heartland, like all those throughout South and Southeast Asia, used not only their imagination but also their personal experience in creating scenes from Buddhist narratives. While the stories depicted are based on classic Indic models, they are set in the context of local terrain, foliage, architecture, social behavior, and material culture. Consequently, the murals serve as ethnographic catalogs of various aspects of Lao/Isan village life in the early twentieth century, including the activities and antics of ordinary people, their dress, rituals, celebrations, and forms of livelihood.

Wat Photharam and Wat Sa Bua Kaeo are particularly rich in such details. At the former, scenes of various livelihoods are integrated into the background of the Buddha's biography. An example is the depiction of the Great Departure, as seen in figures 48 and 49. Just outside the future Buddha's palace, where he is about to take leave of his wife and son to pursue his spiritual quest, are mundane vignettes of village life. In one, a farmer and his water buffalo plow a rice field using a simple plow pulled by water buffalo, just as local farmers did until a few decades ago. Next to it is a pond with people catching fish using local fish traps.

Along with the livelihood activities of the Lao/Isan people, those of other ethnicities can be seen as well. The Chinese occupy a prominent scene at Wat Photharam in a mural depicting a clothing store (figure 51). Shirts, trousers, and underpants hang in an open-air shop, which apparently has attracted a number of interested Lao/Isan shoppers. The shop is staffed by seven women, whose Chinese identity is obvious from their white complexion, straight long hair, trousers, and fitted, long-sleeved bodices. It is likely that all are members of the same family and that their presence and the products they were selling generated considerable excitement among the Lao/Isan community. Their descendants might be the owners of urban enterprises selling motorbikes, cars, and home appliances that today elicit the same kind of excitement.

Throughout the murals, people of various generations can be seen, often in charming and aesthetically sophisticated compositions of three or four figures. An example is the trio of elderly women with bent backs and sagging breasts in figure 52.[1] Figures like this are a common motif in Isan murals and provide information about styles of dress. Until several decades ago, many older women wore no upper garment except on special occasions such as Buddhist holy days, when they wore a length of cloth draped over one shoulder and covering the breasts when they went to the *wat*.

In vivid contrast to the above scene is the cluster of young women in figure 50, who have erect postures and graceful physiques, and are dressed in fitted long-sleeved blouses with a cloth draped over the shoulder. They also wear the local version of the tube skirt (*phasin*), as seen in the Lao/Isan vertical patterns.

Also seen here are numerous varieties of the typical Lao/Isan skirt, or *phasin*, with its distinctive woven vertical pattern. Women's upper garments could be as minimal as the breast cloth mentioned above. For special occasions, younger women might favor a fitted, long-sleeved blouse with the cloth draped over it. Such clothing, generally made of silk, was reserved for merit-making activities at the *wat*, while cotton garments were worn every day.

Ordinary males are usually depicted wearing an indigo farmer's shirt with farmer's shorts and/or a checkered loin cloth (*pha khao ma*) covering the lower body. Often their thighs are densely covered with tattoos, a practice that even two or three generations ago was considered a hallmark of masculinity (figure 53, from Wat Pa Rerai). Women considered men with tattoos to be more desirable mates because they had demonstrated patience, endurance, and the ability to withstand pain. In contrast, the figures of spiritually highly evolved males, such as deities, heroes, and their attendants, commonly wear long-sleeved shirts and the Central Region *chongkraben* (a long piece of cloth wrapped around the waist and between the legs so as to resemble trousers).

◄ **FIGURE 48.** Farming scene. Detail of Great Departure scene, Wat Photharam, Maha Sarakham. ภาพการทำนา วัดโพธาราม จังหวัดมหาสารคาม

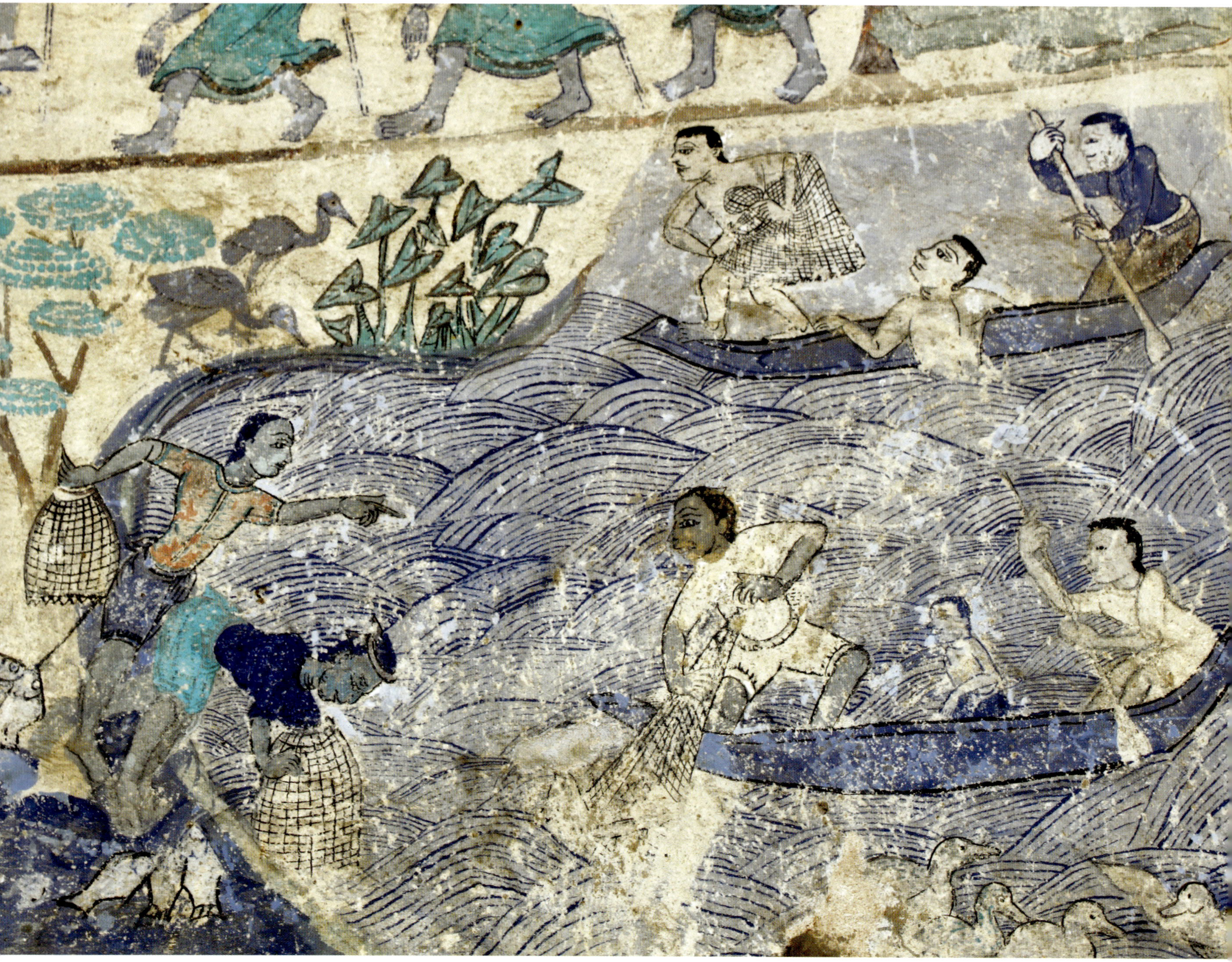

Children are seen in the murals, but not as frequently as one might expect given the large size of families during premodern times. A century ago, birth and death rates were both much higher than they are today, and both births and deaths are depicted in murals. An example of the former is the birth of Nang Sida in the *Pha Lam Sadok* murals at Wat Ban Yang (figure 55). A woman is shown kneeling or squatting and grasping a rope, as was customary, while her attendants massage her abdomen to aid in the delivery. The tiny figure of a newborn infant is seen in the arms of another woman. Nang Sida's mother can be identified as a deity by the jewelry and crown that she wears.

Funeral scenes are also found in Isan murals, the most common being that of Chuchok in portrayals of the *Vessantara Jataka*. Often a procession is seen carrying his body in a sling or coffin to the cremation site, accompanied by monks and laypeople. He lies face up with his hands tied together on his chest in a *wai*, the customary gesture of respect (see barely visible figure in funeral pyre, figure 56). Another local Buddhist practice depicted is the pouring of lustral water over a monk on the occasion of his elevation in rank within the Sangha. As seen in figure 54, from Wat Pa Rerai, water is poured into a wooden trough that has been carved in the form of a *naga* and bored with holes that serve as a drain. The monk sits beneath, and as the laypeople pour water into the trough he is sprinkled with the water that falls through the holes.

Buddhist festivals seen in murals invariably include processions of the faithful carrying offerings to the Sangha and exuberant musicians and dancers. The quintessential Lao musical instrument, the bamboo reed mouth organ (*khaen*), is accompanied by long drums. Sometimes seen as well are the Central Region gong circle and xylophone (*ranat*), occasionally even being carried in procession. The ubiquitous presence of these lively and uninhibited lines of people, not only dancing but

◄ **FIGURE 49.** Fishing scene. Detail of Great Departure scene, Wat Photharam, Maha Sarakham. ภาพการหาปลา วัดโพธาราม จังหวัดมหาสารคาม

▶ **FIGURE 50.** Young women carrying water from well. Wat Ban Lan, Khon Kaen. ภาพหญิงสาว หาบน้ำจากบ่อ วัดบ้านลาน จังหวัดขอนแก่น

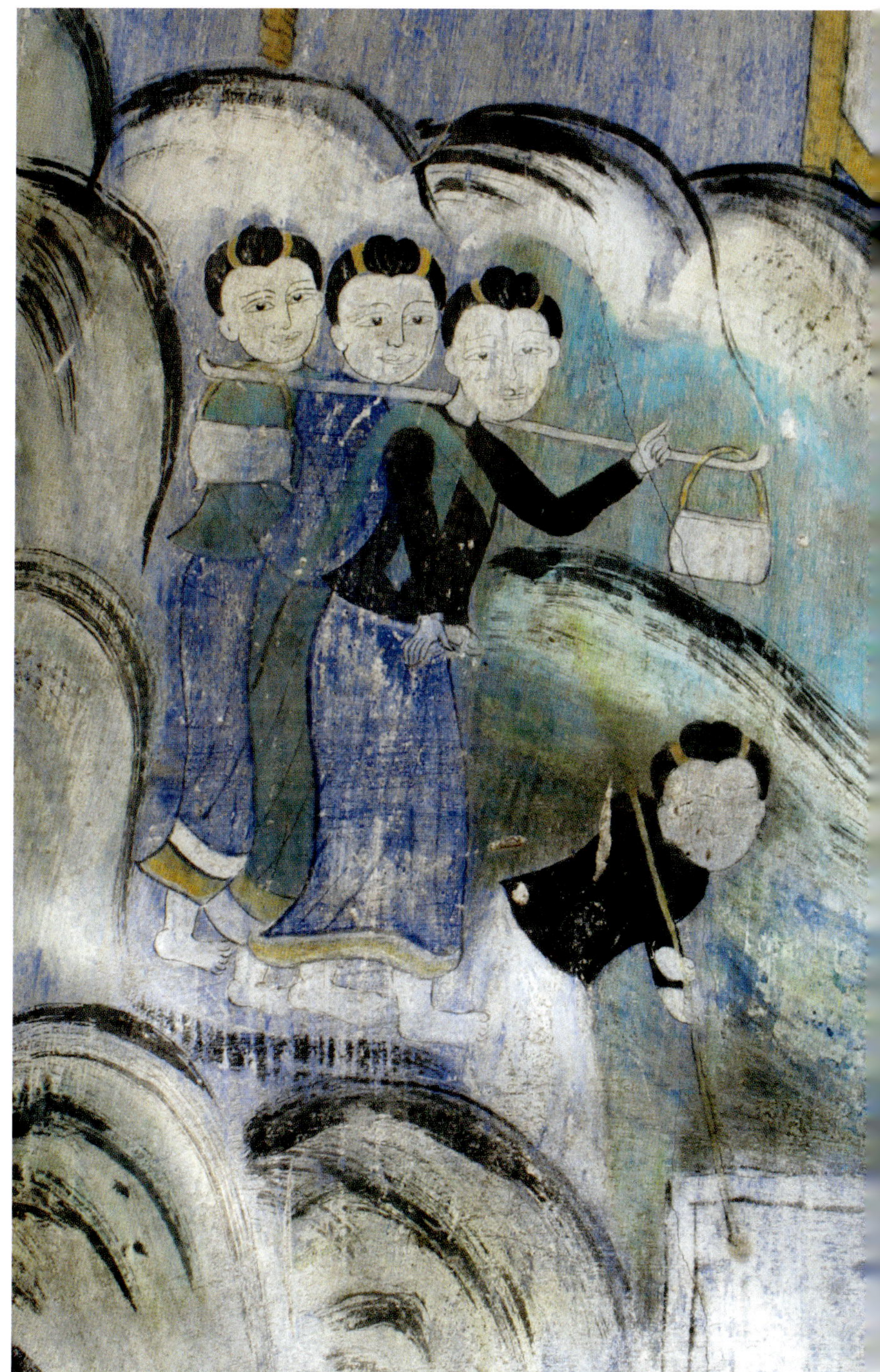

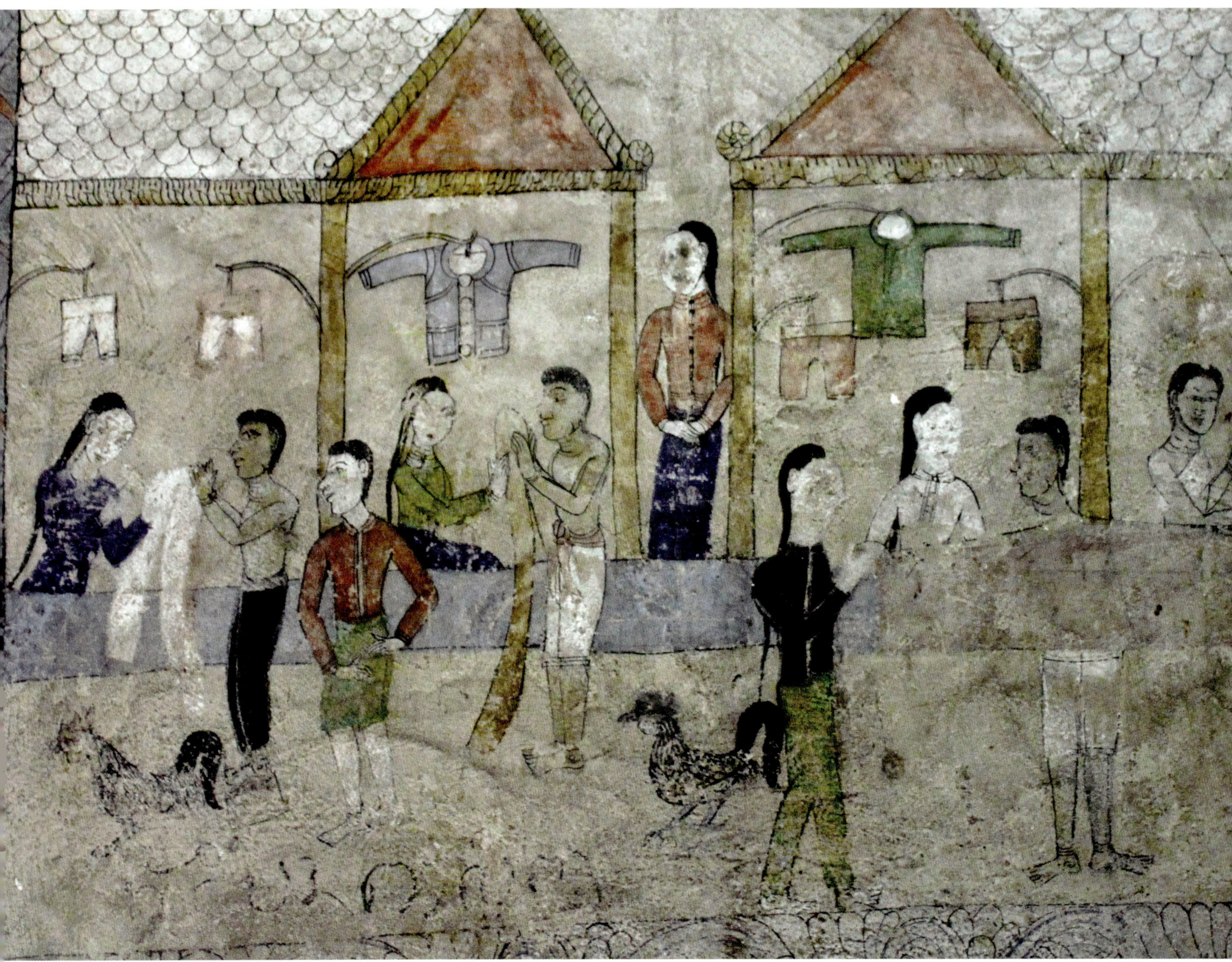

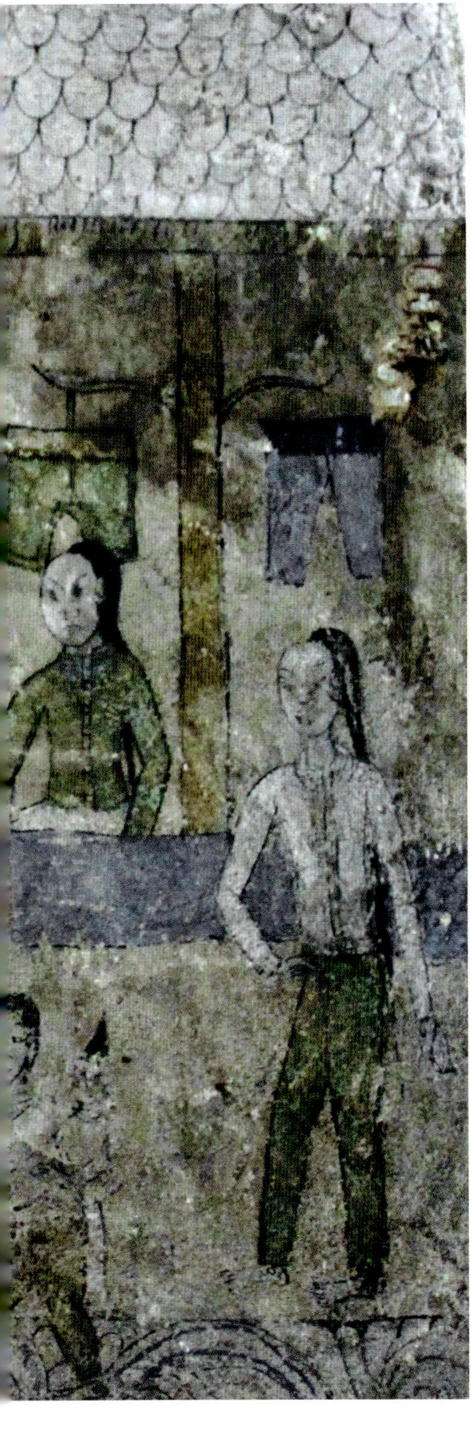

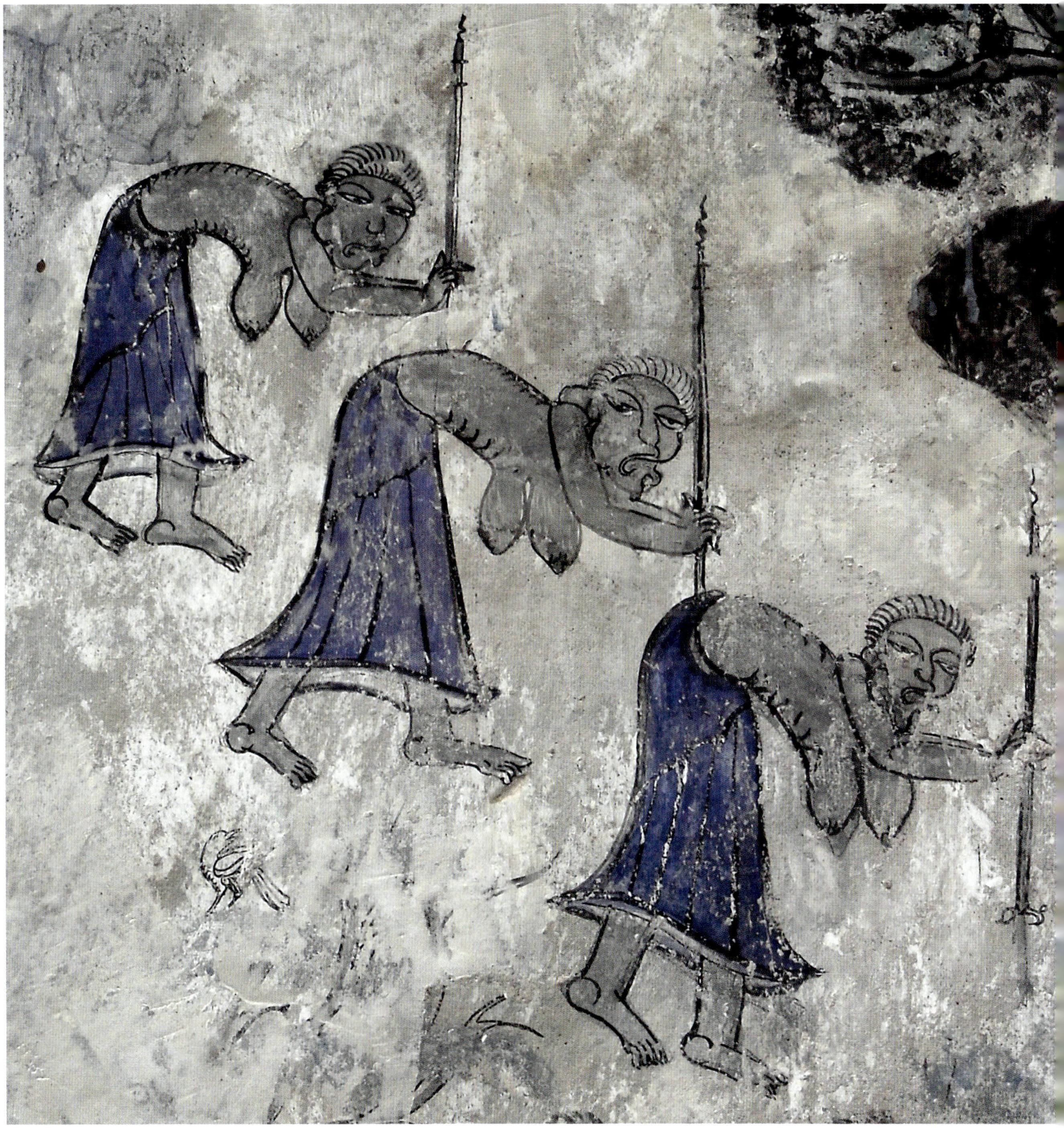

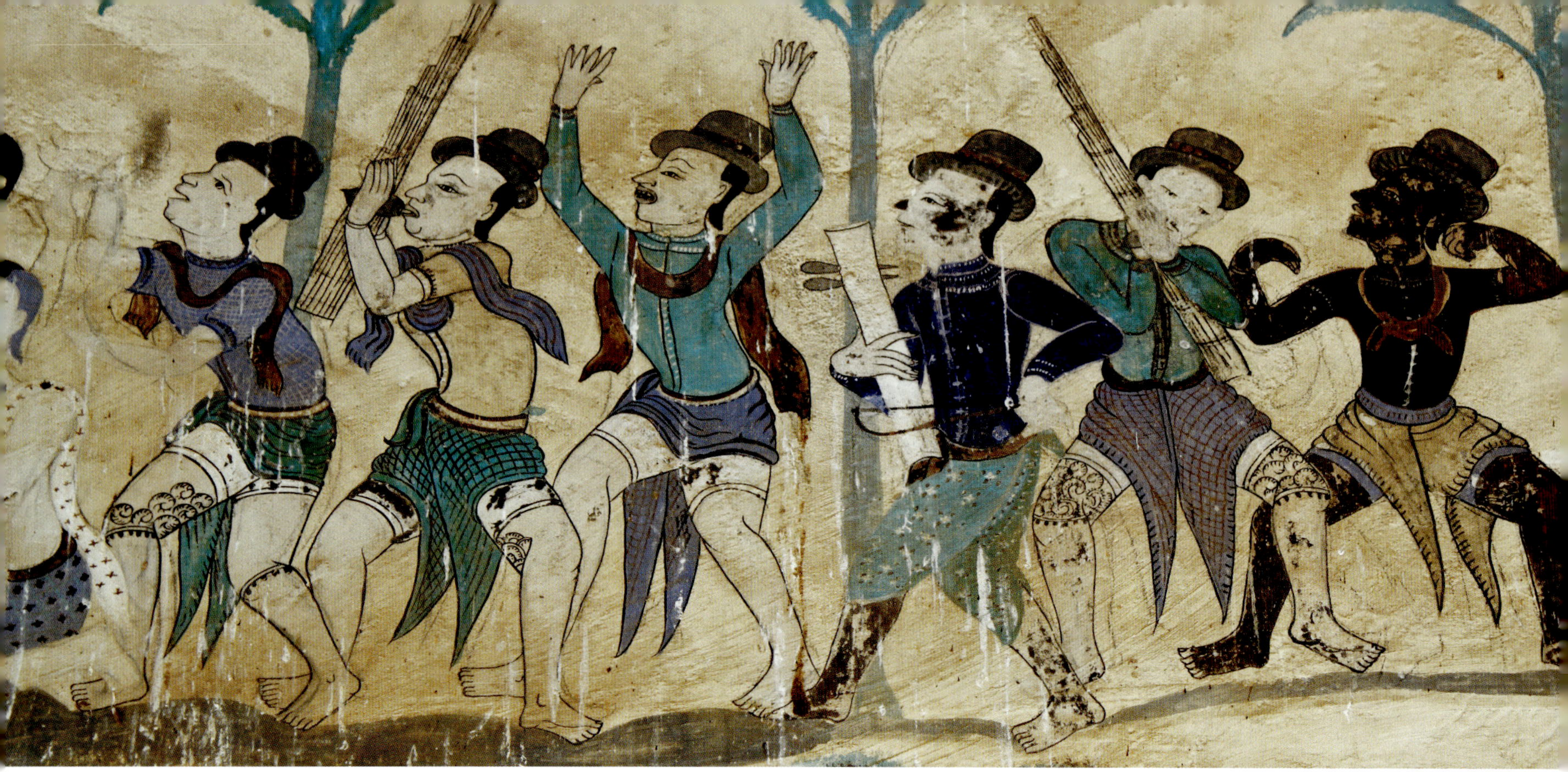

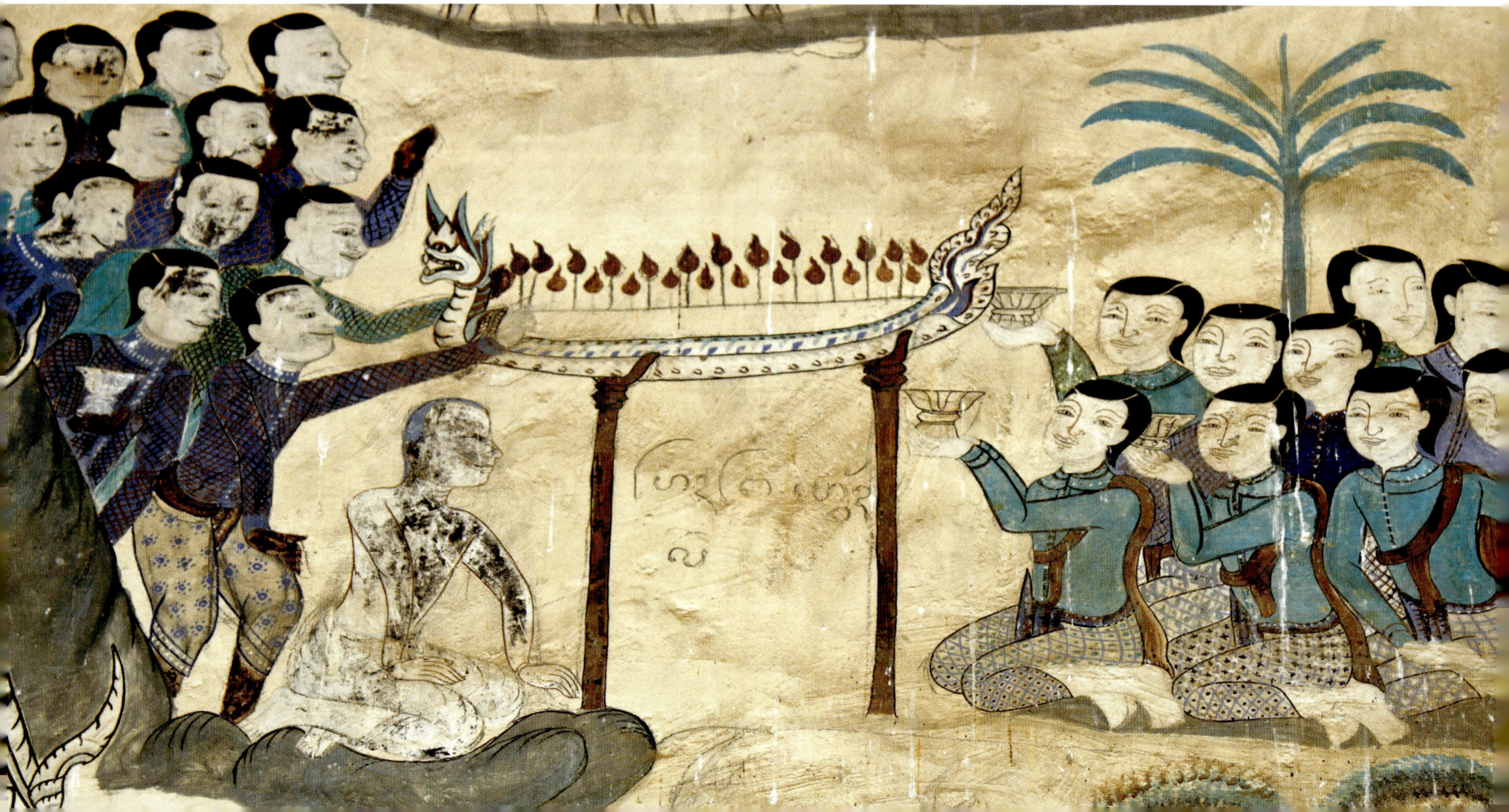

sometimes also drinking and flirting, demonstrates the central role they played—and still play—in Buddhist festivals.

In addition to these depictions of daily labor, life and death, and religious festivities, a little-known prognostication game can be seen at Wat Chai Si. The game involves a tug-of-war between two teams to predict and determine the amount of rainfall for the coming rice growing season (figure 57). This ritual takes place in mid-April during the Songkran festival, which marks the traditional Thai and Lao New Year, and is laden with implications of fertility and renewal. Teams compete in a series of events in which there is not only vigorous back-and-forth tugging on a rope, but also much tossing of sand and water, cheering, and sexual horseplay. Team members come and go, the teams grow larger, and the audience joins in the fray. Theoretically, the women are supposed to win the majority of events, in order to ensure sufficient rainfall, but the result is often less important than the process.[2]

NOTES

1. Such female figures are often part of a mural's *mara vijaya* scene, in which the Buddha overcomes Mara's temptations, which include the demon's seductive daughters, who are then transformed into old hags.

2. Lefferts (n.d., 1) describes these events in detail and notes that Thai-Lao villagers in the Isan heartland use a large wooden mortar as a pivotal point around which the rope is wrapped. His essay notes that the tug-of-war calls to mind the Angkor Wat motif of the Churning of the Ocean of Milk and that it "poses questions about the diffusion of mythic motifs and rituals between populations [that is, Thai-Lao in modern Isan and Khmer in twelfth-century Cambodia] usually seen as distinct."

PREVIOUS PAGES

◄ **FIGURE 51.** Chinese merchants. Wat Photharam, Maha Sarakham. พ่อค้าจีน วัดโพธาราม จังหวัดมหาสารคาม

◄ **FIGURE 52.** Elderly women. Wat Khon Kaen Nuea, Roi Et. หญิงชรา วัดขอนแก่นเหนือ จังหวัดร้อยเอ็ด

OPPOSITE

◄ **FIGURE 53.** High-spirited festival celebrants. Note the tattoos on the men's legs. Wat Pa Rerai, Maha Sarakham. รอยสักบนขาผู้ชาย วัดป่าเรไร จังหวัดมหาสารคาม

◄ **FIGURE 54.** Lustral water ceremony. Wat Pa Rerai, Maha Sarakham. พิธีฮดสรง วัดป่าเรไร จังหวัดมหาสารคาม

FOLLOWING PAGES

► **FIGURE 55.** Childbirth scene. Wat Ban Yang, Maha Sarakham. ภาพการคลอดบุตร วัดบ้านยาง จังหวัดมหาสารคาม

► **FIGURE 56.** Funeral procession for Chuchok's cremation. Wat Ban Yang, Maha Sarakham. ขบวนศพชูชก วัดบ้านยาง จังหวัดมหาสารคาม

► **FIGURE 57.** Tug-of-war ritual. Wat Chai Si, Khon Kaen. เล่นชักเย่อ วัดไชยศรี จังหวัดขอนแก่น

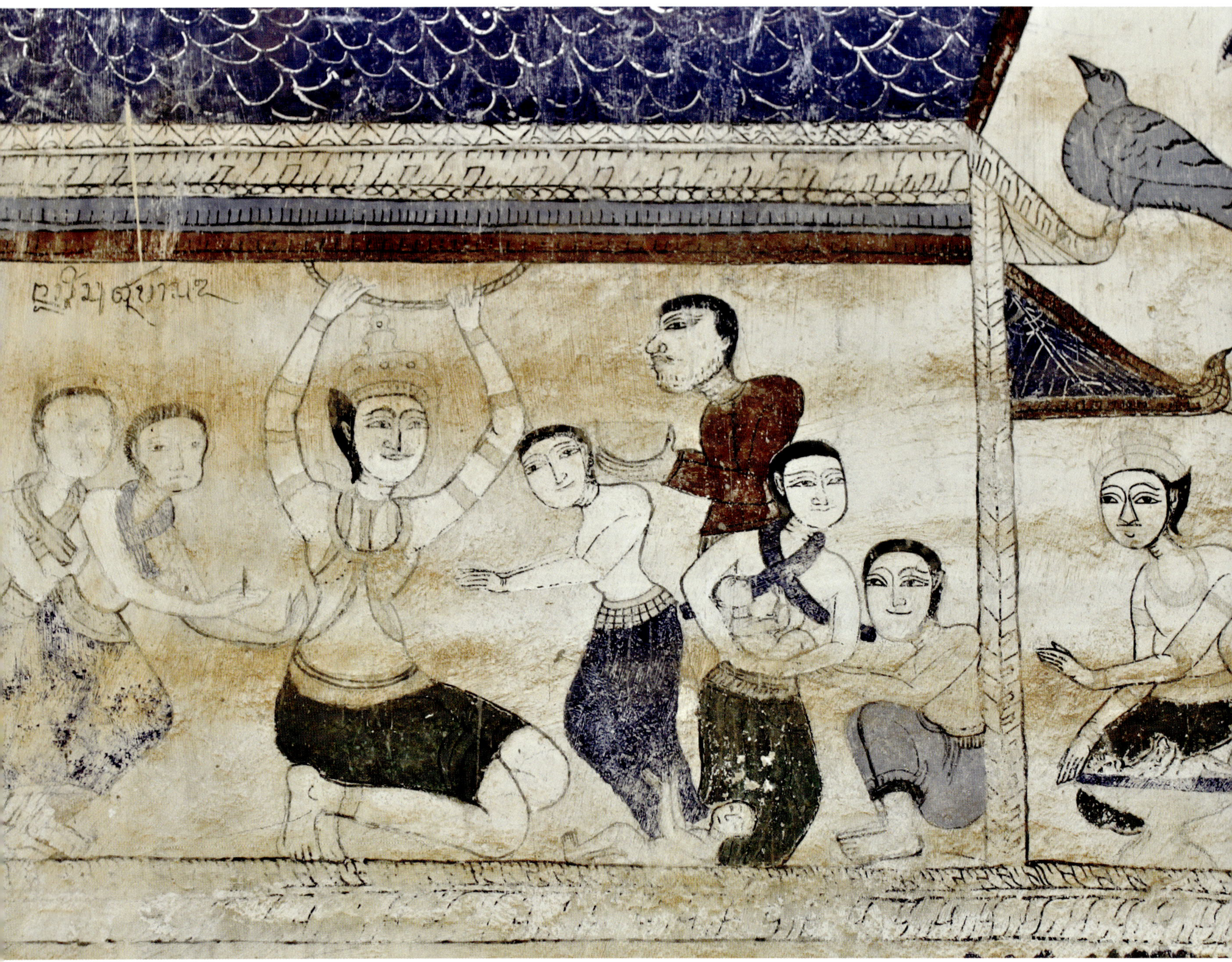

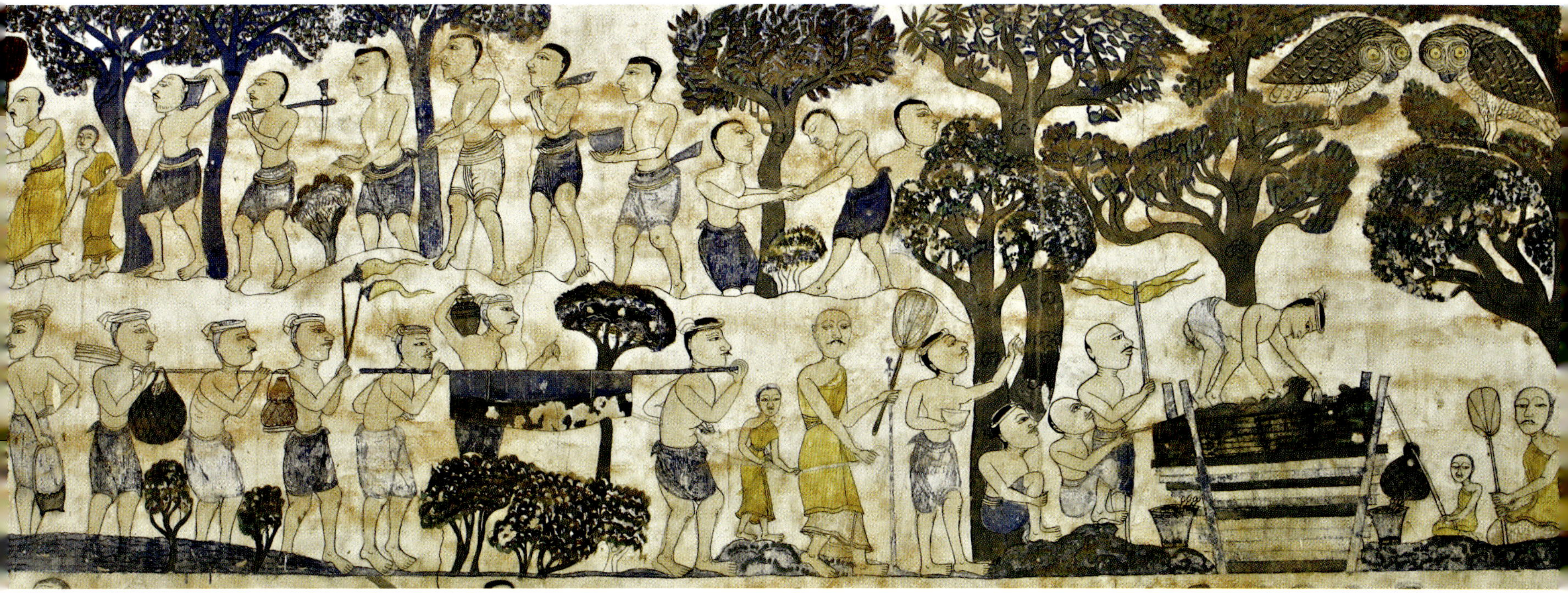

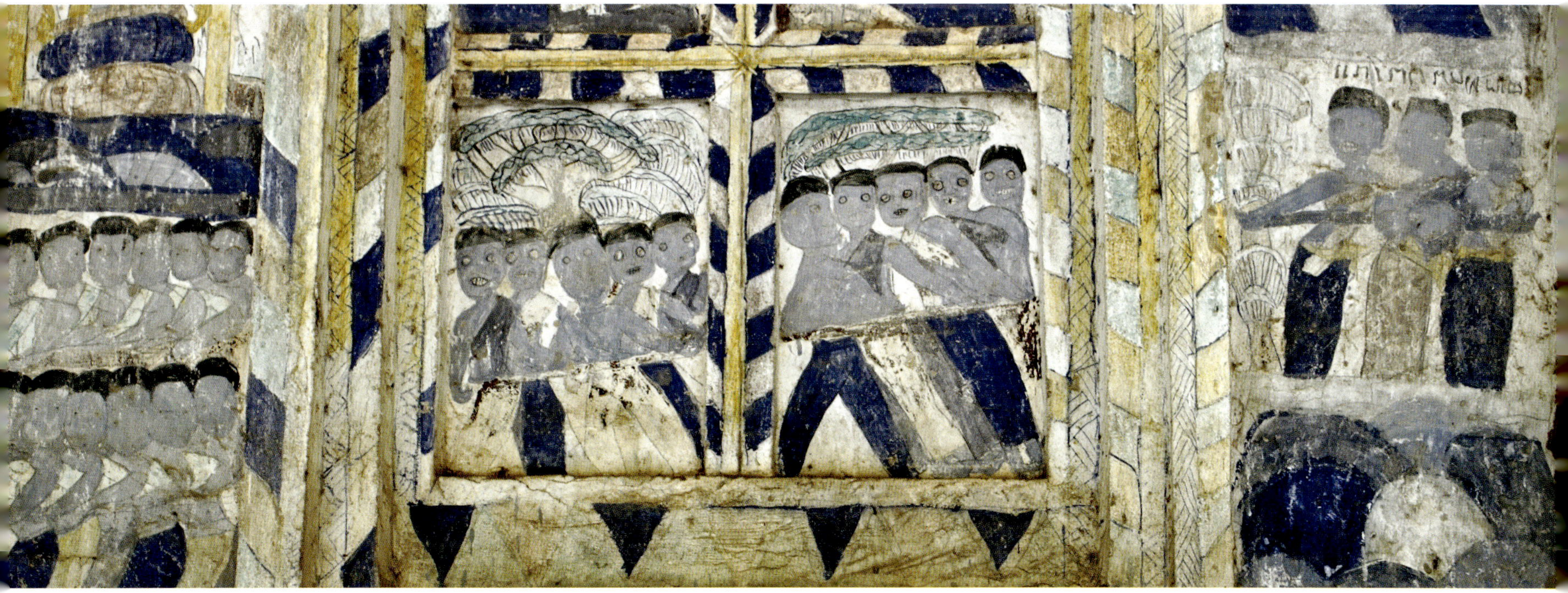

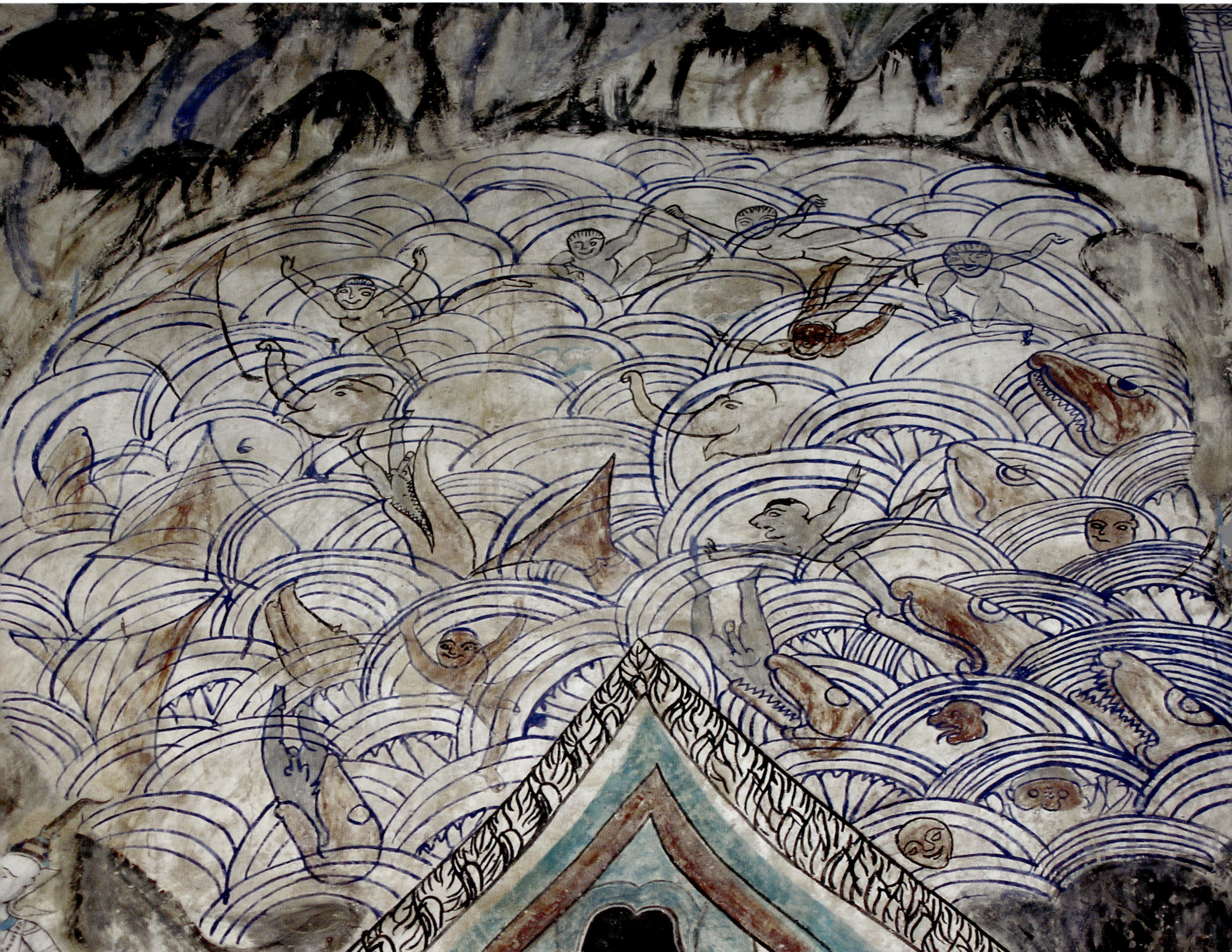

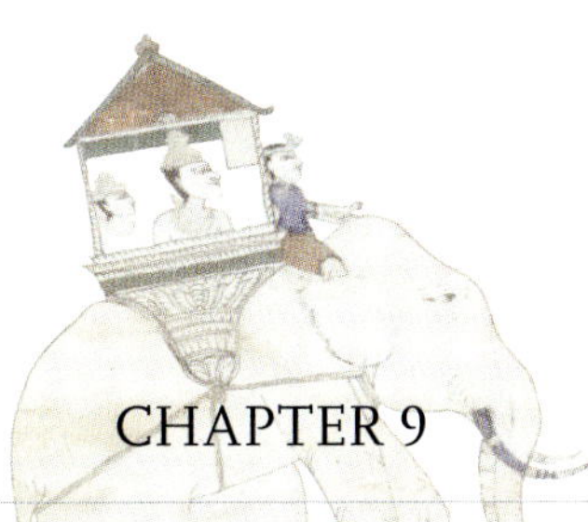

CHAPTER 9

EROTICISM, BAWDINESS, AND BUFFOONERY

As the tug-of-war ritual described in the previous chapter demonstrates, the Isan people find depictions of sexual interplay both interesting and delightful. Similarly, a considerable part of folk literature and entertainment throughout the country includes references to sexual activity and bawdy jokes based on clever puns. Nidhi Eoseewong, a well-known Thai scholar, notes that various forms of singing which accompany ordinary activities like harvesting and boating are filled with sexual innuendoes; he suggests that they once may have been connected with fertility rites. Thai court poetry is also famous for its references to sexual encounters, ranging from rather explicit descriptions to narrative passages referred to as "wondrous scenes" (Nidhi 2005, 29–32). The latter are poetic descriptions of natural phenomena, including earthquakes, storms at sea, lightning, rainfall, and the interactions of bees and flowers, as codified metaphors for erotic activity.

In the same vein, Buddhist murals in every part of the country usually include scenes of flirting, courting, and more-or-less explicit depictions of lovemaking that take place on the periphery of the drama being enacted. In Central and Southern Thai murals such activities are generally confined to the lower registers, where genre scenes of the common people are found, although minor deities are occasionally seen flirting in the heavens. In Isan heartland murals, such activities can be found at any level.

These scenes, while candid, are not so much erotic or pornographic as they are bawdy, fun-loving, and often aimed at communicating certain attitudes toward the subjects depicted. An example is Wat Ban Yang's depictions of the Great Departure, in which the future Buddha leaves his wife and newborn son, as well as his concubines, in order to pursue his path to enlightenment (figure 59). If we take a closer look at the somewhat voyeuristic portrayal of the concubines, we cannot help but notice their exposed breasts and genitalia, a convention used to identify the figures as persons unworthy of respect.

Similarly bawdy details can frequently be found in portrayals of the enlightenment. The future Buddha, seated beneath the *bodhi* tree, is besieged by Mara, the lord of delusion, and his warriors. Below, the earth goddess Nang Thorani wrings out her hair into a torrent that sweeps away Mara's demonic-looking warriors, who are gobbled up head first by gigantic ravenous fish. A particularly robust example can be seen in figure 58, a detail from Wat Khon Kaen Nuea in Roi Et province, where the warriors are being consumed head first and their lower bodies, drawn with exaggerated genitalia, protrude from the mouths of the fish.

This penchant for bawdiness is a ubiquitous part of Isan village entertainment, celebrations, and festivals. Traditional *molam* singing and shadow plays are laced with earthy humor in the form of word play and ribald interchange. The dry season rocket festival, which includes processions of dancers, *naga*-shaped floats, and villagers carrying pairs of copulating dolls with exaggerated genitalia, is a prime example of an agricultural fertility rite based on sexual symbolism intended to bring rain. On this occasion, and at processions for ordinations and other religious merit-making festivities, participants (mostly men, but some women as well) generally drink home brew or cheap commercial whiskey as they dance and sway, with fluid hip and hand movements, to the rhythm of drums and gongs.

Scenes like this appear in countless murals, like those of the carousing men seen in figure 60 from Wat Ban Yang. They often exhibit sexually bold behavior that would be unacceptable in everyday life—the men sometimes wrapping their legs around the women or fondling

◄ **FIGURE 58.** Detail of *mara vijaya* scene. Wat Khon Kaen Nuea, Roi Et. รายละเอียดภาพ มารวิชัย วัดขอนแก่นเหนือ จังหวัดร้อยเอ็ด

FOLLOWING PAGE

➤ **FIGURE 59.** Great Departure. Wat Ban Yang, Maha Sarakham. มหาภิเนษกรมณ์ วัดบ้าน ยาง จังหวัดมหาสารคาม

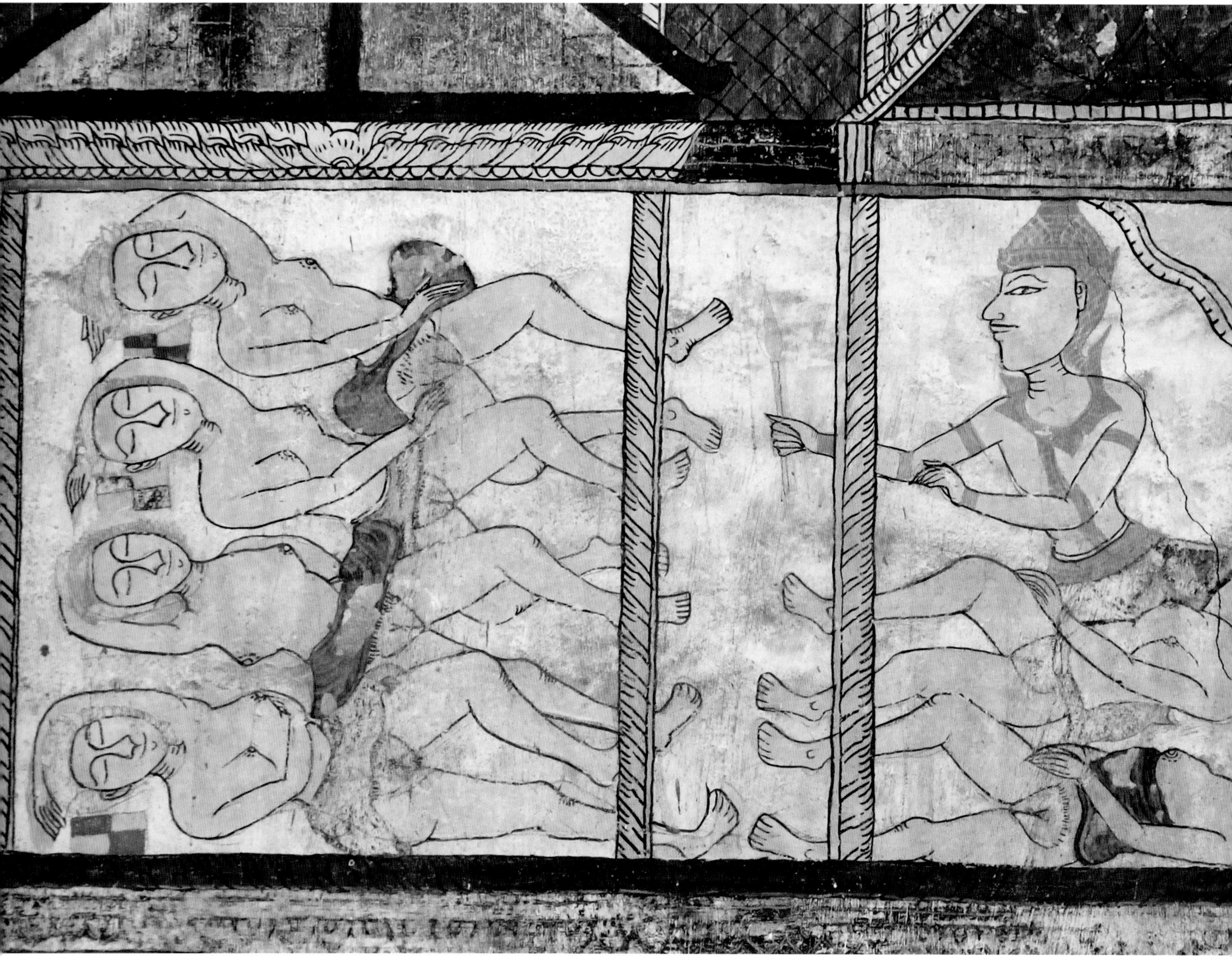

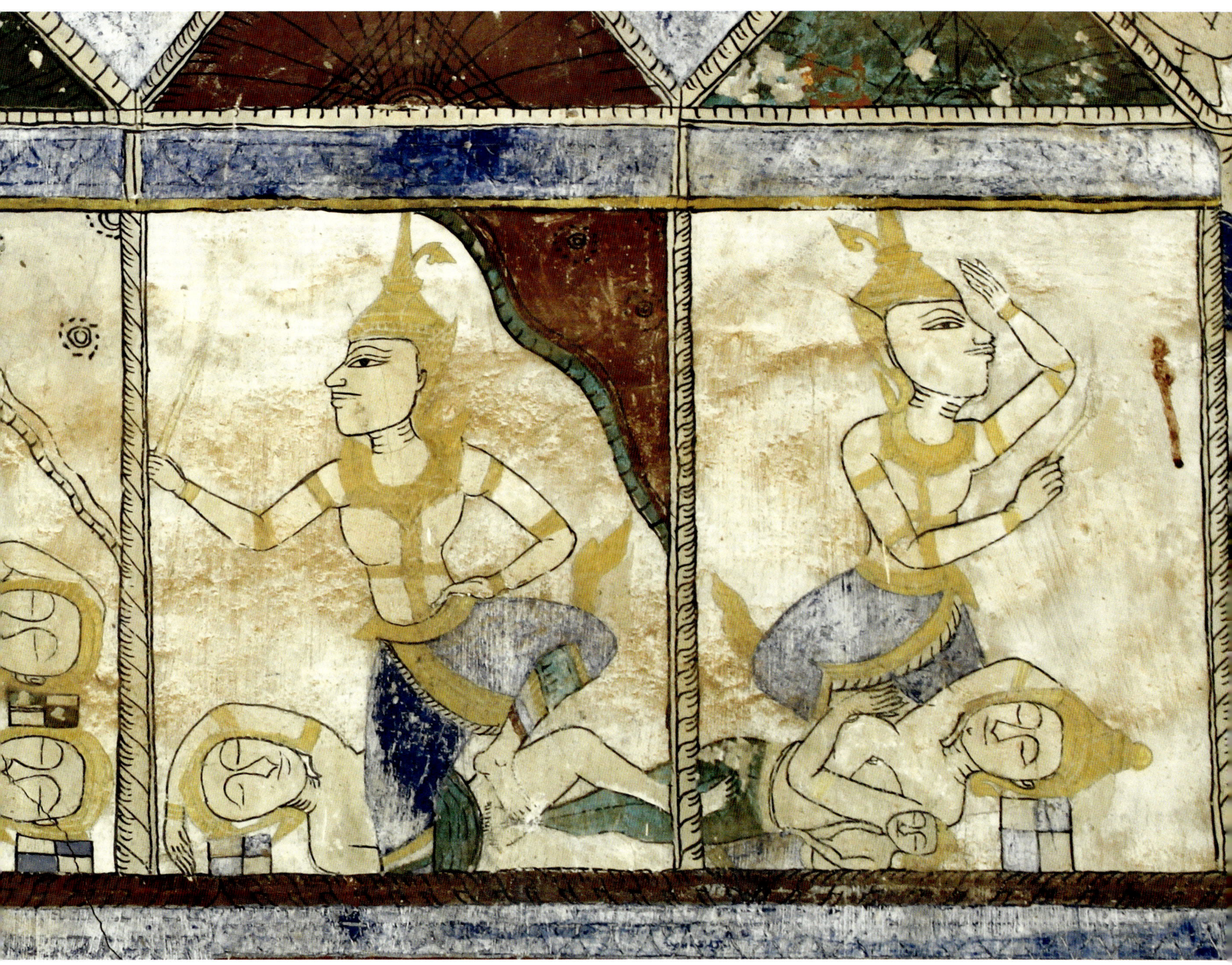

their breasts—with the women resisting, acquiescing, or sometimes reciprocating. Do such portrayals represent actual behaviors, as inversions of customary inhibitions, that occur during certain merit-making occasions? Or are they the hyperbolic expression of the full fun and joy that participants feel during these times of exuberant celebration, as they experience relief from the drudgery of everyday life and find hope in the effect of their merit-making? Either way, what is certain is that these spirited scenes are attention-getters that sustain the viewer's interest. The element of surprise is always present; when perusing a mural, one is never sure when such details might occur.

Other varieties of bawdy expressions occur as well. An example concerns the relationship between Chuchok's wife, Amittada, and their neighbors. The old Brahman truly loves his lovely young wife and treats her so well that their conjugal bliss evokes envy and disharmony among neighboring couples. The tensions come to a head when the other wives retaliate by taunting Amittada. While in Central Region murals the neighbors' antics are limited to pinching the unfortunate young woman, in Isan they go much further. At Wat Ban Yang (figure 61) they

insult her by "mooning" her, lifting their *phasin* (skirts) to expose their bare buttocks. At Wat Sanuan Wari (figure 62), they not only lift their skirts but also urinate at her. Such portrayals evoke sympathy toward Amittada and Chuchok, who, rather than being monochromatic icons of good or evil, are tinged with a range of moral, human hues.

On the other hand, Chuchok's demise is often depicted with great fun and gusto. Isan painters seem to relish portraying how his uncontrolled craving leads him to consume such a massive amount of food that his stomach bursts open, causing him to die. One way to do this is to draw a bystander pointing to the Brahman and his bulging midriff. A clever caption can add even more emphasis to this crucial incident, as seen in the enthusiastic use of alliteration at Wat Sanuan Wari. It reads *"thong phram taek tum tai,"* a rough approximation of which might be, "and the Brahman, his belly bursting open with a bang, bit the dust" (figure 63).

All of the examples above illustrate the Lao/Isan love of bawdy, slapstick humor in every aspect of life, including the teaching of Buddhist stories and ideals.

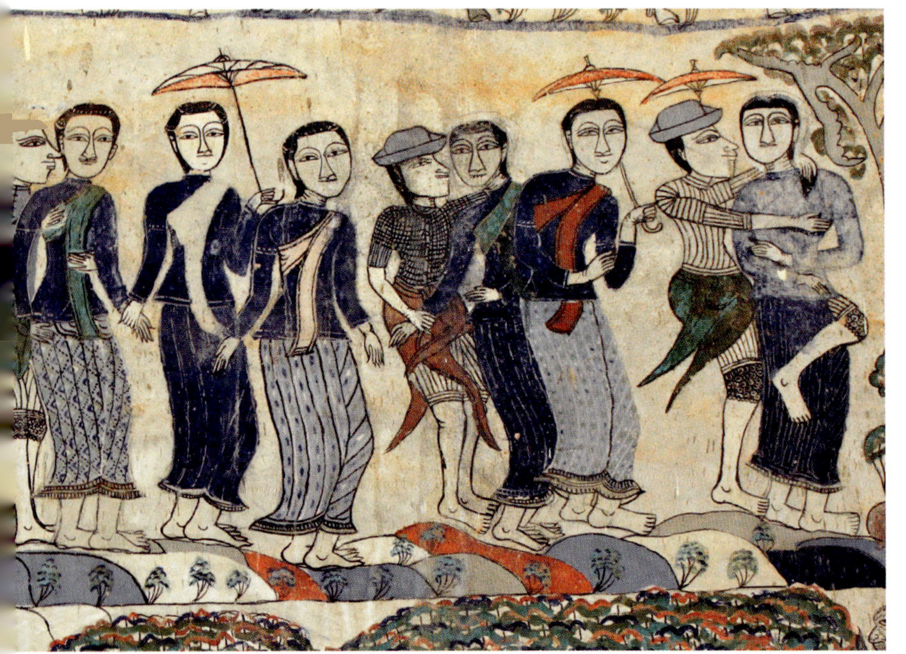

◀ **FIGURE 60.** Procession including carousing men. Wat Ban Yang, Maha Sarakham. ภาพขบวนคนที่มีขี้เมาอยู่ด้วย วัดบ้านยาง มหาสารคาม

▶ **FIGURE 61.** Amittada being taunted by jealous neighbors. Wat Ban Yang, Maha Sarakham. อมิตดาถูกเพื่อนบ้านที่อิจฉาด่าว่า วัดบ้านยาง จังหวัดมหาสารคาม

FOLLOWING PAGE

▶ **FIGURE 62.** Amittada being taunted by jealous neighbors. Wat Sanuan Wari, Khon Kaen. อมิตดาถูกเพื่อนบ้านที่อิจฉาด่าว่า วัดสนวนวารี จังหวัดขอนแก่น

▶ **FIGURE 63.** Chuchok's death by gluttony. Wat Sanuan Wari, Khon Kaen. ชูชกตายเพราะตะกละ วัดสนวนวารี จังหวัดขอนแก่น

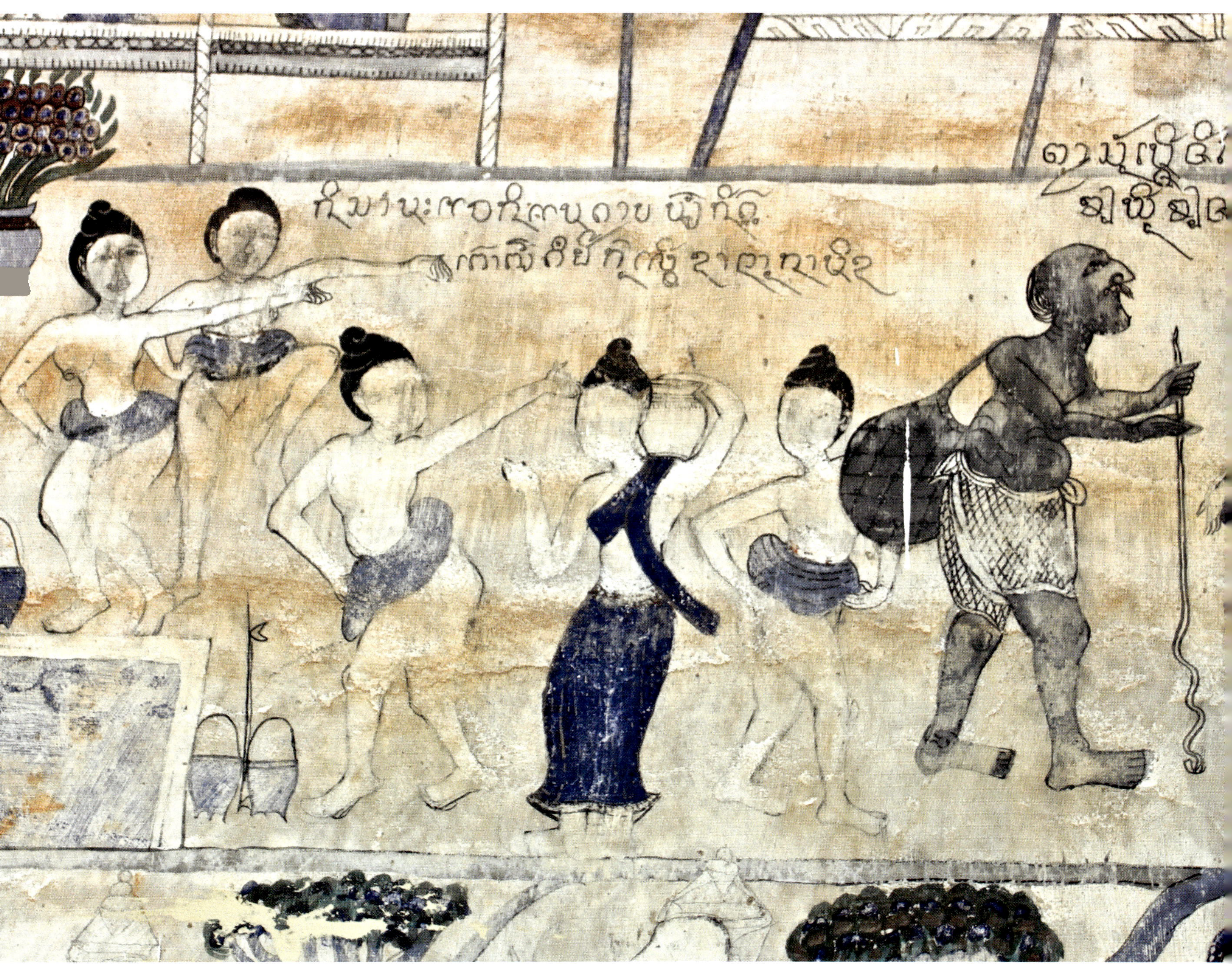

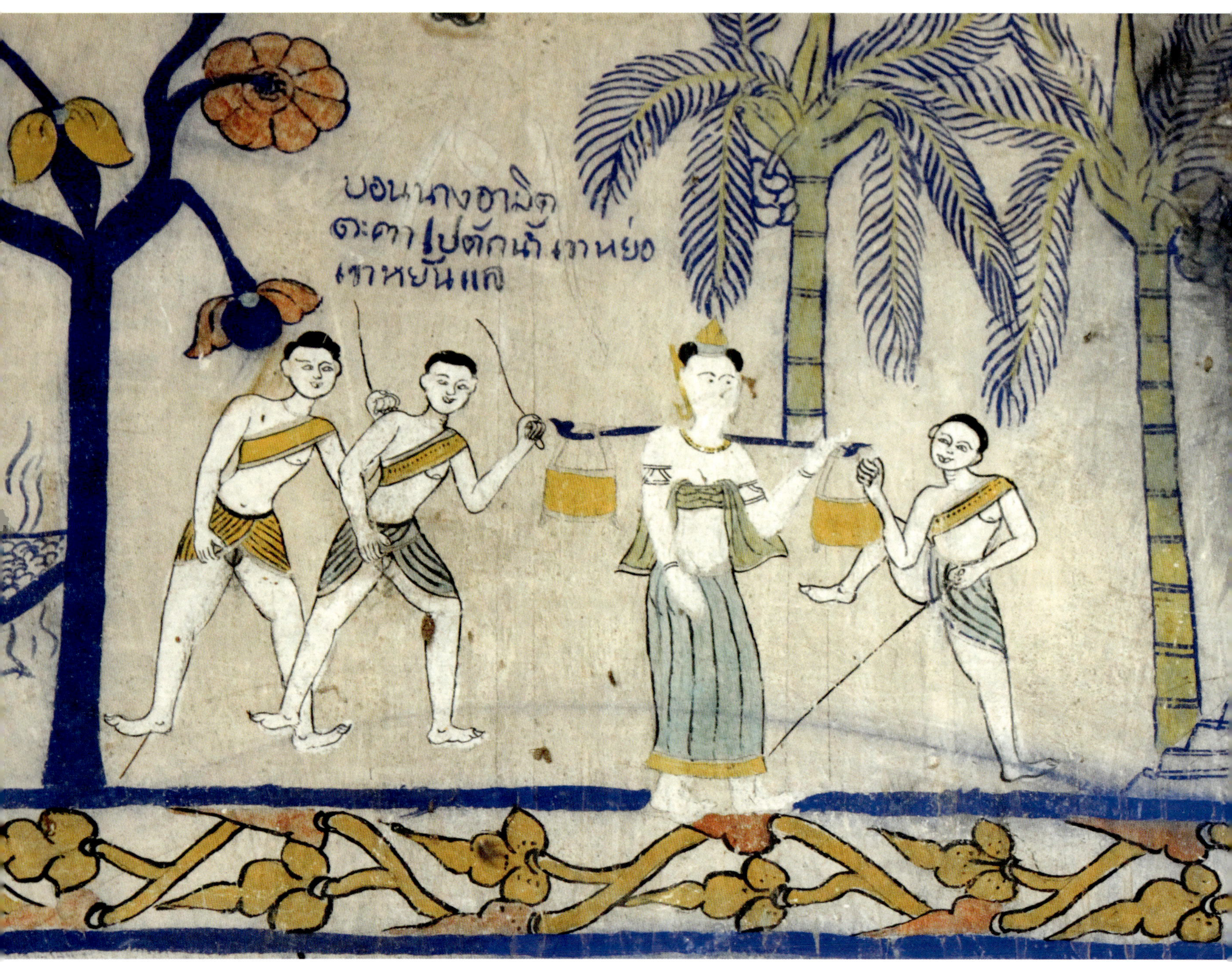
บอนางฮามิต
ตะคาเปตักนั่เขาหย่อ
เขาหยันแล

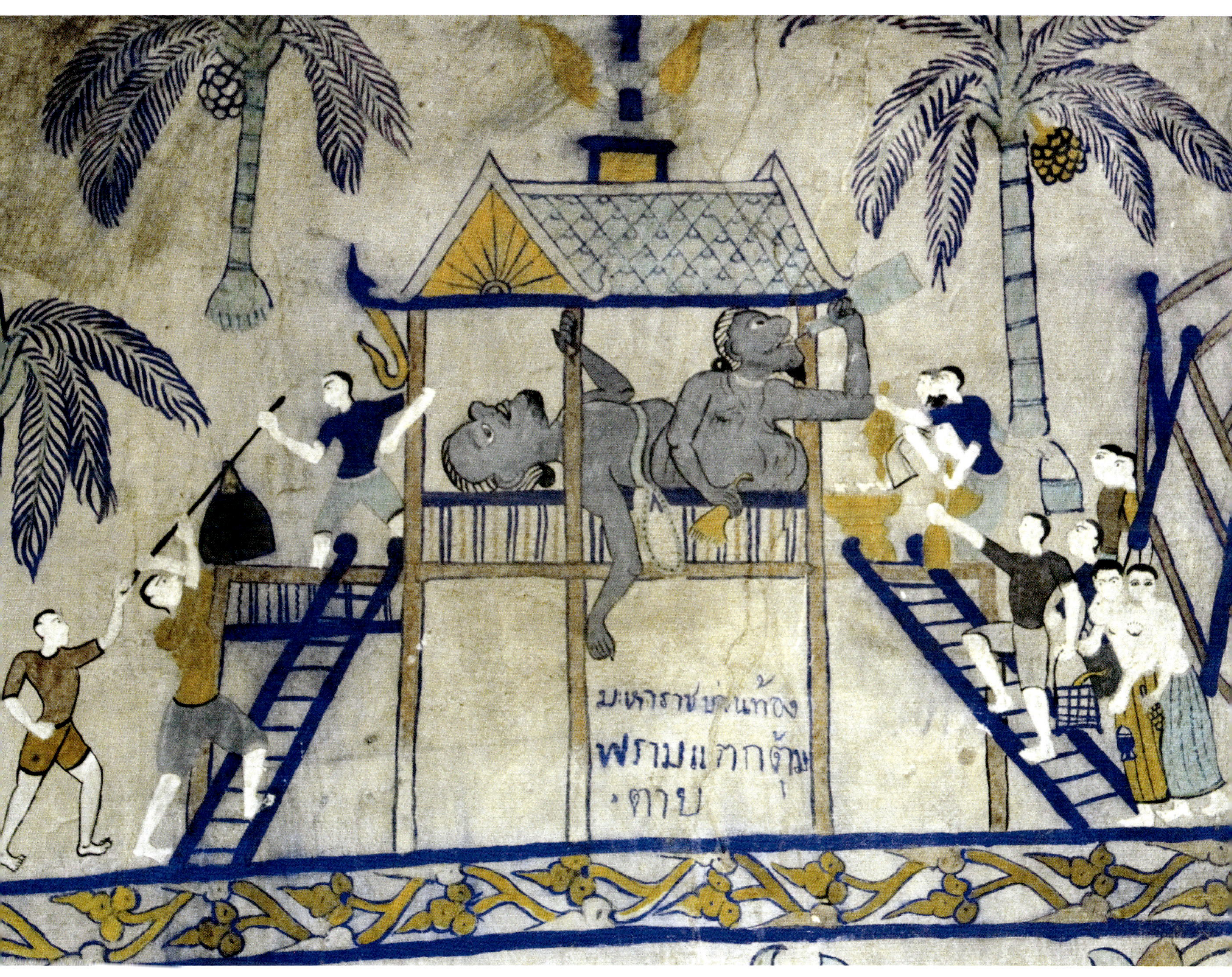
มะหาราชบ่วนท้อง
ฟรามแทกต้ม
ตาย

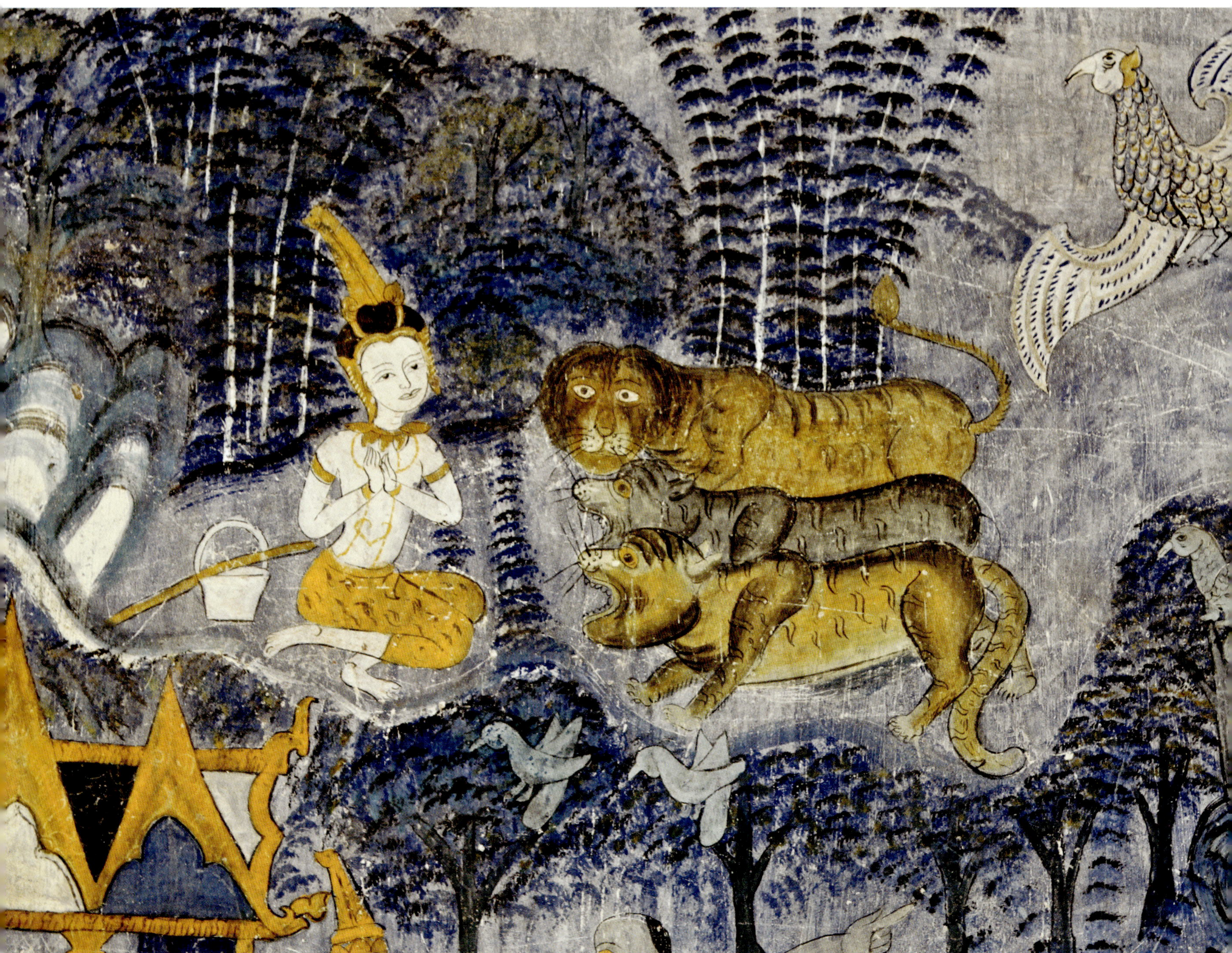

CHAPTER 10

CONCLUDING REMARKS: PAINTING AS PILGRIMAGE

The previous chapters have described the essentials of a group of Buddhist murals found on the exterior of ordination halls in the Isan heartland. We have seen the unique role they play in transmitting essential Buddhist teachings, which they do by depicting not only religious stories but also local participation in the enactment of these stories. In this way the murals take the viewer on a Buddhist pilgrimage. Like all pilgrimages, this one is educational and experiential, participatory and transformative. As reflections of local practice, these murals, through their lively down-to-earth and sometimes earthy details, invite and sometimes entice the viewer to enter into the reenactment of local texts that propound the Buddhist Dharma as understood by the Thai-Lao of northeast Thailand.

For many years scholars, Buddhist monks, and local villagers failed to see the value of these humble murals and the architecturally diverse buildings on which they are painted. Even as Pairote and Wiroj were documenting these works and lobbying for their preservation, demolition and neglect continued. In recent years, however, several efforts at preservation have increased awareness of their value. The first was the Siam Society's renovation of the Wat Sa Bua Kaeo *sim* roof, completed in 2001. Others were the Fine Arts Department's construction of a new roof at Wat Sanuan Wari and Maha Sarakham Ratchaphat University's project to preserve Wat Photharam and Wat Pa Rerai by encouraging the involvement of local villagers.[1] At the same time, several new books in Thai have been published and are bringing these murals to the attention of a wider audience.

These developments are encouraging signs that appreciation of these local cultural forms is growing. We support the initiation of more such efforts, as well as further research into murals in the Isan heartland and other parts of the northeast.

NOTES

1. The university received a grant from the US Ambassador's Fund for Cultural Preservation in 2008.

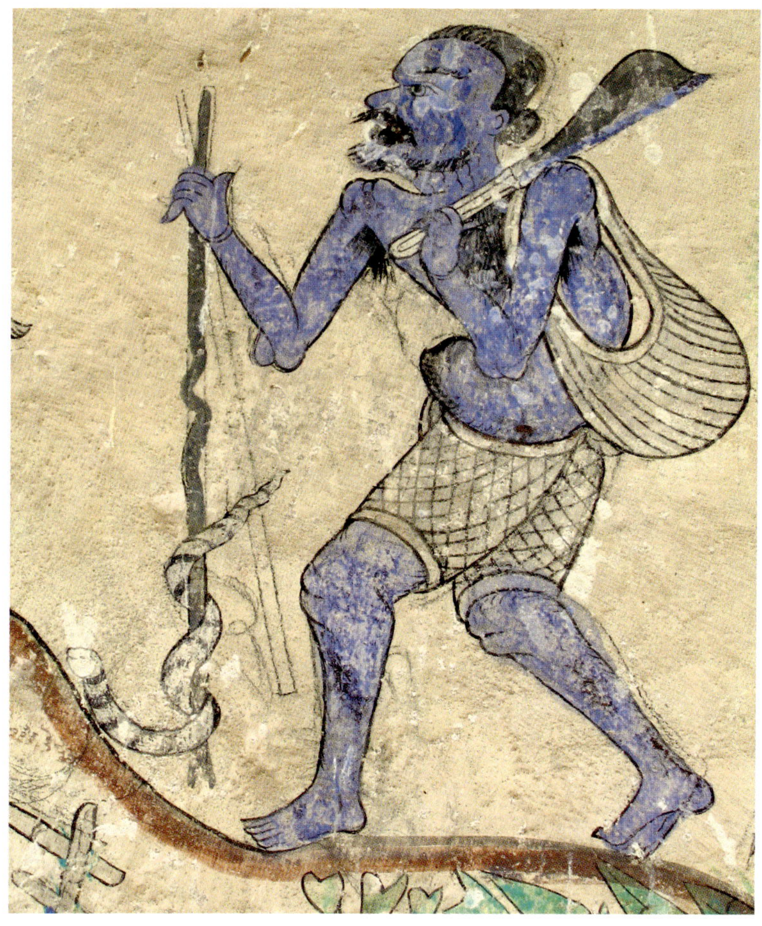

◄ **FIGURE 64.** Matsi encountering forest creatures. Wat Ban Lan, Khon Kaen. พระนางมัทรี ทรงพบสัตว์ร้าย วัดบ้านลาน จังหวัดขอนแก่น

▶ **FIGURE 65.** An unusually handsome version of Chuchok. Wat Ban Yang, Maha Sarakham. ภาพนี้วาดชูชกได้งามเป็นพิเศษ วัดบ้านยาง จังหวัดมหาสารคาม

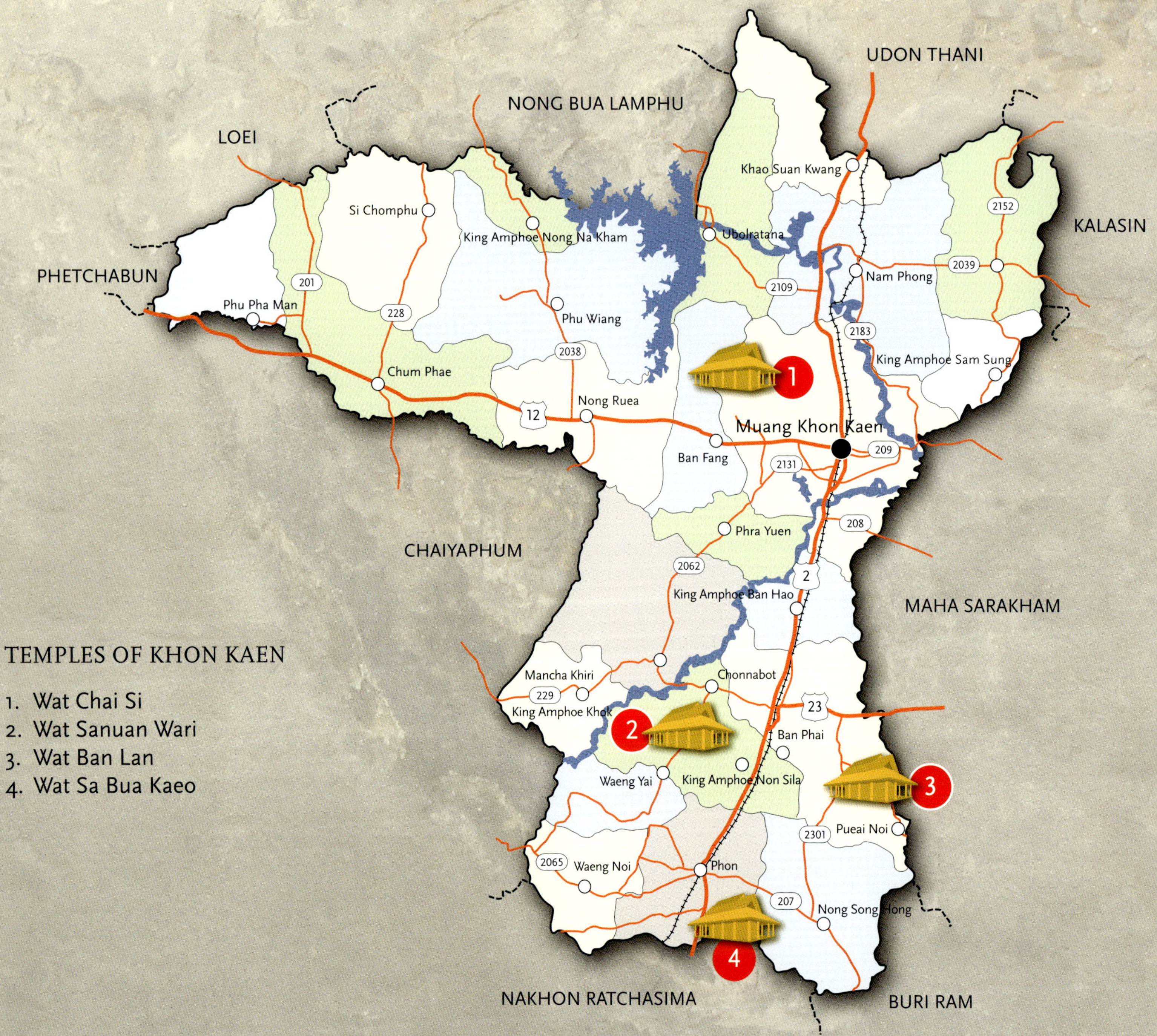

TEMPLES OF KHON KAEN

1. Wat Chai Si
2. Wat Sanuan Wari
3. Wat Ban Lan
4. Wat Sa Bua Kaeo

APPENDIX 1

MAPS OF KHON KAEN

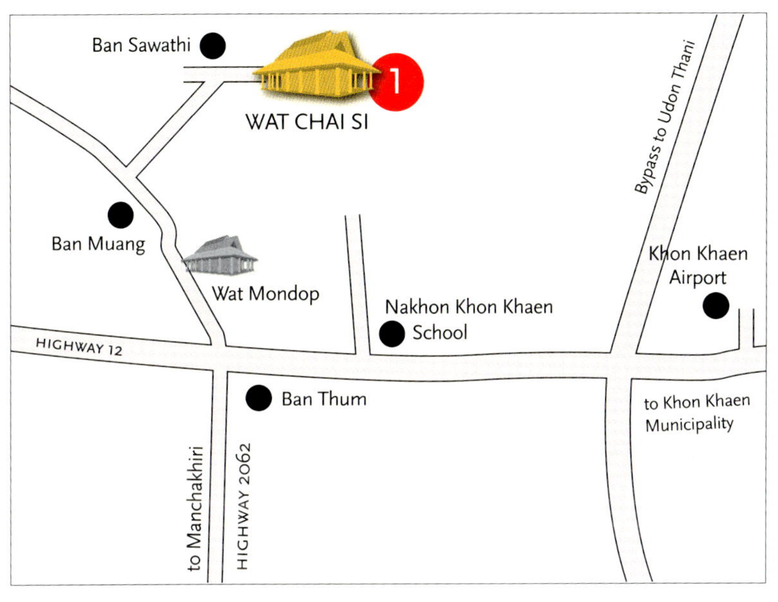

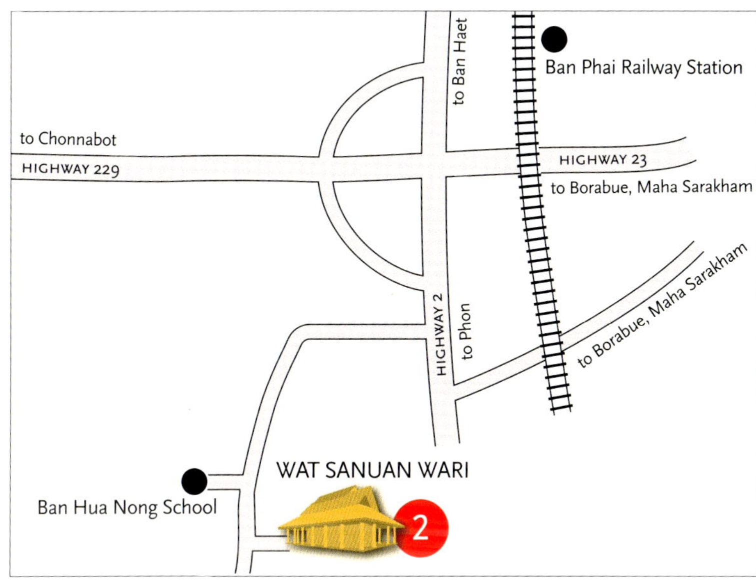

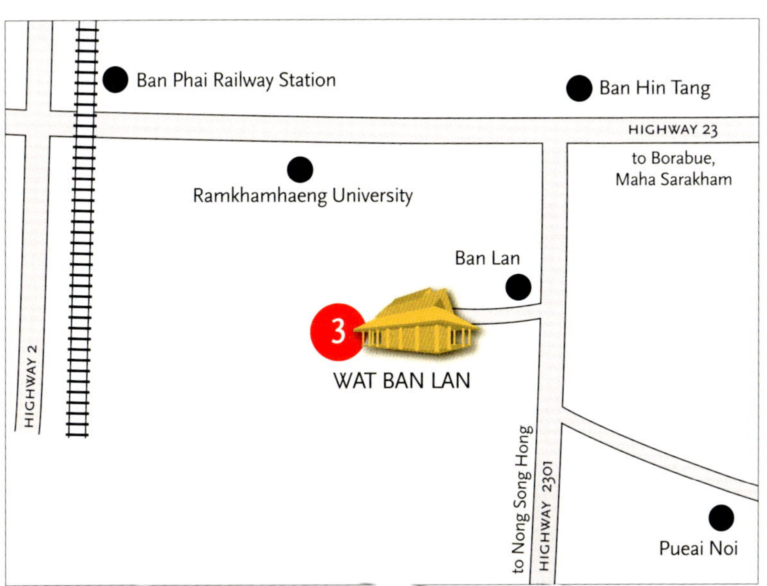

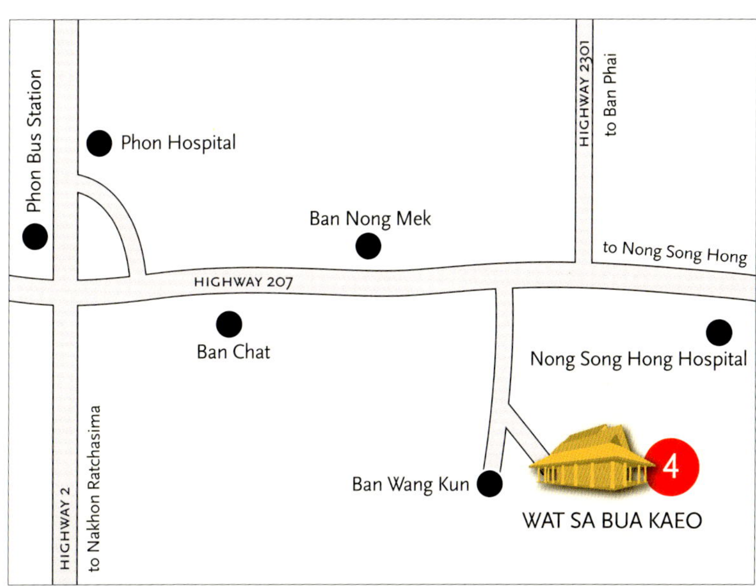

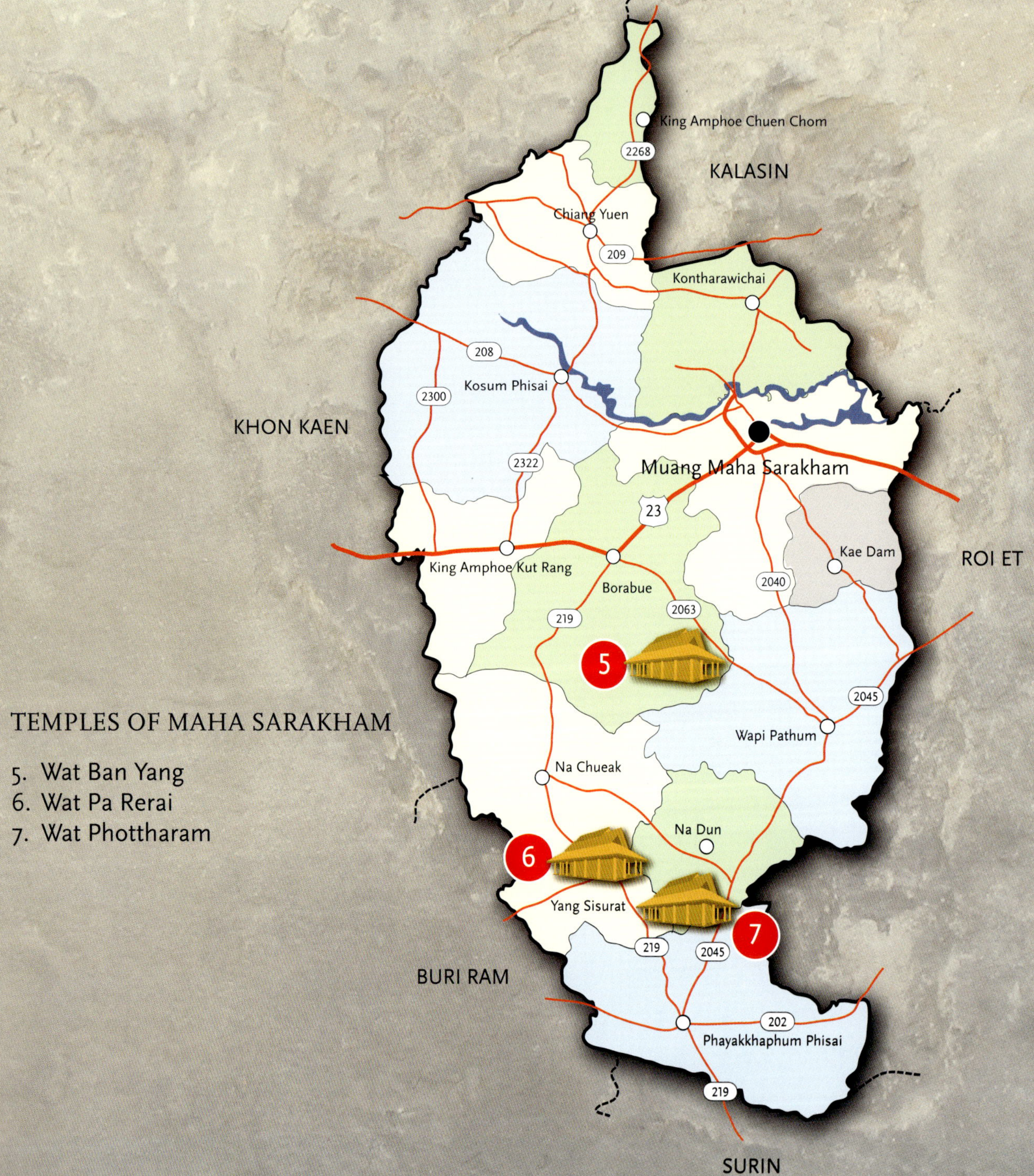

TEMPLES OF MAHA SARAKHAM

5. Wat Ban Yang
6. Wat Pa Rerai
7. Wat Phottharam

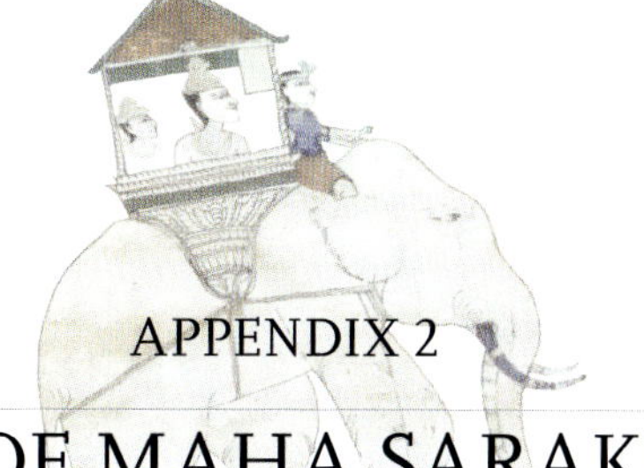

MAPS OF MAHA SARAKHAM

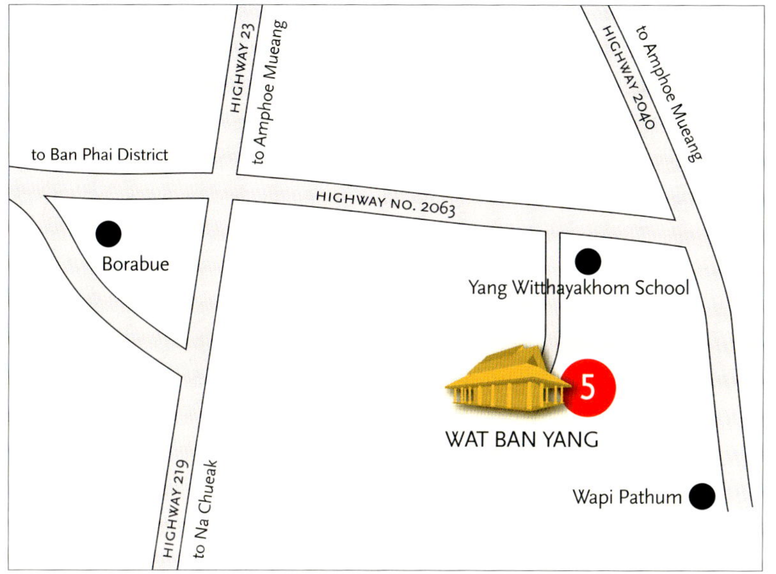

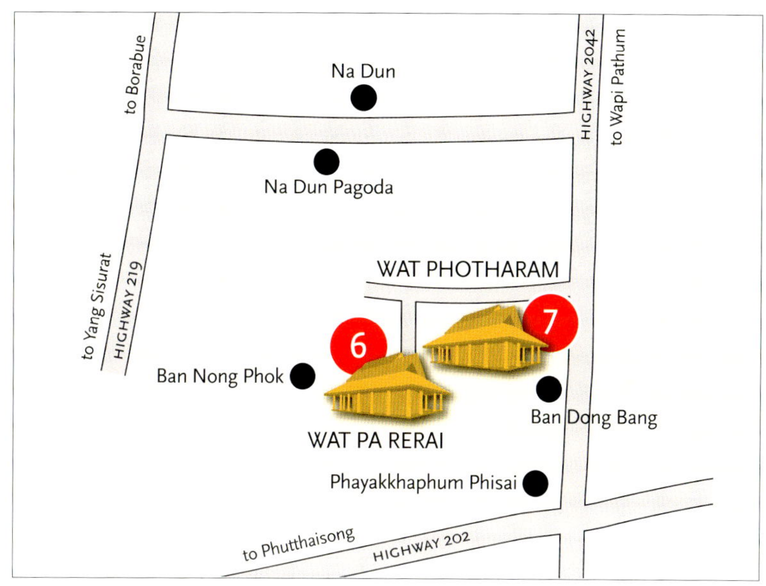

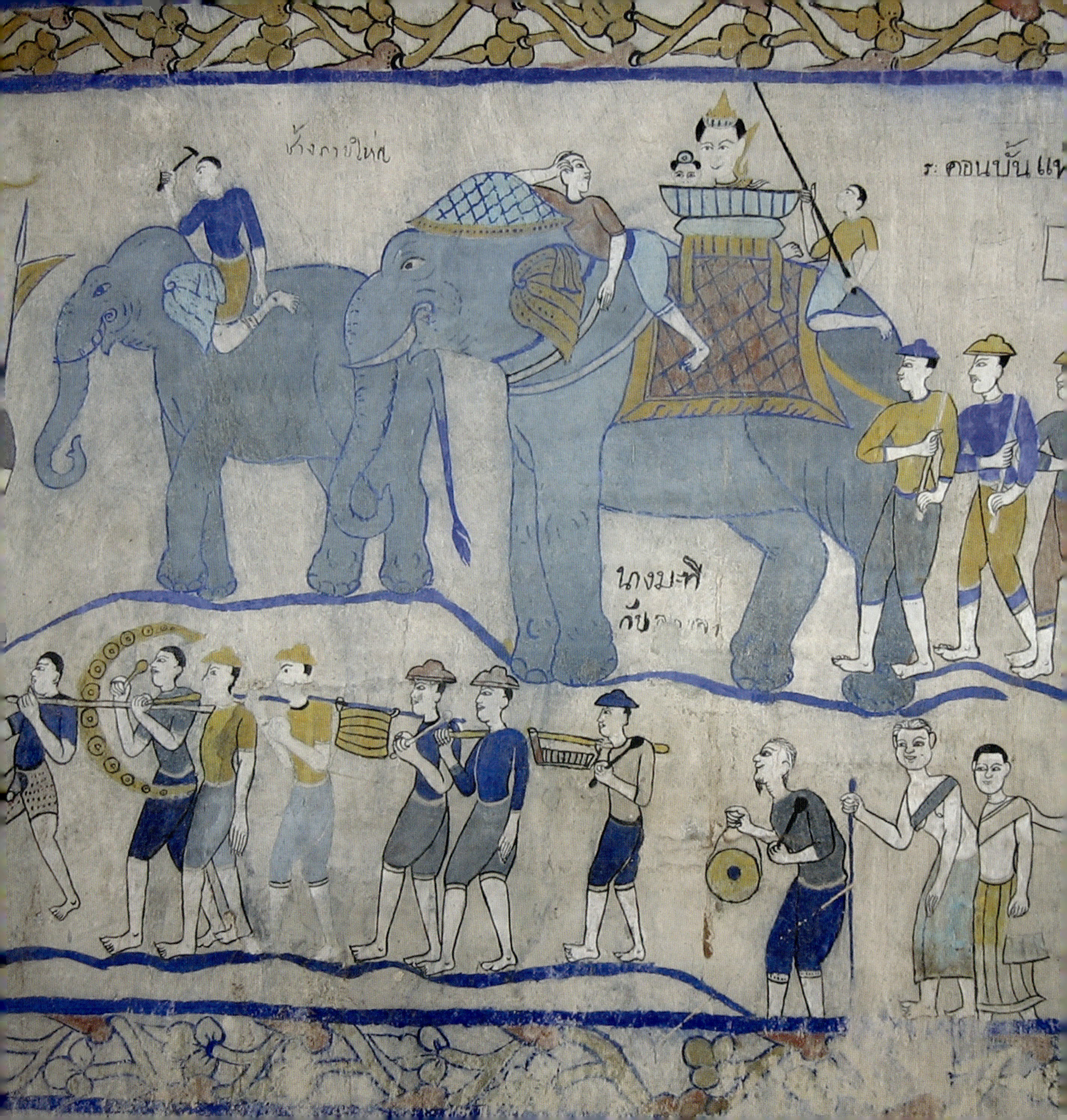

ช้างกายใหญ่
ร: คอนปั้น แท
นางมะที
กับลูกเขา

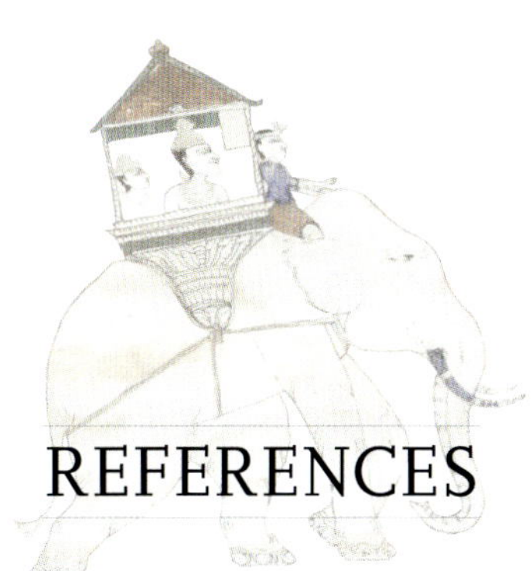

REFERENCES

Apivat Prichaprasasna. 1986. วรรณกรรมอีสาน พระลัก-พระลาม [Isan Literature: *Phra Lak–Phra Lam*]. Bangkok: Thai Khadi Sueksa Institute.

Boisselier, Jean. 1976. *Thai Painting*. Translated by Janet Seligman. Tokyo: Kodansha International.

Brereton, Bonnie Pacala. 1995. *Thai Tellings of Phra Malai: Texts and Rituals concerning a Popular Buddhist Saint*. Tempe, AZ: Arizona State University, Program for Southeast Asian Studies.

———, and Somroay Yencheuy. 2007. "Traditional Shadow Theater of Northeastern Thailand (*Nang Pramo Thai*): Hardy Transplant or Endangered Species," *Aseanie* 19 (June): 13–143.

Buddhaisawan Chapel. 1983. Mural Paintings of Thailand Series. Bangkok: Muang Boran Publishing House.

Cadet, John. 1971. *The Ramakien: The Thai Epic*. Tokyo: Kodansha International.

Cate, Sandra, and H. Leedom Lefferts, Jr. n.d. "Becoming Active/Active Becoming: Prince Vessantara Scrolls and the Creation of a Moral Community." Unpublished manuscript.

Chob Disuankok. 2007. วรรณกรรมพื้นบ้านสินไซ [Sin Sai: A Folktale]. Khon Kaen: Samnak kansueksa thesaban nakhon Khon Kaen.

Chumdej Dejphimol. 1988. "การศึกษาเรื่องหนังประโมทัยในจังหวัดร้อยเอ็ด" [A Study of "Nang Pramo Thai" Shadow Puppet Theatre in Roi Et Province]. Master's Thesis, Srinakharinwirot University.

Cone, Margaret and Richard F. Gombrich. 1977. *The Prefect Generosity of Prince Vessantara*. Oxford: Clarendon Press.

Decha Siriphat. 2006. รายงานวิจัยการศึกษาลักษณะและรูปแบบจิตรกรรมฝาผนังอีสานกับการพัฒนาจิตรกรรมไทยร่วมสมัยอีสาน [Research on the Design and Form of Isan Murals and the Development of Isan Modern Thai Painting]. Bangkok: Thai Culture Commission.

Gerini, G. E. 1892. *A Retrospective View and Account of the Origin of the Thet Maha Ch'at Ceremony*. Bangkok: Sathirakoses-Nagapradipa Foundation. (Orig. pub. 1976.)

Ginsburg, Henry. 1989. *Thai Manuscript Painting*. London: The British Library Board.

Gittinger, Mattiebelle, and H. Leedom Lefferts, Jr. 1992. *Textiles and the Tai Experience in Southeast Asia*. Washington, D.C: The Textile Museum.

Gosling, Betty. 2004. *Origins of Thai Art*. Bangkok: River Books.

Jaiser, Gerhard. 2009. *Thai Mural Painting. Volume 1: Iconography, Analysis and Guide*. Bangkok: White Lotus.

Kamala Tiyavanich. 1997. *Forest Recollections: Wandering Monks in Twentieth-Century Thailand*. Chiang Mai: Silkworm Books.

———. 2003. *The Buddha in the Jungle*. Chiang Mai: Silkworm Books.

Lakkhana Chindawong, ed. 2000. สิมที่มีฮูบแต้มในจังหวัดร้อยเอ็ด [Sim that Have Murals in Roi-Et]. Roi-et: Nuay Anurak Singweatlom lae Thammachat.

Lefferts, H. Leedom, Jr. 2004. "Village as Stage: Imaginative Space and Time in Rural Northeast Thai Lives." *Journal of the Siam Society* 92:129–144.

———. 2006/2007. "The Bun Phra Wet Painted Scrolls of Northeastern Thailand in the Walters Art Museum." *Journal of the Walters Art Museum* 64/65:99–118.

———. n.d. "Churning the Sea of Milk with a Mortar and Pestle: High Art in Village Northeast Thailand." Unpublished paper.

มหาชาติสำนวนอีสาน [The Isan Version of the *Vessantara Jataka*]. 1988. Bangkok: Fine Arts Department.

Miller, Terry and Jarernchai Chonpairot. 1979. "Shadow Puppet Theatre in Northeast Thailand," *Theatre Journal* 31 (1): 293–331.

Napat Sirisambhand and Alec Gordon. 1999. "Thai Women in Late Ayutthaya Style Paintings." *Journal of the Siam Society*, 87 (1&2): 1–16.

Nidhi Eoseewong. 2005. *Pen and Sail: Literature and History in Early Bangkok*. Chiang Mai: Silkworm Books.

Pairote Samosorn. 1989. จิตรกรรมฝาผนังอีสาน [E-Sarn Mural Paintings]. Khon Kaen: E-sarn Cultural Center.

Phra Ariyanuwat Khemachari Thera, ed. 1975. พระลักพระลาม รามเกียรติ์ (สำนวนเก่าของอีสาน) [*Phra Lak–Phra Lam: Ramakien* (Old Isan Version)]. Bangkok: Sathian Koset-Nakhraprathip Foundation.

Phra Lak-Phra Lam: A Previous Life of the Buddha. Vo Thu Tinh's abridged translation of the manuscript from Wat Kang Tha, Vientiane Wat Oup Mong frescoes (1938) by Thit Panh. http://www.seasite.niu.edu/Lao/otherTopics/PhralakPhralam/index.htm

Phra Sanprasert and Luang Si Amonyan. 1974. พระรามชาดก [*Phra Ram Chadok*]. Bangkok: Kasemsan.

Prathet Patchangkhata. 1998. จิตรกรรมฝาผนังวัดป่าเรไรย์ บ้านหนองพอก ตำบล ดงบัง อำเภอนาดูน จังหวัดมหาสารคาม [The Mural Paintings at the *Sim* of Wat Pa Rerai at Ban Nong Phok, Tambon Dong Bang Amphoe Na Dun Maha Sarakham]. MA thesis, Thai Studies, Mahasarakham University.

Renard, Ronald D. 1999. "On Wat Sa Bua Kaeo." *Journal of the Siam Society* 87 (1&2): 121–122.

Reynolds, Frank E. 1991. "Ramayana, Rama Jataka, and Ramakien: A comparative Study of Hindu and Buddhist Traditions." In *Many Ramayanas: The Diversity of a Narrative Tradition in South Asia*, ed. Paula Richman, 50–66. Berkeley: University of California Press.

Roveda, Vittorio and Sothon Yem. 2009. *Buddhist Painting in Cambodia*. Bangkok: River Books.

Somkiart Lopetcharat. 2000. *Lao Buddha: the Image and its History*. Bangkok: Siam International Book Company, Ltd.

Sommai Premchit. 2001. มหาเวสสันดรชาดก: วิเคราะห์ทางสังคมและวัฒนธรรม [The *Maha Vessantara Jataka*: A Sociocultural Analysis]. Chiang Mai: published by the author.

Somroay Yencheuy. 2002. สินไซ [Sin Sai]. Khon Kaen: Siriphan Offset Printing.

Sonthiwan Intralib. 1994. *Thai Traditional Paintings*. Bangkok: Amarin.

Sumali Ekchaniyom. 2006. ฮูบแต้มในสิมอีสาน [The Murals of Isan *Sim* (Ordination Halls)]. Bangkok: Matichon Books.

Supoj Suwannaphukdi. 1990. "การศึกษาจิตรกรรมฝาผนังวัดสนวนวารีพัฒนาราม บ้านหัวหนอง ตำบลหัวหนอง อำเภอบ้านไผ่ จังหวัดขอนแก่น" [A Study of Mural Painting of Wat Sanuan Wari Phatthanaram, Ban Hua Hoing, Tambol Hunong, Amphoe Banphai, Khon Kaen]. MA thesis, Thai studies, Srinkharinwirot University.

Suriya Samutkupt, Pattana Kitiarsa, and Nanthiya Phuttha. 1991. "บุญ ผเวสของชาวอีสาน: การวิเคราะห์และดีความหมายทางมานุษยวิทยา" (Bun Phawes of Isan: An Anthropological Interpretation). Ekkasan prakop nithatsakan. Khon Kaen: Khon Kaen University, Faculty of Humanities and Social Sciences.

Suriya Samutkupt, et al. 1992. หนังประโมทัยของอีสาน: การแพร่กระจายและ การปรับเปลี่ยนทางวัฒนธรรมในหมู่บ้านอีสาน [Northeastern Shadow Play: Cultural Diffusion and Transformation in Rural Villages of Northeast Thailand]. Khon Kaen: Faculty of Humanities, Khon Kaen University.

Swearer, Donald K. 2004. *Becoming the Buddha: The Ritual of Image Consecration in Thailand*. Princeton: Princeton University Press.

Thiva Supajanya and Srisakra Vallibotama. 1972. "The Need for an Inventory of Ancient Sites for Anthropological Research in Northeastern Thailand." *Tonan Ajia Kenkyu* [The Southeast Asian Studies] 10 (2): 284–97.

Tirapong Sarapan. 1994. จิตรกรรมฝาผนังสิมวัดมัชฌิมวิทยาราม อำเภอบ้านไผ่ จังหวัด ขอนแก่น [Murals of Wat Matchim Witthayaram, Ban Phai District, Khon Kaen Province]. MA thesis (Thai Studies), Srinakharinwirot University.

Vo Thu Tinh. 1972. *Phra Lak Phra Lam: Le Ramayana Lao et les fresques murales do Vat Oup Moung, Vientiane*. Vientiane: Editions Vithagna.

Utong Prasasvinitchai. 2008. ซ่อนไว้ในสิม ก-ฮ ในชีวิตอีสาน [Hidden in the Sim: An A–Z of Isan Life]. Bangkok: Fullstop Publishing.

Wajuppa Tossa and Margaret Read Macdonald. 2004. นิทานพื้นบ้านกับ การเล่านิทาน: นิทานพื้นบ้านไทยและอังกฤษ [Folktales and Storytelling: Thai and English Folktales] (in Thai and English). Maha Sarakham: published by the author.

Wat Mai Thepnimit. 1983. Mural Paintings of Thailand Series. Bangkok: Muang Boran Publishing House.

Wat Thong Thammachat. 1982. Mural Paintings of Thailand Series. Bangkok: Muang Boran Publishing House.

Wat Yai Intharam. 1982. Mural Paintings of Thailand Series. Bangkok: Muang Boran Publishing House.

"What is a Naive Painter?" http://www.daprix.com/barto

Wilson, Constance M., ed. 2009. *The Middle Mekong River Basin: Studies in Tai History and Culture*. Northern Illinois University Monograph Series on Southeast Asia Number 9. DeKalb, Illinois: Northern Illinois University, Center for Southeast Asian Studies.

Wiroj Srisuro. 2003. "Isan Sims: Ordination Halls in Northeast Thailand." In *The Buddhist Monastery: A Cross-cultural Survey*, ed. Pierre Pichard and François Lagirarde, 131–148. Paris: Ecole Française d'Extrême-Orient.

———. 1993. สิมอีสาน [Sim Isan]. *Isan Sim: Northeast Buddhist Holy Temples*, Bangkok: Toyota Foundation, Maeka Press.